Émigré

95 Years in the Life of a Russian Count

A Memoir by
Paul Grabbe

With Alexandra Grabbe

Advance Praise for *Émigré*

"The Russian Revolution, with the collapse of all civil, social and moral authority and the exile of an entire elite, is a tragedy whose consequences have not ceased to roil the world, just as its stories never cease to amaze. Paul Grabbe's odyssey, however, is something more: It is a remarkable testament to the power of the human spirit to overcome one of the most wrenching of life's challenges, the abrupt loss of one's world. Ripped as a teenager from the glitter and privilege of a Russian aristocrat, miraculously escaping the Bolsheviks with his family, he battles to make a new life in a new world, waiting on tables, shoveling ore in a gold mine, and enduring hunger until he achieves security and makes peace with his fate. It is a gripping tale wonderfully told, with a rich cast of surprising characters and a series of enthralling adventures."

—SERGE SCHMEMANN
Author, *Echoes of a Native Land: Two Centuries of a Russian Village*
Member Editorial Board, *The New York Times*

Praise for *Windows on the River Neva*

"It magnificently recreates the life and times in which Paul Grabbe grew up."
—HARRISON SALISBURY,
formerly *New York Times* Moscow Bureau Chief

"To find the literate and elegant reminiscences of a man whose father was so close to the tsar is very rare indeed."
—EDWARD CRANKSHAW,
British authority on Russian literature

"Grabbe's perceptive recollection of growing up is a near masterpiece of understatement, of insights into the relations between children and parents, of the collision of the two worlds of children and adults. With the deft, clear, short strokes of the master painter, he portrays his own mental, physical, and emotional development effectively and eloquently."
—PROFESSOR JOHN PARR, Ph.D.

"It's not your average run-of-the-mill revolutionary memoir. Paul Grabbe describes his life with such honesty that the book should appeal to anyone twelve and above."
—BOB ATCHISON of Alexanderpallace.org

Other Books by Paul Grabbe

MINUTE STORIES OF THE OPERA (1932)
With Paul Nordoff

WE CALL IT HUMAN NATURE (1939)
With Gardner Murphy

THE STORY OF 100 SYMPHONIC FAVORITES (1940)

OUTDOORS WITH THE CAMERA (1941)
With Joseph E. Sherman

STORY OF ORCHESTRAL MUSIC AND ITS TIMES (1942)

THE PRIVATE WORLD OF THE LAST TSAR (1984)
With Beatrice C. Grabbe

Table of Contents

You pronounce a name, but it is not known to anybody.
He was famous on the banks of another river.

Czeslaw Milosz

Forward

MY FATHER WAS born in St. Petersburg, Russia, on February 14, 1902. I didn't know how much he missed his country until I read this memoir. None of us knew, not even Mother.

After Dad's passing, I assumed responsibility for his affairs. At the top of a closet, I found a Yardley's soapbox. Inside were dozens of keys. What surprised me was their age. Some were so old they had rusted. Others had neat little labels in Russian. The keys must have opened doors in Russia. Dad had carried them during his travels, unable to accept the fact that he would never return to his country.

Twenty years ago I visited St. Petersburg with my husband. The first thing we did was hike across the city to Dad's former home. It was easy to spot because of the family crest, carved into the side of the building. I sat down in the inner courtyard, rancid with the smell of urine, and studied the weeds growing under three ancient fruit trees. An empty vodka bottle lay beneath the bench. I imagined Dad walking past, holding his tutor's hand, as they snuck off to see another Western at the neighborhood theatre. How hard it must have been to have revolution destroy his world, hard and heartbreaking.

People from all walks of life came to his memorial service in 1999. They remembered Dad as a gentle, kind man who happened to have been born a count. When an artist painted his portrait in the seventies, she put a harlequin pattern in the background, having perceived his uncanny facility for adaptation, a quality necessary for survival after revolution.

—Alexandra Grabbe

Preface

IN 1942, I went to the Library of Congress to see if my books on music, psychology, and photography were listed in the card catalogue. They were all there in the stacks. Strangely enough, however, under my name, I found a book I had not written, the memoirs of my great grandfather, General Count Paul Grabbe, published a century earlier. In the introduction, the other Paul Grabbe said he had always regretted not knowing more about his ancestors, and so he decided to write a memoir in the hope descendants might learn about his life.

This encounter across a hundred years was a revelation. From then on, I began to collect what information I could about my past and undertook the writing of my own memoirs. Part I, *Windows on the River Neva,* was published in New York in 1977 and, in translation, in St. Petersburg in 1995. Part II, *Danish Interlude*, describes the four years I spent in Denmark after the Revolution. I have also recorded my adventures in America, and keep the papers here in my study until the day they, too, can be published.

My life has spanned almost a century now. I hope that the insight that comes with such a life will inspire those who happen to chance upon these pages. Some of my experiences were ordinary, some extraordinary. All happened as I recount them here.

Paul Grabbe
Wellfleet, Massachusetts
December 1997

PART I

Windows on the River Neva

1

ST. PETERSBURG, early in the twentieth century, was a special world. My part of it must have been quite special, too. Father was a Cossack general, an imposing man, with his uniforms and handsome blond mustache. As a child, I took my family's position and material wellbeing for granted. It seemed natural to be fussed over by governesses and tutors. Until I went to school, I rarely saw any other children besides my older brothers. That may explain why nannies became so important. They served as playmates.

There was one nanny to whom, people say, I was devoted. Her name was Pasha. In 1905, Mother asked her to come to France with us. Pasha refused. She couldn't bear to leave Russia, even for a short time. When we boarded the train without her, I felt bereft.

During the night, Father shook me by the shoulder. "Wake up, Pavlik,"[1] he said. "There's been an accident. We have to change trains." Slowly I opened my eyes and watched him reach for my bathrobe. It was dark red, wooly, and warm.

Father hoisted me to his shoulders. He opened the door and went down some steps. Outside, the moon was shining. I could see quite a distance. Our train had stopped in the middle of a field. He walked past the locomotive, which emitted sparks and was making a dreadful hissing sound. Soon we reached more railroad cars. He carried me into a compartment like the one we had just left.

"Here we are," Father said, lowering me into the berth. "Sleep well."

As he tucked me in, I caught a glimpse of Mother at the door.

The next day we arrived in Cannes and moved into a suite at the Elysée Palace Hotel. I gathered from what Mother said that something of which she disapproved was happening back home in St. Petersburg. Later I found out we had left Russia's capital in order to escape the riots, strikes, and insurrections that threatened revolution. Since Father's military duties required his presence on the Riviera, Mother had decided to join him there until things quieted down.

Another family from Petersburg was staying at the same hotel. Mother called on them and took me along. When we knocked on the door, the Saburov boys sat on the floor, absorbed in some game with a locomotive. I wanted to play, but they said no. They wouldn't let me touch their electric train. I thought this wasn't right and said so. Still, they refused. To settle the argument, their mother suggested, "Show him your other toys." Then she turned to Mother and added something about my hair. I heard her say, "Isn't it about time?"

I was dressed, as usual, in skirts. My hair was long and curly. It was the way well-to-do little boys were supposed to look. Customarily, at three or four, they were given a crew cut, and short trousers replaced the skirts.

In the morning, the hotel barber appeared at our door.

"I have instructions to cut your hair," he said.

I turned to my new nanny. "Where's Mother?"

"Out shopping. Before leaving, she said you were old enough for short hair."

The nanny forced me to sit in a chair. She held me firmly while the barber went *snip, snip, snip.* I yelled and kicked, but nothing helped.

A little later, I watched the maid sweep up my beautiful red ringlets. Then Mother returned. She had bought candy. I refused to eat it.

Dressed in short pants and jacket, I went down to the hotel garden and wandered alone among the palm trees. I wanted to share my pain, but there was no one around, not even my brother Nils, off at the beach.

That afternoon Mother took us to a local theater to see *Around the World in Eighty Days.* The first act seemed to go well enough, but, in the second, a band of Indians attacked the travelers. There was gunfire—*bang, bang, bang*—and a commotion on stage. Terrified by the sudden noise, I burst into tears.

"Don't cry," Mother pleaded. "It's only make-believe."

But the tears kept streaming down my face. I had to be taken back to the hotel before the end of the performance.

AT DINNER, I protested Pasha's absence by refusing dessert. Mother summoned my favorite waiter.

"*Regardez-moi ces éclairs!*" he said.

I shook my head. No, no, no, I gestured, although I loved French pastry.

The waiter produced a fruit basket.

"*Peut-être une orange ou une clémentine?*"

Mother peered at me with distress. "It's unnatural for a child not to want dessert," she told the nanny.

Parting from Pasha was hard. Never again could I give my affection to any other nanny or governess. Much harder would be parting from Russia later on.

2

RETURNING TO St. Petersburg after trips abroad or summers in the country was always a joy. I liked to wake up early, stretch out in the comfortable berth, and savor the sensation of being whisked through space. I loved the swaying of the railroad car and the rumbling as the train sped along. At dawn, I would reach for the shade, raise it halfway, and peer outside. In the fall, a typically bleak, northern landscape would meet my gaze. Marshes alternated with patches of leafless trees under a heavy sky. Abruptly the trees would end, and we would race past sodden fields that extended as far as the eye could see. A desolate landscape, but so familiar. To me, those marshes and fields were a welcome sight. They meant I was almost home.

Soon the train would reach Nikolayevsky Station. Mother would take Nils and me by the hand and walk us along the platform to an exit where our carriage would be waiting. We would be driven along Nevsky Prospect, across the Fontanka Canal, and on toward our apartment. Once inside, Nils and I would run through all the rooms to make sure nothing had changed. We would throw open cupboard doors and call to each other in excitement as we rediscovered familiar toys.

My family lived on a quiet street in an affluent neighborhood. Mokhovaya was only two blocks long. At the intersection stood a tall policeman whom Nils and I had nicknamed Pyotr Arsenich. We waved to him whenever we went by.

Directly across from our building there was a small chapel with a faded blue façade and narrow windows, outlined in gold. An icon was embedded in the wall over the entrance. I liked to sit by the window of our playroom and watch the parishioners who came to pray. I knew them by their clothes: shopkeepers, servants, factory workers. Some hesitated on the threshold and crossed themselves before entering.

Occasionally, a man would walk up the street, pause to take a bottle from his pocket, and hit the neck against the wall. I worried the jagged glass might cut his mouth as he emptied the bottle in several quick gulps. At first I thought he was drinking water. One of the servants explained it was vodka.

I wondered how this chapel happened to be on our street, wedged between two larger buildings. No one in our household seemed to know. One day I overheard Mother saying, "If only that chapel could be torn down. It only attracts undesirable people."

My bedroom windows opened onto a courtyard. I used to watch everything that went on below: the handyman—*dvornik*—chasing a stray dog or arguing with the knife grinder; our cook, off to the market; the scullery maid, Vasilisa, hurrying across the yard.

I had mixed feelings about Vasilisa, who spoke with peasant-like directness and could be quite blunt. Once I accidentally dropped a coin into her dishpan and asked her to retrieve it.

"You dropped it in. You get it out," she said with a look of disapproval. "Nothing is in there to bite you."

Knowing Vasilisa could be trusted, I fished the coin out of the greasy dishwater.

Sometimes our cook left early in the morning, before I woke up. Upon his return, choosing the right moment, I would sneak into the kitchen. I was not supposed to venture into that part of the apartment, but went anyway in order to hear Danila talk about his life, and especially his hobby, horse racing. He was always so friendly.

From my window, I sometimes caught a glimpse of a chimney sweep up on our roof. I would watch him lower a brush down a chimney, bring it up, then lower it again. He was covered in soot. Even his face was sooty. The chimney sweep did not seem quite real. It was almost as if he had jumped out of one of my storybooks.

When I think of my childhood home, I see our playroom, with the multicolored maps on all four walls. In one corner, our teddy bear; in the other, our carousel; spread out on the floor, the tracks for my trains. I used to squat for hours, trying to make two trains run simultaneously in opposite directions without colliding.

I see my brother Nils, four years my senior, at the piano. I hear him playing Schubert. Nils only touched the grand piano in the ballroom when Mother asked him to play. He hated to perform for people who had no interest in music, but Mother usually got her way. She liked to show him off in front of guests. "It's easier to play than to argue," he explained.

Our canary liked Nils's music. At the first note, the bird hopped onto

20

its perch, cocked its head, and began to sing. Its gay song carried right through the closed doors into the *prokhodnaya*, a large passageway, which suggested a gymnasium, and no wonder. Along the walls were various kinds of athletic equipment: parallel bars, a ladder, a pole for climbing, a trapeze. Father was quite a gymnast. In his youth, he had excelled in sports, especially figure skating and horseback riding.

Our lunches were served at an oval table in the *prokhodnaya*. During these meals, we sometimes heard the muffled sounds of hammer and saw, of carts unloading in the courtyard, of unfamiliar voices shouting back and forth. As children, we didn't pay much attention to the background noise. Later we came to understand its origin: Father's hobby, the renovation of buildings. Few people within his circle knew about this activity. Most considered him primarily a military man, a view reinforced by his already impressive career. Though still in his mid-forties, he was a colonel and aide-de-camp to Grand Duke Mikhail Nikolayevich, patriarch of the Romanov family.

My grandfather had introduced them during a campaign in the Caucasus. Subsequently, the grand duke's sons, Aleksander and Sergei, had invited Father to the Far East. Father's sociability made him a pleasant companion. It was on this trip that he met the tsarevich, who was to become Tsar Nicholas II.

Years later, the old grand duke remembered his sons' friend as an amiable young man and asked for his services. Father had accepted at once, and was to remain at the post for twelve years, until I was nearly eight years old. As everybody knew, Father was destined to achieve higher rank but in reality, his main interest was construction. Within the limitations imposed by his military duties, he gave himself to this activity with relish.

When home on leave, Father would spend hours in his study, examining blueprints and scribbling figures on a pad. Sometimes I watched from the divan in a corner of the room. I was allowed to sit there on the Bokhara rug if I kept quiet.

Once, he took Nils and me to a building site. Father pointed out what various workers were doing. "How's Dunya these days?" he asked the foreman.

"Much better, Your Excellency," the foreman answered, pleased that Father had remembered his wife's name.

We could see how much Father enjoyed talking to the men. I was beginning to realize he had a faculty for getting on with people. It hurt that he didn't treat us the same way. Maybe that's why I felt a little jealous of all those construction workers.

One day Father told us that, in his youth, he had envisaged a career in engineering. It was not to be, however. His father had gambled away not only what money he had, but his wife's fortune as well. Everyone in the family looked to the maternal grandmother for support. Father counted on her to finance his schooling, but Countess Elizaveta Alekseyevna Orlova-Denisova had her own ideas about his future. When he told her that he wanted to become an engineer, she said firmly, "No. I will not allow it. You must join the Guard Cossacks, the regiment in which my husband began his career."

Recalling this scene, Father described his grandmother as imperious.[2] Apparently, her manner discouraged all argument. In her eyes, only two careers were suitable for a young man of good family: diplomacy or a commission in a regiment of the Guards. Since there was no other source of money, Father had yielded to her wishes.

At twenty-eight, he married Mother. Her dowry, which included several old city properties, revived his interest in construction. Here was an opportunity to try his hand at remodeling to produce income. Father had realized that what the city needed was not additional housing for the rich, but modern apartments for the rapidly growing sector of middle-income workers. He was one of the first in St. Petersburg to act on this insight.

In making over 26 Mokhovaya Street, Father created a thirty-room apartment on the second floor of what had been a six-story Baroque-style stone mansion. Our apartment, comfortable and spacious as it was, seemed modest in comparison with some of the other homes in our neighborhood. I remember, in particular, a townhouse up the street to which I was taken every Sunday for dancing lessons. The Tolstoys had two children: a boy my age, Seryozha, and a girl, Dalechka, who was a little awkward and rather shy. Were those visits ever fun! After the lessons and the refreshments, we scattered in a wild game of hide-and-seek. Discovery followed discovery: silent rooms whose occupant, a maiden aunt, was away; backstairs, which, for some reason ran only from the third to the fourth floor; mysterious passageways. I looked forward to Sunday because those afternoons allowed me to see other boys and girls, an opportunity that did not occur often. Within my parents' milieu, it was customary for children to play only with siblings and cousins.

Even at 26 Mokhovaya Street, we were limited in our contacts. Our U-shaped apartment was divided into three separate worlds, each opening onto a different side of an inner courtyard. At one end were the pantry, the kitchen, and quarters for the menservants. Here lived Danila and his two assistants; Yegor, the butler; a footman; Father's orderly; and the chauffeur, Vlasyuk. I liked to linger in the pantry and chat with them.

Among the servants, Yegor was top man. Appropriately formal in demeanor, he seemed remote and cold. During short family absences, Yegor was left in charge of the household. It was through him that Mother learned of any problems affecting the staff. He was also the one who kept her current bottle of Chateau d'Yquem locked up and guarded her Huntley and Palmer gingersnaps. I, too, liked these cookies, but was not allowed to have any. They came from England and were said to be expensive. Whenever I tried to run off with a handful, Yegor usually caught me. He was vigilant, hard to circumvent.

After the evening meal, Yegor would withdraw to his quarters with the other servants. Unless summoned, they would not reappear until morning.

In the center of the U lived Mother and Father, each with a bedroom, bathroom, and study. Their quarters were separated from the rest of the household by the intervening living, dining, and guestrooms. Because my parents used a separate entrance and staircase, I had only a vague idea of their comings and goings.

Our ballroom was also located in the center of the U. On two of its walls, facing each other, were enormous mirrors in white frames. Under one of the mirrors stood the grand piano, covered with a red silk throw. There were draperies at the windows, a large bronze chandelier, a row of delicate white chairs.

The ballroom was used mainly for children's parties. Right before Christmas, a huge fir was set up in the middle, its top a little to one side of the chandelier. Nils and I spent hours decorating the tree with ornaments, gingerbread men, and little baskets filled with raisins and nuts. We also fastened to the branches small candleholders, each containing a brightly colored candle.

Mother invited several cousins and a few other children, including

Dalechka and Seryozha, to our Christmas party. Yegor would arrange the presents on small tables, then hide them under linen tablecloths. After he had lit the candles, we were allowed to enter, and the tablecloths were removed.

I never saw anyone dance in the ballroom except the *polotyory*, two men who came once a month to polish the floor. *Polotyory* means floor rubbers, and that's exactly what they did. Once wax had been spread on the parquet, each man attached a brush to his right foot and the pair moved along rhythmically, side by side, with their hands clasped behind their heads for better balance. After each stroke of the brush, they jerked their bodies sideways in a little dance-like movement. I liked to watch them work. When they were through, the parquet glistened.

The children's quarters were located at the opposite end of the apartment from where the servants lived, across the courtyard. Nils and I shared this wing with governesses or tutors, and three maids, including Mother's lady's maid, Emilia. The children's quarters had its own bathroom and an anteroom leading to a separate entrance and stairs. The anteroom marked the end of our domain. At that spot, an invisible line separated us from our parents' world. Children were not supposed to venture beyond the anteroom unless properly attired and on best behavior, but this regulation was not strictly enforced. To insist would have seemed too rigidly Germanic. The implicit constraint remained, nonetheless.

All told, our apartment housed twenty people. To feed everyone cost fifteen rubles a day—at the time, the equivalent of seven dollars and fifty cents.

When the food bill rose steeply, we knew Danila had lost at the races or taken to the bottle. Arguments and recriminations followed. Then everything went on as before, until the next relapse. There was never any thought of parting with Danila. His father and grandfather had cooked for the family. As a boy, Danila had been sent to France where he had learned to combine French and Russian cuisine, a skill that made him proud.

Every day after dinner, Danila would confer with Mother in her study on the next day's menu. Sometimes I listened in on these conversations, concealed behind a curtain. In this way, I learned about the servants' menu. Their food was simpler, less expensive. This information surprised me.

"Why is what the servants eat different?" I asked Mother.

"We must stay within our budget. Their food is every bit as nourishing as ours."

I did not know what the word *budget* meant, so said nothing. I was too young to challenge Mother, who usually ended such a conversation by saying we weren't rich.

My parents made such a fuss about economizing small sums that I began to believe they were hard-pressed for money. I don't know how many times I heard Father say, "Even the tsar puts out the lights when he leaves the room." Every fall, when I was being fitted for the clothes Nils had outgrown, I was reminded of the need to save. Since neither of us received an allowance, we had to haggle with Mother every time we needed money for a toy, a record, a book. This situation was demoralizing. It tempted me to help myself to candy, to small change, to anything desirable that was within reach. I pried open closets and bureau drawers. On occasion I even borrowed from the servants.

Once, at Christmas, Mother's oldest brother gave me a five-ruble gold piece. I knew there were more coins where that one had come from, so, instead of thanking him, I said, "May I have another?"

Uncle Sasha looked startled, but pulled a second gold piece from his pocket.

Later, Mother scolded me. "If you had saved what he gave you last year, you wouldn't have had to ask for more."

Save! Don't spend! Economize! These admonitions still ring in my ears. Not until my early teens did I realize that my family was quite well off. Then I felt I had been misled.

3

MOTHER'S FATHER, Nikolai Aleksandrovich Bezak, had risen to high rank in the civil service under Alexander III to become Minister of Post and Telegraph. His wife, Maria Feodorovna, was the only daughter of a landowner whose holdings included thousands of acres of woodland in the Upper Volga. Grandmother was a widow. Her sons often came to dinner. I enjoyed these evenings because the tenor of their conversation was always irreverent.

"Our government is paralyzed, morally bankrupt!" Uncle Kolya would exclaim. "It should be pouring millions into rural education. The peasants must be taught to read."

25

"No, no, no. I disagree," Uncle Sasha interrupted, spearing his fork into a breast of chicken. "Not peasant education. These *muziks* are brutes, no better than ordinary cattle. They can't be educated."

Father was seldom present. I don't know whether he felt unable to cope with his brothers-in-law or if their criticism of the government made him uneasy. Certainly he must have thought them irresponsible, people of whom one must beware lest they damage a career.

As a boy, I did not realize how eccentric Sasha was. He spoke in a high-pitched voice, alternating between Russian and French, but using each language with polished precision. My uncle had graduated with honors from the University of St. Petersburg and even served in the prestigious Chevalier Garde, but what really fascinated him was travel. Twice a year, he would set off for far-off continents, always on the fifteenth of the month, with his itinerary planned to the smallest detail. He let nothing get in the way of these voyages. When he was ordered by a commanding officer to be present at the annual regimental parade, he resigned rather than change plans.

Once Sasha, back from a trip to Africa, presented Mother with a box of chocolates. Kolya, who lived directly below us, had also joined us for dinner.

"How are you, my dear?" Sasha asked Mother as Yegor carried in the first course. "Looking lovely, as usual."

Kolya picked out a chocolate cream and popped it in his mouth. When he went for another, Mother tapped his hand playfully.

"Was your trip eventful?" Kolya asked.

Sasha smiled, and a disdainful look spread across his face. "In Kenya, they told me direct travel to Guinea was impossible. So I pulled out a map, drew a line, and said, 'This is the route I intend to take.'"

I would have liked more details, but did not dare interrupt. At the turn of the century, the only feasible way to cross Equatorial Africa from Lake Tanganyika was via canoe on the Congo River. Such a trip must have taken courage, if not foolhardy daring, an aberration of Bezak ability.[3]

"On the way back, it turned out we were late for a train connection in Greece. I rented a locomotive to catch up. If they can do it in Jules Verne, so can I," Sasha added, helping himself to a second puff pastry.

Kolya turned to Mother and said, "When the curtain rose on the first act of *A Life for the Tsar*, there was you-know-who, in his usual place."

Sasha had a favorite seat at the Imperial Marinsky Theatre: front row, third from center, right. To ensure its reservation, he employed a man who did nothing but stand in line and purchase tickets.

Sasha's employees all had unusual jobs. While traveling around the world, John Kirby, his English companion, kept a record of the type, make, and number of each locomotive. If a train happened to be pulled by a locomotive already on the list, the occasion called for champagne.

Mr. Kirby had another duty. While Sasha remained in his steamship cabin or hotel suite, the Englishman socialized with the ladies, then reported back on his conquests. How do I know? Mother talked rather naively about it.

Her second brother was much more complex. Everyone used to talk about his sharp tongue,[4] but all I remember was his kindness. Nikolai Nikolayevich, a tall, thin, distinguished looking fellow with a courtly manner, spent several months of the year in Paris. Mother told me, "He's a scholar, specializing in French civilization," but I thought of him as plain old Uncle Kolya, who brought such incredible toys at Christmas: huge teddy bears, electric trains, our carousel.

Although Sasha and Kolya always fussed over their sister, seldom did they include her in serious conversation. In fact, they treated her like a child, maintaining she had no mind of her own. Mother always defended herself whenever they teased her. Often her responses were approximate, but she didn't care. The same approach did not work too well in running a household.

At times Mother seemed to have a knack for making decisions that made no sense. If we were to appeal to Father to right some wrong, he would take her side. After the grand duke's stroke, Father spent most of his time in Cannes. During trips home, he preferred not to get involved with household squabbles. This attitude left us feeling trapped. Nils withdrew. My reaction was healthier: I threw tantrums.

I still remember one such occasion, after Mother had refused to let me have more gingersnaps. "I simply cannot stand such wild behavior," she declared. At the hallway door, she paused and added, "Before you were born, I so hoped for a girl."

I must have violently repressed my feelings of resentment, dismay, and anger. I retaliated in any way possible. Once, in the German resort of Bad Homburg, disappointed to have been excluded from a party, I hid in a wing of the hotel until late at night. Surely Mother was suffering as she had made me suffer. Surely she would welcome me back with open arms. Not at all: I received a scolding and was sent to bed without dessert.

Resistance to Mother became more intense as time went on. During the quarrels that ensued, we would not speak for days. After a while, Mother would say she couldn't stand people with long faces, and proposed that we kiss and make up.

Now that I'm older, I realize Mother had a number of very serious problems beyond those created by Father's prolonged absences. Perhaps the mental handicap of my brother George was one too many. George was eight years older than me. Our parents had taken him from doctor to doctor, all over Europe. He had had many operations, but nothing helped. His mental age remained that of a not-too-bright five-year-old.

My brother had a most unusual mathematical skill. Today such a person is called an idiot savant. The family discovered George's strange ability after he asked for calendars for Christmas. When given any date in any year, he could correctly name the day of the week on which it fell. He volunteered the answer without even a moment of hesitation.

As it became apparent that medicine would be of no help, Mother sought out Christian Science and became one of the first Christian Scientists in Russia. Perhaps her new faith helped bring about what must have been a difficult step. I was still small when she decided it would be better for George to live with an attendant, apart from the family. Grandmother offered to keep him at her apartment, so Nils and I seldom saw our brother, except during the summer.

4

OUR COUNTRY ESTATE was located near Smolensk, about two hundred miles west of Moscow. When we went to Vasilievskoye in June, we took the night train from the capital. By noon the following day, we would arrive in Tiomkino. From the window, I caught sight of the chubby stationmaster, standing on the platform to greet us. Makar Savelich, who also distributed mail for the region, kissed Mother's hand, then, with pomp, escorted the family outside where three troikas were waiting. The first, drawn by white horses, was presided over by Foma, dressed for the occasion in a black tunic over a white shirt, with a red feather in his cap. Mother usually traveled in this carriage with Nils. I followed in the second, accompanied by a governess or tutor. Other members of our party, such as Emilia, rode in the third. There was also a cart for the luggage. Danila and Yegor had already gone down the day before to make sure everything was ready for our arrival.

We were all tired, but excited on this final lap of the journey, twelve miles that seemed to last forever. It took two whole hours to travel from Tiomkino to Vasilievskoye, bumping along over an incredibly rutted and uneven dirt road. At first the road stretched through fields of rye that seemed endless. We passed through two villages, deserted but for children and a few older people. Everyone else was off working in the fields. Dressed in ragged clothing, the children stood in the doorways of their *izbas*—log cabins with thatched roofs—and watched our progress with curious, sullen stares.

Once, after torrential rain, the mud in one of the villages was so deep that the horses had to strain to get the carriages through. Our new French governess felt affronted. Was taking her along these roads some kind of practical joke? Perhaps this was the way Russians expressed their sense of humor? Apparently it was hard for her to believe roads could be in such bad condition.

After the second village, I knew we were almost home. We rode through the gates and circled the pond in front of the manor. At that point, with Foma setting the pace, all three carriages moved forward at top speed. Foma pulled up in front of the veranda with a flourish. He liked panache.

Mlle. Labouré was incredulous. Here, in remote, provincial Russia, ostensibly in the middle of nowhere, stood a handsome, two-story mansion set off by carefully landscaped grounds. *"Mais ça, c'est un château!"* she exclaimed.

Her surprise was natural. Vasilievskoye could easily have been taken for the home of some grand seigneur, elsewhere in Europe. The house had a certain elegance, perhaps due to the warmth of color in its sandstone exterior. The classical simplicity of its design was characteristic of the Palladian style favored by Charles Cameron, a Scottish architect popular in Russia in 1800.

The manor had large, airy rooms with high ceilings, decorated in pastel-colored designs and lit at night by Alladin lamps. They were surprisingly bright, even brighter than our electric lights in the city. In the attic Father had installed a large reservoir for storing water, pumped up manually from below. By force of gravity, it flowed through pipes to the two bathrooms and the pantry. Rainwater from the roof was also collected in the reservoir. Drinking water came from a spring. Even so, it had to be filtered and sometimes boiled due to the risk of cholera and typhoid.

On each side of the manor sat a guesthouse. Behind the one to the left stood a separate structure that contained the kitchen and the servants' quarters. On the right were the stables, shielded by shrubbery and trees. Here we kept a dozen or more horses, Nils's pony, and my donkey. Nearby were the greenhouses, lodging for the head gardener, a vegetable garden. Still farther off was the home of our steward. The dairy farm lay beyond that.

Vasilievskoye was named for the man who built it: Count Vasili Vasilievich Orlov-Denisov. I like to think that he influenced my life. Born on the Don, and son of a Don Cossack general, he himself became a general at thirty-one. The times seem to have brought out his abilities. Two of his exploits deserve mention. The first occurred in 1809. Russia was at war with Sweden. In one of the final battles, Orlov-Denisov led several regiments of Cossack horsemen across the frozen Gulf of Finland at night during a snowstorm, taking the Swedish army by surprise.

When Napoleon moved on Russia, Orlov-Denisov, who had retired to Vasilievskoye, was recalled to duty, and engaged the French troops as they passed through the area. The two small cannons that flanked the manor served as a reminder of that time. He also captured Marshal Murat's field kitchen, which was stored in our barn for many years until Father gave it to a museum.

The second outstanding incident in Orlov-Denisov's career came after Napoleon's army had captured Moscow. In an early morning surprise attack, Orlov-Denisov led his Cossack cavalry as the horsemen galloped toward a French camp at Tarutino. By this action, my ancestor turned the tide, touching off the retreat from Russia. Subsequently, he was designated a hero of the Napoleonic war.

Father marveled at Orlov-Denisov's daring and praised his dash, resourcefulness, and courage. "A remarkable man," Father would exclaim.

What I admired most about this ancestor was his independence of spirit. As Tolstoy portrayed him, Vasili Vasilievich was not impressed by rank or power. I wanted to be like that. To fend off Mother's arbitrary ways, I had discovered the need to make up my own mind.

DURING THE FIRST nine years of my life, I spent every summer at Vasilievskoye. One of my earliest memories takes place at night. I lie in bed but cannot sleep. The oppressive silence makes me apprehensive. Out of the darkness comes the mournful sound of a church bell. After one lonely stroke, there's a pause. Then I hear the bell again and again. It must be ten o'clock. I continue to hold my breath. There's a cemetery behind the church, and I'm afraid of cemeteries. Who knows what ghosts or other furtive creatures might be lurking there. I've heard about them from Emilia. She says the souls of the departed linger for forty days. And now the bell has stopped ringing. Cautiously I bring my head out from under the covers. All I can hear is the familiar clamor of the frogs out in the pond.

In another vision from the past, I see myself with rod and line, walking to the river. I spent many happy hours on the riverbank, perched high up in a tree. I cast my line. I have a bite. The excitement of the moment runs through me like an electric shock. I jerk the rod. Sometimes I catch the fish. Sometimes it gets away. What matters is the happiness I feel sitting there, on that branch, with the leaves rustling around me.

I liked to be alone and sought out secret hiding places. One of my favorites was in the ravine between the house and the river. A narrow bridge of white birch led across the ravine to a gazebo. Down below, the ravine was thick with bushes and vines. I managed to hack my way through this underbrush and build a little playhouse. I felt safe there. Mother was allergic to the vines.

I spent most of my time outside. One morning, after breakfast, I set off with the small rifle that Father had given me, my first firearm. As I came down the alleyway, I spotted a sparrow perched in a linden tree. I took aim, pulled the trigger. For a few moments, I thought I had missed. Then I noticed blood dripping from the branch. I felt revolted. The sparrow had been a living creature. I had not meant to kill it, not even to hurt it. I only wanted to test the new rifle.

Often I went exploring, following paths, curious to know where they might lead. One day I walked as far as I could go and reached a fence. Far away, on the horizon, stood a house that belonged to the Petrovs, our closest neighbors. They had two children my age. Once Mother took us to call, but there was no further contact. When I asked her to arrange for me to play with the children again, she did not answer. Later I learned the Petrovs were rural gentry, a different social milieu. "They're provincials," Mother told me later. "We would have nothing to talk about." That was the end of that, although I did continue to go to the edge of the estate and gaze across the field at that distant house.

EVERY MORNING I would race our fox terrier to the vegetable garden. Koubik loved strawberries, too, and was adept at picking off the ripe ones. I tried to get there first, but didn't care who won. What mattered was our complicity.

On the way back, I would stop to chat with Foma, a burly man with red hair and searching eyes. Proud to have been chosen as head coachman, he was meticulous in keeping carriages and horses in tip-top shape. Foma knew about many things, not only horses, but fishing and the weather. He was the one who told me that for use in a troika, horses had to be trained to pull together. "The outer horses have to pull sideways," he explained. "When horses are harnessed three abreast, the center horse, which is the largest, must be taught to trot while the outer horses gallop, and to walk when they trot."

After the stables, I would make a detour past the greenhouses. Mother had forbidden me to go inside. The prohibition made filching the fruit all the more tempting. If I found a window open, I would squeeze through and help myself to grapes and peaches.

The steward gave me a baby pig on my Name's Day. I called my pet Svinyusha, an endearing term for "little pig." I built a small enclosure near the kitchen door and fed Svinyusha apples. When I talked to him, he would grunt back as if to show he liked my company.

A week or so before our departure, Danila served roast pig. With disgust, I refused to touch the dish, lest I be eating one of Svinyusha's brothers or sisters. After the meal, a sudden foreboding made me rush to the enclosure. Empty! Svinyusha was gone. I stormed into the kitchen. Danila admitted that he had indeed cooked my pet...at my mother's orders.

Stunned, I slipped out of the house and ran to the ravine, consoling myself with the thought that no one could find me there. The solace I found in the Russian countryside helped. When I came home, I had bitten all my fingernails.

Much of the time I was left to myself. Nobody minded if I wandered off. I was likely to find some mushrooms for Danila to put in a pie.

VASILIEVSKOYE SEEMED made for entertaining, and, as Father told us, when Vasili Vasilievich brought his beautiful bride there in the 1800s, the estate was the scene of many parties. Now there was no social life at all and few visitors.

An infrequent caller was Father Arkadi, the rosy-cheeked priest from the Russian Orthodox Church outside Vasilievskoye's gate, built by Orlov-Denisov for the people on the estate and the neighboring villages. I remember Father Arkadi as an awkward man who was horribly dull and sipped tea noisily from the saucer. Mother felt that, if she had to receive him, one visit each summer was more than sufficient.

Another guest was Makar Savelich the postmaster who would use the post office telephone to invite himself over on the pretext of delivering the mail in person. Mother found his pushy joviality offensive, but looked forward to his visits because he always came primed with gossip, having steamed open the mail. Although he never acknowledged actually reading our correspondence, the oblique references made his snooping obvious.

"Times certainly are uncertain. I do hope the plans of your esteemed brother Nikolai Nikolayevich work out to his complete advantage, and, I might say, satisfaction," Makar Savelich declared after a letter from Uncle Kolya informed us of his decision to resign from the Ministry of the Interior.

The postmaster would also share local gossip: "Your maid Katyusha has certainly found herself a fine young man. What? She hasn't told you that she is to be married? I do declare. Well, well. You must not let her know I mentioned it."

Although indignant, Mother could not resist listening, and, when she asked Father to have a word with Makar Savelich, she did so only half-heartedly. She wasn't sure it was desirable to cut off this avenue of information altogether. Father's mail went to Cannes, so he was not inclined to reprimand the man. There was another reason for his reluctance. Father often told us the story of why he had a certain fondness for the postmaster:

"One winter I traveled to Vasilievskoye to check some repairs. On the way back, the train was delayed by a snowstorm. I found myself stranded for several hours at the station. As usual, Makar Savelich was in an expansive mood. Over a glass of tea, he confided an ardent desire for a child.

"'I hope your wish is granted,' I said sympathetically, as I warmed myself in front of the potbellied stove.

"'Alas, God has apparently not so decreed.' The postmaster's eyes then fell on a copy of *La Vie Parisienne*, which Father had been reading. 'May I?' Makar Savelich asked, picking up the magazine and leafing through the pages. The pictures featured showgirls, suggestively disrobed. 'An-h-h!' he sighed. 'What a collection of beauties! We have nothing like it in Russia.'"

Father suggested that the postmaster keep the magazine.

The following winter Father again had to make a hurried trip to Vasilievskoye. The postmaster greeted him, beaming. "Your Excellency, I cannot tell you how indebted I am," he said effusively.

"Indebted?"

"The magazine you left me with those pictures. With your help, God has been kind. Yes, just three months ago my wife presented me with a son. I beg of you, Your Excellency, since, in a manner of speaking, you had a part in this, please do us the honor, the great honor, of being the child's godfather."

IN HIS BELIEF in God's goodness, Makar Savelich was not so different from the peasants. As they saw it, God took a hand in their lives. If you lived a good life, God treated you well. If you didn't and God was angry, there might be some way to placate Him.

We saw the peasants every day but seldom exchanged words. Sometimes our fire engine was called in for a village fire. The fires occurred at night. The men would pump furiously, but with little result. We would watch the blaze consume first the thatched roofs, then the walls of the log cabins. The owners seemed resigned to their fate. "It must be the will of God," they would say.

Once in a while a group of men from one of the two villages visited Father with a petition or a grievance. Their words were respectful but their tone, surly. They might want to borrow an agricultural tool or request permission for cows to cross a meadow. Father always remained on the defensive no matter what the nature of their business was.

Peasant women were around more often than the men. Many were hired by the day to work in the gardens. I remember how they used to rake up grass clippings. Colorful in their ankle-length dresses and bright head-scarves, they would move along in unison, holding wooden rakes. They often sang as they worked. Some threw bantering remarks at Nils and me, which we tried to return in kind. Mother did not seem to know how to relate to them, so if she happened to be present, everybody felt ill at ease.

Most of the congregation of Vasilievskoye's church came from the village of Godnevo, across the river. We saw peasants at mass every Sunday, but had very little contact. I knew no peasant children in all my summers at Vasilievskoye. The only child my own age with whom I ever played was Vanya Semyonov, the steward's son.

One day Vanya approached while I was fishing. He climbed up on the branch, sat down nearby, and cast his line next to mine. Neither of us spoke for several minutes, then he said, "The fish aren't biting much today, are they? Maybe there's going to be a thunderstorm." The remark broke the ice.

We went around together a good deal that summer, but, just as his family was socially and intellectually removed from the outlook and interests of the peasants, so was my family's lifestyle, concerns, and point-of-view on a different plane from that of the steward's family. Somehow a distance, a constraint separated us. A closer relationship never developed.

I came to understand the nature of this gap several years later when I received a letter from my former friend. It began, *Your Excellency, I take the liberty of writing to beg you to grant me a request.* Vanya explained he was applying to a technical school and that my recommendation would help with admission. What a disappointment to be addressed as *Your Excellency* by someone with whom I had climbed trees, gone fishing, gathered mushrooms. For the first time in my life I realized I was cut off from some people through no will of my own. Even in the world of children, it seemed, there were inferiors, equals, and superiors.

I didn't answer Vanya. I could do nothing to help without the cooperation of my parents, and they couldn't have been more indifferent. "His father dictated that letter, and it should never have been addressed to you in the first place," Mother said with a contemptuous scowl.

NILS REMAINED my most frequent companion. We liked each other although his unemotional approach to life was very different from my spontaneity. We rode our bicycles, went rowing on the river, played croquet. He usually beat me at croquet, as he did at other games, making me feel inadequate.

What we had in common was an appreciation for music. Even in his early teens, Nils played the piano well. He could pick up almost anything by ear and read music with ease. I had none of these skills and feared I could never acquire them.

I felt inferior to Nils socially as well. My good-looking brother cut a fine figure with his dark brown eyes and curly black hair. I had ears that protruded and hair so red that once a boy yelled, "House on fire!"

Nils knew five languages, including Latin. I couldn't spell, even in Russian. My brother excelled in mathematics. I didn't. He had an amazing memory and stayed abreast of current events, reading not only the newspapers of the Right, but those of the Left, too.

Everything seemed to come easily to my brother. How could one struggle against such superiority? Finding no answer, I felt defeated and was aware that an undercurrent of hostility ran through our relationship. I repressed my anger, but it surfaced when Mother boasted about Nils. I was convinced she preferred him to me.

OUR ACTIVITIES at Vasilievskoye seldom included George. Perhaps we did not know how to behave with him or what to say. He lived on the first floor with Surem Gerasimovich Chilingarov, a man hired by my parents as his companion. Physically normal, our older brother was unable to conduct a conversation. In our eyes, he was just one of those facts of life that must be accepted. To explain his condition, Mother told us a nurse had dropped him on his head when he was a baby. We never questioned this story.

AT VASILIEVSKOYE, it sometimes rained for days on end. As soon as the bad weather broke, everyone rushed outdoors. The reappearance of the sun called for a celebration, usually a picnic. Some old peasant would claim to know the exact location of buried treasure. Adults and children would set off, some in carriages, some on horseback. We'd eat lunch, seated around a tablecloth spread on the grass, then begin to dig in the hope of finding a cache of silver coins. Towards evening, we would return home empty-handed, but pleasantly exhausted. On one such expedition, an accident occurred—a horse kicked Koubik. Our fox terrier died before we could get him home.

At noon the next day a solemn procession started off from the house. First came the footman, Dourakov, carrying a box with Koubik's remains. Mother followed with George, Nils, and me. Her Christian Science visitors trailed behind with our French tutor and Chilingarov. At a respectful distance came Foma, the servants, the gardeners, even a few peasant women attracted by this unusual event. The procession moved across the birch bridge to one of the pond's islands, where a gravesite had been prepared. Monsieur Honorat delivered a short eulogy in French, trying, without success, to share our grief as Koubik was buried.

That same afternoon, I came upon Monsieur Honorat in the garden. He seemed to be examining something. He had caught a large fly and, slowly, methodically, was tearing it apart, piece by piece. I hurried past, pretending not to have noticed. I was fortunate Monsieur Honorat took his frustrations out on an insect rather than on me. Luckily I didn't have to avoid him for long.

Several days later Father sat us down after dinner and made an announcement: "We won't be spending the summer here anymore. For a number of years I've been selling arable land to peasants on the installment plan. Now I have sold what was left of the estate, together with the manor house and grounds, to a rich merchant from Moscow. Vasilievskoye is too costly to keep up," Father added when he saw the look on our faces. "I need the money for my remodeling projects in the city."

The news came as a shock. Vasilievskoye had become our second home.

As I think back on those summers in the country, I realize there was a special quality about the place, a quality I absorbed from everything around me: the birch trees and fragrant linden; the country people who worked on the estate; my Russian nanny, Pasha.

AND SO CAME the time to say good-bye. It was a bright September day. Our luggage had been piled near the front entrance. Nils and I ran down the corridors to say a final farewell to each room. When we were ready to leave, we sat down as a family group, according to Russian custom, for a moment of prayer. "*Noo, s'Bogom*"—"God go with us"—Father said, making the sign of the cross and standing up. Silently we piled into the waiting troikas. The staff gathered in front of the veranda and removed their hats. Nils shouted, "Good-bye! Good-bye!" Foma flicked his whip and we were off. The bells on the horses' harnesses jingled softly.

Autumn came early that year. The beech trees were already shedding their leaves. At the end of the first mile, we neared the ravine. I noticed that the vines had turned crimson. As we drove on, I caught a final glimpse of the manor house. I did not know then that I was saying good-bye not just to Vasilievskoye, but to a lifestyle.

The interior of the manor house would soon burn. Father heard that, as if to chide him for selling his ancestral home, the merchant had set the mansion on fire to collect insurance. The Revolution finished off the rest. The trees were chopped down, the greenhouses were smashed, and before long there was little left. All that remained was the memory.[5]

5

"FRESH AIR IS good for you," Mother would say as she marched me off every morning with a governess or tutor. I objected to these walks, just as I balked at swallowing a spoonful of cod-liver oil before lunch. Then Mikhail Dimitrievich Kryzhanovsky came into my life, and everything changed. In fact, I could hardly wait to get outside.

My new tutor wanted to become an actor. Brimming with an enthusiasm for the performing arts that neared reverence, he confided when we met, "My brother is a tenor at the Imperial Opera. Someday I'll play Lopatkin in Chekhov's *Cherry Orchard* and Khlestakhov in Gogol's *Inspector-General*."

This attitude contrasted sharply with that of my parents who thought of actors as not quite reputable, a prejudice common in Russian society at the time. They had hired Kryzhanovsky based on the recommendation of a woman married to one of Father's fellow officers. Later I heard a rumor that Mikhail Dimitrievich had had an affair with her, a detail Mother must have ignored.

Mikhail Dimitrievich blurred his Rs and kept running out of cigarettes. I found these peculiarities endearing. After a while, I thought up a special nickname for him, an affectionate diminutive: Koukoulya.

My tutor was supposed to help with my studies. After I turned ten,

Mother arranged for me to take an examination at the nearby gymnasium so she could check up on my progress. She was unpleasantly surprised when I flunked the exam. Apparently, Koukoulya had failed to teach me to spell or to recite the Ten Commandments in proper order, or to trace the course of the Gulf Stream on a map. I couldn't have cared less. Koukoulya told fabulous stories. No sooner were we out the door than I would ask, "So, what happened?"

"Where did we leave off?" he would say before launching into the next episode.

The story I remember the best lasted several months and involved a lottery winner. With the prize money, the man bought a traveling circus, rented a barge on the Volga, loaded the tent, performers and animals onto it, and went floating down the river. He stopped with his troupe in all the towns and hamlets along the way. Before every performance, some harrowing event would occur: the barge would crash into the pier, toppling the cage that held the bear and allowing it to escape, or the tightrope walker would fall in love with a local peasant girl and fight the villain to whom she was betrothed, or panic would break out after the tent caught fire.

Koukoulya walked fast. Sometimes at a crucial juncture, he would stop in front of a theater and examine the billboard. "Wouldn't you like to see this picture? Sounds good. It's about outlaws in the Wild West."

I would have preferred he finish the story, but knew I had to wait. He was already reaching into his pocket to purchase tickets. Koukoulya couldn't resist the cinema. He showed a naïve delight in what was presented on the screen. In 1911, motion pictures were a novelty. Neighborhood theaters opened in all the residential sections of St. Petersburg. Some ran continuous performances. Their programs changed every week. I don't think we ever missed a show. Father and Mother knew nothing of these expeditions, and I was careful not to reveal what was going on.

Sometimes, when rain or snow forced us to stay indoors, Koukoulya did get around to covering more serious subjects. Instead of using a textbook, Koukoulya tried to introduce each subject through an event that captured my imagination: "About a thousand years ago, there lived a prince who ruled the Kievan state. His name was Sviatoslav. Sviatoslav was a man of great energy: brave and resourceful, quick as a panther. During his campaigns, he slept out-of-doors, using his saddle as a pillow. He spent much of his time fighting the Khazars. They were nomads from the steppes: Mongols, who harassed his state. Eventually, he beat them off and broke their power. I must say, in one respect, he was quite different from any other ruler Russia ever had." Koukoulya paused suggestively. "Sviatoslav abhorred stealth. He never tried to take his enemies by surprise." Again Koukoulya paused. "Instead, what do you suppose he did?"

"I don't know. What?"

"He sent messengers to his enemies to announce his arrival."

This story made a deep impression. The practice of letting people know when they had trespassed or offended, and you were on the move against them, had definite appeal. I made up my mind that, as an adult, I, too, would wage war this way.

At the time the Scriptures were taught in every school in Russia. Koukoulya used a textbook for my lessons in *Zakon Bozhyi*, the Law of God. During one study session, I began to fidget as he started to read from the Old Testament. I examined the picture of a benign old gentleman in flowing robes who seemed to float on a pellucid cloud, no doubt the artist's concept of God in the act of Creation.

"Do we have to read the Bible?" I blurted out when Koukoulya paused to catch his breath. "It's boring."

"Some of the sentiments are quite beautiful, quite worthy of your attention." He picked up a copy of the New Testament, and began to leaf through. "Here for instance: *Blessed are the humble, for they will inherit the earth.*"

Blessed are the humble! I liked the idea immediately. It put the powerful, the arrogant, the haughty in their proper place. It was a warning against self-importance, and a reminder of how very frail and vulnerable man is. These thoughts did not occur to me until much later, but, even as a little boy, the precept felt right. It suited my temperament and experience.

"Maybe you've heard these teachings of Christ in church."

"In church?" I murmured, trying to recall.

Every Sunday morning during winter, Mother took Nils and me to the Sheremetievs' private chapel. Apparently, she saw no inconsistency in being a Christian Scientist and joining us there. Several families had a standing invitation. I attended mass willingly in order to hear *a capella* singing. Russian church music has a serenity and fullness of emotion that can be very moving. I also enjoyed the mansion, with its fine view of the

Neva. There was a large ballroom in which we romped, a two-story high library, and many nooks and crannies to explore. We had to take an elevator to reach the chapel on the third floor. Behind the choir alcove, a spiral staircase of wrought iron led to a landing where the bell ringer sat, holding the ropes to half a dozen bells. I liked to watch and listen as he rang them in the manner traditional to the Russian Orthodox Church. The sound was so joyful.

Unfortunately, no one had bothered to explain the service to me. I had been made to understand, however, that every night before bed, I must to recite my prayers—the Lord's Prayer and a special prayer for the Virgin Mary—or else God would surely strike me down with thunder and lightning. On my eleventh birthday, I decided it was foolish to mumble prayers, simply to get through them. Surely, God would not punish me if I stopped this meaningless ritual? Gathering up my courage, I climbed into bed and went to sleep. In the morning, I ran to Koukoulya's room and tugged at his shoulder until he opened one eye.

"Guess what! Last night I didn't say my prayers and nothing happened."

"What exactly did you expect?" he said with a yawn.

6

"LOOK AT THIS," Father exclaimed, setting his glass of coffee down on the table. He held up the *Peterburgskaya Gazeta* so we could read its bold headline: "Titanic Sinks. Many Feared Lost."

"What a tragedy," he mused. "Of all things, hitting an iceberg. Who would have thought?"

"Certainly not the captain," said Nils. "He claimed even God couldn't sink his ship."

"That's arrogance for you. Tempting Providence." Father took another swallow and lowered his voice. "Never wise to do that."

Nils and I exchanged glances. Whenever Father used that tone of voice, we knew he was about to broach a difficult subject.

"By the way, we're bringing Grandmother over. A bed will be set up in the playroom. She'll be staying a few days…until she gets well. Mother thinks we can take better care of her here, but she may have pneumonia. Stay out of the playroom, at least for now."

That afternoon, our end of the apartment became strangely quiet.

People approached the playroom door on tiptoe, opening and closing it softly. They spoke in whispers. Doctor Grouss came and went. Soon he was back again. Around three in the afternoon, Mother entered the room. I did not see her come out for hours, although I kept a close watch. Emilia brought her supper on a tray. When the door opened, I caught a glimpse of Grandmother, shielded from the light by a screen. With each breath, she made a strange raspy noise. The door shut before I could get a better look.

I went to find Nils. "Grandmother must be very sick," I said.

"She may die," he commented laconically.

"Die?"

"Of course. That's what usually happens when the elderly catch pneumonia. They die."

I recognized the matter-of-fact way my brother had of expressing himself, which exasperated me at times. I didn't like to hear him say Grandmother might die, as if he didn't care. Nils was as fond of her as I was. Of that I was certain. How could he not be? She was so thoughtful, so kind, always gentle with George. And yet, she could be firm, but never arbitrary. When there was a quarrel or a misunderstanding, Grandmother would listen to all sides. In the summer, at Vasilievskoye, I used to go to her end of the house if puzzled or bothered by something. She seemed to like being sought out. Not always, of course. Not when she sat at her desk, peering through horn-rimmed glasses at a book or article.

Grandmother spent a great deal of time reading. Books, newspapers and magazines—French, Russian, English, even German—were everywhere: in the bookcase, on the table near her armchair, even on the floor. If she was immersed in a book, I knew not to disturb her. At other times she would listen, ask questions, and talk to me about all kinds of things. Many topics were beyond my grasp, such as why she liked certain authors or what it meant to be civilized or how the words we use can affect behavior—like the English word, *fairness*, for instance. "It's an English concept, a good one," she had said. "We could use a little *fairness* in Russia, but there isn't even a word to express it."

But now Grandmother was sick. She might even die.

Before dinner Kolya arrived. I saw him take out a handkerchief and dab at his eyes, as if he didn't want anyone to notice his tears.

That evening I went to bed feeling troubled. Around me in the darkness, I imagined unfamiliar and menacing forces. The night seemed heavy with foreboding. I tossed for a long time before falling asleep.

In the morning I found the playroom door open. Grandmother was no longer there. Emilia stood near the window.

"Where's Grandmother?" I asked.

"In the ballroom. Maria Feodorovna, God rest her soul, died last night."

Instead of saying *died* Emilia used the gentler way Russians have of referring to death: *Ona skonchalas*, an expression that derives from the verb *konchat*, to finish, and carries the idea that a woman has completed her stay on earth.

She turned on her heels and left. I stayed, trying to sort out my feelings. I had never experienced death before. I was aware, of course, that people died when they got old or had an accident or became very ill. To be sure, Koubik had died at Vasilievskoye, and his death had been a shock, but no person I knew had ever passed away.

I hurried to the ballroom and immediately noticed the grand piano had been pushed to one side. In its place carpenters had installed a raised platform. On the platform, I saw an open coffin in which Grandmother lay, eyes closed. Mother sat nearby with Kolya and Uncle Fedya, their younger brother from Kiev. They were talking in whispers and, at first, didn't notice me.

I looked at Grandmother's face. In life, it had always been so animated. I wondered where people went after death. I became aware of the silence in the room, the solemnity of the occasion, the presence of death not five feet away.

Seeing Grandmother in her coffin brought back a story I had read earlier in the week: *Viy*, a fearsome tale Gogol wrote about a seminarian who falls into the clutches of a witch. As I stood there, the details flooded back. With a shudder, I pictured the devastated church, the icons askew, and the bat-like creatures arrested in their flight by the coming of day, grotesquely immobilized around broken windowpanes.

Mother's voice broke into my reverie: "Here you are, Pavlik. You may go and kiss Grandmother."

I did not want to kiss a dead person, but how to avoid it? Acutely ill at ease, I stepped up to the platform and followed orders. Grandmother's forehead was cold. I felt grateful when Mother rescued me: "Don't just stand there. Go have breakfast."

THAT DAY AND the next, people came to pay respects. They looked solemn, offered condolences, and stayed only a short time.

Toward evening, Sasha arrived from abroad. He sat beside the coffin for a long while with his head bowed low, saying not a word.

Then came the day of the funeral. First there was a short service at the apartment, conducted by an elderly priest who walked with a cane. Afterwards some men in black appeared, as if out of nowhere, and carried the coffin downstairs. We put on our coats and followed. The pallbearers placed the coffin in a hearse, drawn by two black horses. Slowly it began to advance. We followed on foot. Traffic parted for us. Pedestrians crossed themselves as the cortege passed.

The bracing April air felt good, and faces brightened perceptibly. Except for the immediate family, most of the mourners acted jovially, as if they were taking part in a not-too-unpleasant social occasion. They greeted each other, moving from group to group. Some did not live in Petersburg and wanted to take full advantage of an opportunity to exchange the latest gossip.

After a long walk, we reached *Alexandro-Nevskaya Lavra*, a monastery on the outskirts of the city. Within its grounds was a cemetery. Nils read aloud the names of celebrities in politics, theater, the arts. He pointed to a bas-relief of a seagull on one grave. "Over there, that's where they buried Komissarzhevskaya, a talented actress who died young of smallpox. She's famous for her portrayal of Nina in Chekhov's play."

Before internment, we attended a funeral service in the church behind the cemetery. A choir of forty monks sang beautifully. The Russian Orthodox funeral service is called *otpetvaniye*, singing off. It ends with a mournful prayer.

As I watched the pallbearers carry the coffin outside, I wondered why I wasn't crying. Others were. Kolya cried, so did Nils and Mother. On the steps, she shot me a reproachful look.

By the time we reached the burial site, it had begun to snow. After a short service at the gravesite, the pallbearers placed the coffin next to my grandfather's crypt in a red granite mausoleum. It was simple and solid looking.

I felt very tired and glad to be driven home in Father's new Renault.

7

MR. BOYLE AND I came upon each other soon after Grandmother's death. The meeting was not an auspicious one. I had just climbed up to the exercise bar and was trying to figure out how to get down when I became aware of someone's presence.

"Why not jump?"

The English words startled me. I swung around, piqued by the mocking tone. A man with bright blue eyes stood near the door, a faint sardonic smile on his thin lips. Of medium height, he wore a tweed jacket and was perhaps in his mid-thirties.

"Why not jump," the man repeated, this time with a suggestion of finality, as if expecting to be obeyed.

I made not a move, staring down at him.

The stranger said slowly, "But I can see you're a coward."

I watched him turn and leave. At the time I knew little English, but understood it well enough to get the point: I had just been insulted. Now angry, I called to Nils, in the next room. He helped me to the floor.

"Who's that man?"

"An Irishman. A member of the British colony in Petersburg."

"What's he doing here?"

"I guess he'll be taking care of George now that Grandmother's gone. Last night I overheard Father telling Kolya that Mr. Boyle comes highly recommended by some of Mother's Christian Science friends."

"Well, I don't like this Mr. Boyle."

"Don't worry. We won't see much of him."

"How come?"

"Because he and George will stay out on Kamenny Ostrov. That's what Father said."

Nils was referring to our villa in the suburbs.

We dropped the subject and several months passed. Then summer came. Since Vasilievskoye had been sold, we went to a seaside resort in Estonia, a place on the Baltic Sea called Haapsalu. We all looked forward to our holiday, especially Mother since her best friend, Nini Voyeikov, planned a visit.

Father had rented a villa right on the water, with a comfortable porch, a library, even a billiard room. There was a guest cottage for George and Mr. Boyle. In the main house, the stairs above the second floor led to a glassed-in cupola overlooking a shady garden and the small jetty that extended into the bay. Several canoes and a rowboat were tied up at the jetty.

Those canoes gave me an idea, which I tried out that very afternoon. Whenever the breeze blew from off the sea, I paddled into the bay. I would go almost a mile before turning the canoe around. At that point I would open two umbrellas I had found in the house and coast back to shore, using them as sails. I was delighted by this exploit, my first adventure on the open sea. I went out again and again. Then one day the wind shifted. Hard as I tried, I could not row back. To my great humiliation, Mr. Boyle was obliged to rescue me.

When Mother heard what had happened, she ordered me to learn how to swim before any more canoe rides. "Surely Mr. Boyle will be glad to teach you," she said.

I tried to dissuade her, but to no avail.

Having Mr. Boyle as a swimming teacher did not appeal to me in the least. Granted, he might be good for George as Mother maintained, but there was something about him, a certain callous quality, I didn't like. His sincerity seemed forced. Besides, I well remembered our first encounter. Still, I wanted to be able to use the canoe, so I agreed. It was a decision I came to regret.

Mr. Boyle's method was simple. He took me to a bathhouse at the end of a long jetty. After we had put on our bathing trunks, he simply dumped me in the water. "Sink or swim," he called as I spluttered and struggled. When it appeared that I might sink, Mr. Boyle hauled me out. He gave me about a minute to recover, before pushing me in again.

Finally I was able to convince him to let me rest a few minutes. Once his back was turned, I ran straight to the house. Up the stairs I raced, all the way to the cupola. I slammed the door behind me and locked it. Minutes later, I saw the knob turn. Then that familiar nasal voice said, "Open up."

I wanted to shout, *Miserable cad! Tyrant!* but remained silent as Mr. Boyle would not have understood my Russian, and the right words wouldn't come in English. All I could do was clench my fists. I stood there, dripping wet. To my distress, I heard Mr. Boyle pull up a chair. He was settling in to wait, too.

Several hours passed and a thunderstorm broke overhead. The wind tore at the window frames, and a torrent of rain engulfed the house, but it was the incessant lightning that scared me the most. I felt trapped, crouched in the farthest corner of the cupola, more and more anxious with every thunderclap. Frightened as I was, I held my ground. I had sworn to myself that I would not give the bully satisfaction.

Darkness came, and the storm subsided. I heard Mr. Boyle descend the stairs, presumably on his way to supper. I unlocked the door and tip-toed to my room. I felt abused and angry, not only with Mr. Boyle, but also with Mother for letting him harass me that way. Fortunately summer was almost over. Upon our return to the city, Mr. Boyle accompanied George to the suburbs. I hoped I would never see the Irishman again.

IF MOTHER DIDN'T realize what a difficult time I was having, it might have been because she was preoccupied with her own problems. Although my parents were careful to keep up appearances, I realize now that they were both frustrated in their relations as man and wife. "I was thinking of getting a divorce," she said one day, out of the blue. Mother probably never intended to confide in me, because she quickly added, "But Nini has talked me out of it." I suspect Father of having had an affair, perhaps several, for he was quite dashing, and appreciated a pretty face.

Mother's words led me to conclude that my parents did not sleep together any more. I was too young to grasp the implications, but did register the signs. For one thing, Father's dressing room contained a single bed on which he claimed to rest after lunch. Yet I always found him there in the morning before breakfast.

No doubt Mother felt neglected by Father's long absences. Her feeling of hurt could only have been compounded by the memory of having been a court beauty herself. As lady-in-waiting to Empress Maria Feodorovna, Mother must have drawn many an admirative glance with her petite figure and lustrous black hair.

WHILE WE WERE in Estonia, Father had spent most of his time on a cruise with Nicholas II. His career had taken an upturn after the death of Grand Duke Mikhail Nikolayevich in 1910. Father had become an aide to the tsar, a post known as *fligel adjutant*. "To receive so rare an appointment delighted me," he says in his memoirs. He goes on to describe his first tour of duty:

> ...*Quickly I arranged to have my uniform altered, and went the following day to present myself to the tsar and Her Majesty.... (They) received me most cordially and said they were glad that I would be a member of the suite since they had both known me well for a long time.*
>
> *A few days after my appointment, I was assigned to a tour of duty. I entered my new duties not without pleasurable emotions, leaving for Tsarskoye Selo on the 10 o'clock train. Waiting for me at the station was a troika with three magnificent horses. It brought me quickly to the Aleksander Palace.*
>
> *I took over my duties in the quarters set aside for the duty officer, and at once proceeded to the reception rooms where ministers and other personages were already waiting for an audience. Here, too, I found the skorokhod, a minor court official, who briefed me on the day's program. Without him, it would be difficult, for he is the expert on court procedures and etiquette, knows everything, and alerts one in good time about all kinds of forthcoming events....*
>
> *For the evening meal, I was invited to the Imperial table, and it was flattering ... for it is not all fligel adjutants by any means who are honored with an invitation to have dinner in the tsar's family circle.... At the table were the tsar and the children, while the empress ate reclining on a couch and was alone in having a special vegetarian menu.*
>
> *It is interesting to be at the dinner table in such rare surroundings, forgetting entirely the honor of which one is the recipient, and to observe the Imperial family's unconstrained relations: the casual conversation, simplicity, and cordiality—this is the impression that remains....*
>
> *Service as duty officer did not come often because soon the people at the Chancellery noticed that I enjoyed the special good graces of the tsar, so that my turn to serve was skipped when it fell on days that involved interesting events, especially when there were trips to the Crimea in prospect and only certain officers were assigned.*

Still, there always seem to be intrigues at any Court and also an abominable disease—envy.

It became clear that the tsar preferred Father to the other fligel adjutants once Nicholas had arranged for his new aide to be present on several trips to the Crimea, and to the coast of Finland. The fact is the tsar felt at ease with Father. He was companionable and quite a raconteur. Besides, the tsar knew Father would not overstep his role as military aide by introducing politics or controversial subjects into the conversation.

The next promotion had come four years later.

> *On the 2nd of January, 1914, in Tsarskoye Selo, members of the tsar's suite were gathered to wish their majesties a happy New Year. At the conclusion of the ceremony, the tsar came up to me and said: "We know you well, like you, and are used to your presence, so I'm naming you commander of my Konvoy, and raising you to the rank of major general with appointment to the suite."*
>
> *I cannot express my joy at this unexpected appointment. There was no end to the congratulations I received, but not all, by far, were sincere. Especially offended was the commander of a Cossack regiment who considered himself a candidate for the post.*

The *Konvoy* was an elite Cossack regiment—men recruited from among the most outstanding Cossack troops. It had been organized a hundred years earlier, to guard Tsar Alexander I during the war against Napoleon. In recent times, this duty had been assumed by the Secret Service, and the *Konvoy* served primarily as a military escort, fulfilling a ceremonial role in accompanying the tsar. The *Konvoy*, however, remained directly under his authority through the Minister of the Court, and Father, therefore, had no other military superior—a unique situation.

"I've always wanted to be free of meddling superiors, and now it has come to pass," Father told us.

A parade of the *Konvoy* was scheduled about six months later. He arranged for Nils and me to attend. I still have vivid memories of the palace courtyard at Tsarskoye Selo, lined with *Konvoy* Cossacks, mounted on splendid steeds. Their tall hats of black Persian lamb—*papakhas*—added to their imposing stature. The empress and her daughters stood on the steps leading to the palace. A little to one side, there was a group of notables, and, among them, Nils and I, all waiting for the tsar to arrive at the reviewing stand.

Our ears caught a faint sound as of surf on a distant shore. The sound increased, and soon we could hear the voices of hundreds of civilians and soldiers who lined the avenue, all shouting "Urra-a-a-h!" as the tsar drove by in his Delaunay-Belleville. When the Imperial car appeared, the sound grew to a roar. The car stopped. The tsar stepped out. I had never seen the tsar that close before, nor the tsarevich. They both wore the *Konvoy* uniform. While the tsarevich was helped to his mother's side, the tsar mounted a handsome stallion and placed himself across from the assembled regiment. Then the commands rang out. Column after column, the *Konvoy* wheeled to the right and circled the courtyard. As the *Konvoy* reached the extreme left, it reformed in columns of twenty abreast, each led by an officer. The columns moved forward, past the tsar and the reviewing stand. Leading them all was Father, astride a white horse. In his hand, he held a bared sword. As the first column approached the tsar, Father spurred his horse into a gallop, and, executing a semicircle, took position beside the tsar.

I held my breath as Father performed this maneuver. Nils gripped my arm. We were thrilled. It was the first time in my life that I had been able to observe my father in his military role.

No one in all of Russia had a similar dress uniform: a scarlet tunic, embroidered in gold. At his belt dangled a gold dagger, a gift from the tsar. On his chest were various decorations: the Cross of Saint Vladimir, the French Legion of Honor, Bokhara's Gold Star. On the left side, he wore the white Maltese Cross of the Corps des Pages. People were always turning to look at him. I felt proud to be his son.

There was no doubt he had achieved an enviable position, but his promotion was not an altogether happy turn of events for Nils and me. We saw Father less than ever. His duties kept him constantly busy, and, as tension increased prior to World War I, his schedule at Court became more demanding.

THAT SUMMER a number of official visitors arrived in Russia. The tsar received these foreign notables at Peterhof, a palace on the Gulf of Finland. A bungalow was made available to Father for the duration of the state visits.

Our entire family joined him there, including George and, alas, Mr. Boyle.

The first official visitor after our arrival was Admiral Beatty of Great Britain. As a gesture of solidarity with Russia, he brought the First Battle Cruiser Squadron of the Royal Navy to St. Petersburg. The tsar entertained Admiral Beatty, and he, in turn, held a luncheon on his flagship, H. M. S. *Lion*.

Next to come was President Poincaré of France, his visit another gesture of Allied unity. Father rode at the head of a detachment of *Konvoy* Cossacks, behind the carriage in which the tsar brought the president of France to the palace—a most impressive ceremonial occasion, in my opinion.

At the time I wasn't old enough to grasp the significance of these state visits. I spent my days bicycling around the palace grounds, unconcerned with what was happening around me. Sometimes I would sit on a bench and admire the spectacular fountains. I also went swimming in the Gulf of Finland, played tennis with officers of the *Konvoy*, and took walks with Nils.

MY FINAL ENCOUNTER with Mr. Boyle came while we were at Peterhof. Father was off on a cruise with the tsar. Nini had a home nearby and invited Mother to visit. She left Mr. Boyle in charge of the household. I didn't learn of this arrangement until after her departure and immediately felt threatened. I was even more concerned when I learned she had left instructions for him to give dictation. Since the man could hardly speak the language, I made twice as many mistakes as usual. Mr. Boyle insisted I copy each misspelled word twenty-five times, but this hardship was nothing compared with the tyrannies that awaited me. The Irishman turned out to be a health freak. Every night before bed, he would bring in a dishpan filled with ice water for a footbath. The first two nights, I put up with this sadism, but, on the third, I balked.

"I will not put my feet in that cold water. I simply refuse."

"Oh-h-h-h!" drawled Mr. Boyle. "You won't, won't you?"

"Absolutely not."

"In that case, I will have to punish you."

Mr. Boyle seized me by the shoulders and jerked me forward so that I fell across his knee. Then he reached for a cane, apparently prepared for the occasion, and gave me a resounding whack. Indignant, I let out a yell. No one had ever laid hands on me before, and I swore to myself that no one ever would do so again. My reaction must have startled Mr. Boyle because he loosened his grip. That momentary lapse was all I needed. I wriggled out of his grasp and headed straight for Father's study and a drawer in his desk where he kept his service revolver. Seizing the gun with both hands, I pointed it at Mr. Boyle who had followed me into the room.

"Don't come one step closer."

"Put the gun down," he said.

"If you touch me, I'll kill you," I shouted.

We stood facing each other in complete silence. Several minutes passed. The situation was becoming grotesque. By then, I had calmed down somewhat and knew I wouldn't pull the trigger, although I might have hit him with the butt had he come closer. Mr. Boyle decided not to insist.

When Father and Mother returned, they had a long talk with the Irishman. Then I was summoned. They both wore pained expressions.

"We are very sorry to hear you misbehaved," Father said. "Your Mother and I have decided on a punishment. We are going to send you to school at once, that is, starting in the fall. When you were born, we had you enrolled at the Corps des Pages, but you can't go there until you're thirteen. We'll find some temporary substitute."

8

ONCE BACK in Petersburg, we moved into an apartment provided by the Crown. Located in the barracks of the *Konvoy* regiment, it overlooked the Neva. That same week my parents enrolled me at the Aleksandrovsky Kadetsky Korpus, a school that prepared boys for service as officers in the regular Russian army. Although the teachers seemed pleasant enough, I immediately sensed I might have problems getting on with my classmates. When I got home, I went to find Nils, who was playing Schubert on our new piano.

"How did it go?" he asked.

"Not too well. I don't think I like school all that much."

"Well, what did you expect? It's not the Corps des Pages."

I hadn't known what to expect. I had never been to school before.

"Somehow I feel uncomfortable there," I added.

"Everyone else comes from a less privileged background. That's probably why."

As usual, Nils was right. As soon as my classmates became aware of Father's position at court, they kept their distance. My occasional arrival in a chauffeur-driven car did not improve the situation. Not that they were unfriendly. It was just that differences in status and worldly goods got in our way. I felt isolated. One bright spot was French class. I was the only pupil who already spoke the language. It's not surprising the others considered me the teacher's pet.

"Flaubert, c'est un nom célèbre," Monsieur Flaubert announced with pride as he paced up and down the classroom.

My classmates exchanged glances. One shrugged. The name may have been famous in France, but none of us had heard it before.

"Préférez-vous vivre ici plutot qu'en France?" I inquired after class.

"Je préfère vivre ici," Monsieur Flaubert said, not too enthusiastically. The pale gray eyes peering over his spectacles had a wistful look.

I remained unconvinced. What mattered was that a bond had been created between us. We shared an intense loneliness.

One morning my teacher did not show up for class. I found out that he had called in sick. When he did not appear for several days, I decided to bring him a present to cheer him up. With the three rubles I had saved, I went to Yeliseev's, the best deli in Petersburg, and bought a chocolate cake. Clutching the package under my arm, I set out to find his apartment.

Monsieur Flaubert lived on Vasilievsky Ostrov, in a drab section of the city. After a long search, I located the right street, then the right house number. I climbed three flights of stairs to his apartment. The door was ajar. I knocked anyway. Since there was no answer, I pushed open the door. Clothing, books, and dishes were scattered about. My teacher had been sleeping, dressed in a pink bathrobe. He looked up with feverish eyes, surprised to see me. "Oh, it's you," he said. "Don't come too close. I have a high temperature."

I placed the box on the table and stepped back. I watched as he raised himself in bed, which took effort. His face was flushed, his hair, rumpled.

"I've brought you a present. I got it just for you. I hope you like it."

"Thank you so much," he said with a gracious smile. "Now you had better leave."

"I hope you will get well soon. How do you feel?"

"Not so good."

"Have you seen a doctor?"

"Not yet, but one is coming. You really should go," he said again. "What I have may be contagious."

For a few seconds I stood on the threshold, reluctant to leave. "I hope you get well soon," I repeated and closed the door behind me.

A week later came the announcement that we were to have a new French teacher. Monsieur Flaubert's illness, I learned, was diphtheria. Shortly after my visit, he had been taken to the hospital where he died. I reacted to this news with dismay and sorrow but went about my business as usual. That was a gloomy period in my life. I was just beginning to get used to going to school every morning in the dark. During the winter months, it didn't get light until midmorning. I could scarcely see the streetcar.

Not long after Monsieur Flaubert's death, I learned the mark I had received for good behavior had been lowered. I had been very proud of my high mark and demanded to know why the report card had been altered. My homeroom teacher refused to answer.

That afternoon I reported the incident to Nils.

"I can guess why," he said. "Yesterday Mother was talking on the phone to someone at your school. I heard her say it was odd that you had been given such a high mark. '*It must be a mistake. He behaves so badly at home.*'"

A few days later, in choral class, I lost my voice. Singing had been one of my favorite activities. At about the same time, I discovered I could no longer digest anything. Since the school lunches were making me sick, Mother called the doctor.

Dr. Grouss poked my abdomen, shook his head, and prescribed a daily enema with warm oil. He did not completely overlook the emotional factor, because he added, "Perhaps Pavlik should have lunch elsewhere."

Fortunately, Ella Grabbe Phalen, a newly married cousin, lived near the school and invited me over. I enjoyed going to her apartment and those lunches were delicious.

ONE DAY ELLA took me to a matinee performance of the circus. My favorite act was the jugglers. I watched with fascination as Rossi threw plates into the air until he had nine moving at once.

As soon as I got home, I searched for something to juggle. That very night, I practiced throwing some old tennis balls into the air, first one, then two, eventually three. After a while my juggling improved. I was delighted with this new skill. I only practiced at night, after everyone else had gone to bed. I didn't give my valet, Matvei, a demonstration until my technique was perfect. He whistled appreciation. Here was something no one else in the family could do, not even Nils.

"That's quite a trick," my brother exclaimed, watching me juggle three oranges. I knew he was sincere. Nils could never have learned to juggle, even if he had tried.

My spirits rose and soon my health improved.

IN THE FALL, I started the Corps des Pages. There were sixteen of us in class. One-third were boarders; the rest, day students. Most came from a milieu like my own. This similarity was no coincidence. To qualify for admission, a pupil had to be the son or grandson of a general or civil servant of high rank. He was commissioned an officer after seven years of study and usually entered the Imperial Guard, the elite corps of the Russian army. First the graduate had to apply to the regiment of his choice and be accepted by its officers. Acceptance was based on personality, family background, and character, determined, in part, by the candidate's reputation.

The Corps des Pages was located in the center of the city, around the corner from the Nevsky Prospect. It occupied the Vorontsov Palace, donated by Tsar Alexander I in 1810. Previously, the palace had been the headquarters of the Knights of Saint John, after Bonaparte drove them from Malta. The imposing three-story building was surrounded by a garden with ancient trees and pathways where we younger boys would romp after lunch.

For the first few months, I had to work hard due to my lack of preparation. We studied Russian, French, German, geography, geology, physics, geometry, and arithmetic. Of course, we also had gymnastics and military drill, as well as religious studies. My favorite subjects were Russian and geography, probably because my teachers were outstanding.

Valentin Mikhailovich Pushin would lumber into the classroom at 9:59 and lower himself ponderously into a chair. "Good morning," he would mumble. From an inner pocket would appear pencil and notebook. We would wait while he scribbled some last thought on a pad of paper.

When, at last, Professor Pushin began to speak, his features would come alive and his voice would resonate with emotion. Some of the time he read passages from the Russian classics out loud. Through his teaching, I became aware of Pushkin's felicitous use of language and Gogol's unique writing style. Valentin Mikhailovich inspired me to start reading. Thanks to Nils, who had accumulated quite a book collection, by the time I was fifteen, I had read most of Pushkin, Chekhov, and Turgenev.

The other teacher I remember well was Staff Captain Boris Ivanovich Chizhov, who taught geography. A wiry man in his mid-thirties, Captain Chizhov strode around the classroom, gesturing. What he had in common with Professor Pushin was dedication to his subject. Chizhov would unroll the map above the blackboard, point to a country, and ask us to describe its physical characteristics, climate, and natural resources. "What are the people like? How do they live? What do they believe in?" Without waiting for a response, he would launch into an exciting lecture, which provided the answers.

I admired Captain Chizhov so much that halfway through the school year I took up a collection among my classmates and bought him a small Fabergé Easter egg. Solemnly we presented it to him at the end of class. "How wonderful!" he said with surprise. "I'll wear it on my watch chain."

I did not realize how lucky I was to have good teachers. Had I known, I might not have listened to my cousin Nika, a glamorous officer in the Horse Guards and recent Corps des Pages graduate. "Hey, Pavlik," he said at a Christmas party. "Why work so hard? Grades aren't all that important. It's much better to be sociable than studious. You'll graduate, no matter what."

I took his advice to heart. Naturally, my grades began to fall.

About to fail Russian history, I made an eleventh-hour attempt to pass the examination. The night before the exam, I stayed up late, memorizing one hundred and twenty dates. In the morning, I was able to answer every question correctly. The head teacher shook his head. "Your record couldn't be worse," he said, stroking his white beard. "Yet your answers are correct. I feel there's something not quite right here, but can't figure out what." He conferred with colleagues and gave me a barely passing grade.

My marks soon reached an all-time low. Paradoxically, bad grades enhanced my standing with classmates. They hated *zubrilas*—nerds—and looked up to boys who were athletic or showed initiative. I fitted into the later category.

One fine spring day, I noticed a ledge outside the classroom window, barely wide enough for access. I climbed outside. Soon I found myself on the roof. Glancing below, I caught sight of our homeroom teacher, Lieutenant Colonel Zarzhevski, with an attractive blonde. I rounded up some classmates and showed them the secret passageway. From the roof, we watched the plump colonel, smiling and gesturing as he escorted his lady friend to the street. Up until then, we had all suffered from Zarzhevski's strict discipline. After some of us dropped a hint or two, his attitude changed dramatically.

WHILE I GOT on well with my classmates, I couldn't share their enthusiasm for military matters. Parades, uniforms, and decorations fascinated them. They looked down on service in the regular army as somehow demeaning. I couldn't have cared less about the relative merits of certain regiments and especially disliked military drills.

The drills reminded me of my childhood, and specifically of times when Nini and her husband, Vladimir Nikolaievich Voyeikov, then a colonel in the Imperial Hussars, had come to call. Mother had bought custom uniforms of his regiment and made us wear them every time the Voyeikovs visited her. While Mother and Nini chatted, Voyeikov would line us up and make us march around the room, bellowing orders. I hated him with all my heart. Nils did, too. Voyeikov never came when Father was home, although they had been Corps des Pages classmates.

Lieutenant Colonel Zarzhevski had a hard time teaching me to salute or stand at attention. "Don't you want to be an officer?" he asked.

I didn't. I had decided not to remain in the army beyond the years required for military service. To special friends I had even confided that I intended to spend my life visiting the oppressed and dispossessed of the world as a traveling bishop.

When I mentioned my disinclination for the military, Father said, "But you come from a military background. You are aware that twelve members of our family attended the Corps des Pages? You're the thirteenth. Your grandfather was a general, as were three of your great-grandfathers. We even named you after one of them."

If I had been able to read Paul Khristoforovich Grabbe's memoirs[6] at the time, I might have felt differently about a military career. All the more so if I had realized there was a great deal more involved than marching drills. No one had bothered to tell me about military science or encouraged my proclivity for games involving strategy and planning. I must say, however, that I had come to enjoy the Corps des Pages more every day. I would leave home looking forward to school. When my education was cut short by the Revolution, I regretted being deprived of what had become a true haven.

9

ON A BALMY June day in 1915, Nils and I were on our way to Bogorodskoye, Mother's small estate to the southeast of Moscow. For years we had wondered what it looked like. How would Bogorodskoye compare with Vasilievskoye? Now, at last, we would have an answer. The little bells on the troika's harness jangled faintly as our carriage made a sharp turn and entered the village of Lounino. Ahead of us, the road ended at a tall fence, almost hidden from view by a profusion of lilac bushes in full bloom. We caught a glimpse of a gate and, beyond it, a two-story building of pink sandstone.

"This must be it," Nils exclaimed. "We're here."

We were both in fine spirits, excited to be on our own. Mother had been delayed in the city. Only the French governess, Mlle. Vernier, and my new tutor, Volkov, whom we called Vladimir Aleksan'ch, had accompanied us. I liked him already. I could tell Mlle. Vernier did, too. Nils and I felt we could cope with both of them, especially the pretty mademoiselle who didn't seem to understand much Russian.

As our troika drove along Lounino's main street, Foma had to slow the horses. Pigs, scrawny chickens, and small children scattered on all sides. To judge from the sagging roofs, the inhabitants were poor, yet the village had its own church, set off by a white picket fence. In contrast to the impoverished surroundings, the church had been freshly painted, as had the priest's residence.

Outside the church there was unusual activity. A peasant, wearing a shirt embroidered in red, hammered a nail into the porch steps. A second, on a ladder, had just replaced a broken windowpane. A third was adjusting something in the belfry. A burly man in a dark, flowing vestment stood below, in charge of this work.

"That must be the priest," said Nils. "Let's ask what's going on." Foma stopped the troika so Nils could get out. "*Zdrastvuitye*. Good day to you. We've just arrived to spend the summer at Bogorodskoye. You are Father—"

"Lavrenti. Heard you were coming. Delighted to have you here. As you can see, we're sprucing things up a bit."

"Preparing for a holiday?"

"Oh, no. We're getting ready to receive His Eminence the Bishop. He's coming from Ryazan."

"Here?"

"Indeed, for his annual visit. He should arrive on Tuesday."

Impatient to reach the estate, we climbed back into the troika. When we drove up to Bogorodskoye, Yegor appeared at the door. We barely greeted him, so eager were we to explore the manor house. The terrace offered a nice view of the Oka, flowing from one side of the horizon to the other through low-lying grasslands. A major tributary of the Volga, the river joined the main stream farther east.

While we were standing there on the bluff, a passenger steamer plied past. We saw it stop to let a herd of cattle swim across the river. Then someone with a deep voice said, "Those cows aren't part of the estate. They belong to peasants from the village. They'll swim back before sundown and find their way home."

We turned to face a stocky man with a surprisingly small head, which he bowed a bit too reverently.

"Sidorov, at your service. The hunting here is quite good, especially duck hunting in these marshes." He pointed toward the river. In his other hand, the steward held an Irish setter on a leash. I didn't like the way he gestured or his shifty eyes. What's more, he was addressing Nils, not me. I narrowed my eyes as he continued speaking. "I'd like Your Excellency to accept this little token. I'm sure you will find him to be a splendid hunting dog."

"Thank you. We'll let you know if there is anything we need."

Sidorov appeared disappointed. Apparently, he expected more in the way of thanks. He had no idea that Nils never used a gun, whereas I was just beginning to acquire a taste for hunting. In any case, I was irked that he considered my brother important enough to merit a present.

Nils handed me the leash as soon as the steward had left. "Here.

You take him. You can also have that shotgun Father gave me. Bring us a couple of ducks some day for supper, will you?" While I was petting the dog, Nils added, "Did you notice those wooden cases on the pantry floor, beside the basement door?" He could not restrain an impish grin.

"Cases?"

"Two cases of Mother's wine. You heard what Father Lavrenti said about the bishop." Nils paused. "Why not entertain him when he gets here? Invite the local clergy to supper. We'll have Danila prepare a feast and treat them to some of Mother's wine."

"Sounds like a great idea."

"I'm not so sure about that," said Vladimir Aleksan'ch, who had just joined us outside. "The supper, sure. Why, not? But I don't think it would be right for you to serve your mother's wine without asking her permission first. Just think about it for a moment. The wine isn't yours to give away. It wouldn't be right."

My tutor kept on talking, but we weren't listening, too pleased with ourselves. What made our plan all the more thrilling was the fact that we had hit on a seemingly legitimate reason to appropriate Mother's wine.

The next few days went by in hasty preparation. There were conferences with Danila on the menu, the drafting of a letter of invitation to the bishop, a general tidying up to do.

By then we had explored every inch of the estate and decided we liked it a lot. The house was comfortable, the grounds attractive. It was the kind of place so often featured in Turgenev's stories: a peaceful rural setting, deep in the Russian countryside. There was an apple orchard, a tennis court, a vegetable garden. We had our bicycles and horses for riding. We could go swimming or fishing in the river. On rainy days, Nils could play his piano, and I had the player organ to keep me occupied. Although the estate was smaller than Vasilievskoye, it seemed to answer all our needs. A major difference was the proximity of the two villages. Lounino was practically on our doorstep, yet we were hardly aware of it. Lounino seemed a totally different world.

By Monday, the preparations were complete. The bishop had accepted for himself and six others.

On Tuesday, promptly at six-thirty, he emerged from the church and strode toward the house. With him came Father Lavrenti, the deacon, two priests from neighboring parishes, and two monks. We greeted our guests and led them inside. The bishop was a solidly built man in his mid-fifties, vigorous for his age. He had a dignified manner, but what struck me the most was the benign expression that lit up his face. As we seated ourselves around the table, I noticed he wore around his neck a simple but solid-looking silver cross, suspended from a chain. He often reached for the cross as if to remind himself that, although the setting was secular, he remained a man of God.

The bishop seemed in excellent spirits. He cracked jokes and made no secret of the fact that he was partial to good food. Danila did not disappoint him.

We started with borsch with sour cream. When everyone was served, the bishop bent his head over clasped hands and uttered a short prayer. He spoke softly but distinctly, as if addressing someone beyond our hearing: "Oh God, on Thee do we depend for our sustenance, and Thou givest us our food in good time."

After the prayer, he made the sign of the cross. We followed suit. Yegor chose that moment to serve the *piroshki*, some filled with chopped cabbage, others with kasha.

"Excellent borsch," said the bishop.

"The *piroshki* couldn't be better," added Father Lavrenti.

For the next course, Yegor brought in a platter barely large enough to hold a fifteen-pound fish called a *som*, caught in the Oka that day. It had the snout of a bulldog, the whiskers of a cat, and was garnished with hardboiled eggs, sautéed mushrooms, slices of lemon, and springs of parsley. A sauce béarnaise enhanced the fish. At this point, Yegor uncorked several of Mother's bottles and began pouring wine.

"Ahhh!" exclaimed the bishop. "How did you guess? Chateau d'Yquem. My favorite."

"Glad to hear it," said Nils, rising. He raised his glass and offered a toast.

After the fish came roast duck served with brown rice, baked apples, and green beans. And, all the while, Yegor kept busy filling glasses. Cucumber salad followed the duck. Dessert was a *bombe surprise*. Danila took great pride in this specialty: vanilla ice cream in the form of a large cone with shredded chocolate hidden inside.

Conversation ranged from a discussion of country life and Tolstoy's views on religion, to whether or not the *sterlet*, a species of sturgeon renowned for its caviar, could still be found in the Oka.

"I used to go fishing and still know some of the local fishermen by name," confided the bishop.

The monks listened in respectful silence, from time to time exchanging comments on the food. Vladimir Aleksan'ch also ate in silence, as did Mlle. Vernier. The only time I entered the conversation was to ask Father Lavrenti about duck hunting in the region.

After supper, coffee was served in the living room. Then Nils entertained the guests by playing Chopin. Finally, the Bishop indicated it was time to leave.

"Do take home some wine as a souvenir," said Nils, distributing the bottles that were left in the second case.

"You didn't need to give away all the wine," my tutor said once the door had closed. "Your mother won't be at all pleased."

He was right. Mother arrived with George a few days later and discovered her wine was all gone. She scolded Nils and made me do penance by reading Tolstoy's *War and Peace* aloud every afternoon for a week, but it was Vladimir Aleksan'ch whom she held responsible.

Relations between Mother and my tutor deteriorated fast. Sometimes she spoke to him sharply, almost as if he were a servant. Vladimir Aleksan'ch was an engineering student who had accepted the summer job to pay his tuition. She didn't seem to grasp his equivocal position in the household. He kept his dignity by managing never to talk back. I knew of this unfortunate situation and was genuinely sorry, realizing our prank had contributed to her negative first impression. The fact is I had grown fond of him. There were so many things we liked to do together.

A favorite pastime was waiting in a rowboat near the shore, until a tug pulling several barges passed. We'd row like madmen to catch up, and tie our boat to the dinghy trailing behind the last barge. Then, as we were towed upstream, we would spend the afternoon enjoying the fresh air, the sun, the sense of movement. Eventually, we would untie the rope and let the current carry us back downstream. As the boat drifted, we fished or jumped into the Oka for a swim. We planned our day so we would reach Bogorodskoye in time for supper.

We also played a variant of hide and seek. It went like this: on a scrap of paper, I would scribble a note, designating the location where I planned to leave a second note. I would dash off on my bicycle to the spot indicated. Vladimir Aleksan'ch would wait five minutes, then read the first note and set off after me, also by bike. My companion got into the spirit of the game. At his suggestion, sometimes we would reverse roles. He made a wonderful playmate and was a thoroughly admirable person.

Then the blow came.

Someone told Emilia my tutor had been observed in the garden, making love to the French mademoiselle. That was all Mother needed to hear. Although the summer was not even half over, she fired Vladimir Aleksan'ch and told him to leave on the next train. I knew nothing of any of this until he knocked at my door to say good-bye.

Flabbergasted, I pleaded, "Do you really have to go?"

"I do."

"Can't I persuade you to stay?"

"Afraid not. I have to leave."

We stood there for a moment, looking at each other. I felt baffled and hurt. What else could his departure mean if not rejection?

Vladimir Aleksan'ch shifted his weight to the other foot, before saying, "Unfortunately the situation is such that I have to leave, but before I go, I want to tell you something. I've had it on my mind for a while and may not have another chance."

"Have I offended you?"

"Not at all. It has nothing to do with our relationship." He paused. "Some of the things you do…and I hope we know each other well enough for me to be frank."

I listened, waiting.

"For instance, this business about the wine. Giving away what wasn't yours. A small matter, you may say, but is it really? You've also shared stealing candy, or sneaking into locked greenhouses, or taking loose change. Well, as a friend, I need to tell you, don't do it. Apparently, we differ on what we consider right and wrong. I believe that any wrong you do to others will bounce back and hurt you."

I listened intently, my eyes on his suitcase.

"What I believe is this: when you take what isn't yours, you steal part of yourself, part of your self-respect. That's dangerous. It you twist the truth for your own purposes, you end up a lesser person. What you are doing is chipping away at your self-esteem, when your goal in life should be to grow, to expand awareness so as to become a better person. The choice is yours to make. Do you understand?"

Abruptly, Vladimir Alexand'ch looked away. "It's time for me to go. I've probably already said too much. I'm so very sorry to have to leave you. Believe me."

I followed him outside. "Good-bye," I said as he stepped into the carriage. "I'm sorry, too."

We both waved. In another minute, the carriage had disappeared beyond the gate. Later that afternoon, I pried the truth out of Emilia. For the next hour, I stomped up and down in my room, but the anger, the hurt, stayed bottled up inside.

FROM THAT DAY on I busied myself in various ways, mostly away from home. In the branches of a scraggly oak, I built a treehouse in which I spent hours alone, just ruminating or reading the humorist Averchenko.

It was around this time that I developed a new interest—duck hunting—and found a friend to share it with me: Fedyushkin, Father's orderly. With his thick black beard and long dagger, he looked quite fierce, but was actually gentle and perceptive. He taught me not only how to carry a gun, but also how to clean it, and even how to make cartridges.

Before daybreak, Fedyushkin took me down to the Oka where we dismounted and tied our horses to a tree. We crossed the river in a rowboat and walked about a mile through marshland. There was special stillness in the air. Even faint sounds carried great distances—the sluicing sound of oars in water, the distant jangle of cowbells, a dog's far-off bark. It was still dark when we reached a small pond.

"This place is alive with ducks," Fedyushkin said in a low voice. "Hundreds of them, hidden in the reeds."

As dawn tinted the sky a pale orange, we crouched at the water's edge. Suddenly our ears caught the whistle of ducks in flight. In a moment they would be upon us, flying overhead. The ducks came whizzing past so fast that it took a sharp eye to bring any down. I took aim at a duck that had landed nearby, but Fedyushkin stopped me.

"No, Pavel Aleksandrovitch. Never shoot a duck except on the wing."

"Why not?"

"Because...." He stopped to think. "A duck is a creature of God. It's only right to give it a chance to get away."

The first time we went duck hunting, I had beginner's luck and bagged a dozen.

We returned from these expeditions late in the morning, tired but exhilarated. Usually, there was no one else around. The war had started, and, with the exorbitant price of powder, the peasants could no longer afford to hunt. At first I took along our new hunting dog, but soon changed my mind. At the first shot, instead of leaping forward to retrieve the bird, the setter fled in panic. Sidorov must have known all along. He wasn't the sort to give away anything of value.

We took the shortest way home, past a village, until an unpleasant incident forced us to change our route: a group of peasant boys appeared from behind a shed and started throwing stones. For the first time in my life, I became aware of the peasants' hostility to rich landowners and their sons.

After each hunt, I cleaned my gun. I spent part of every afternoon preparing cartridges for use the following day. To get money for gunpowder, blank cartridges, and shot, I made a fabulous deal with Danila, which, at first, worked to everyone's advantage. He would buy the contents of my bag, and I would use the money to send off to Moscow for ammunition.

One day Danila told me Mother had discovered this arrangement and forbidden him from buying anything more from me.

I located Mother who was on the porch. She put down her book and said with a frown, "You should be glad to contribute those ducks to the household, rather than make some commercial venture out of it."

This was too much. Losing my tutor was injustice enough. To be deprived again so overwhelmed me that I could only stare straight ahead. I walked slowly over to the window and thrust my fist through the pane.

"What have you done?" Mother exclaimed. "Here, let me see. Have you cut yourself?" I extended my bleeding hand. She recoiled at the sight of blood. "Go get a bandage from Yegor. And be sure to tell him that I want that pane replaced at once."

For a long time I had been unable to express my feelings. Apparently, I could only do so by hurting myself. The summer ended on this discordant note.

10

WE RETURNED to Bogorodskoye in 1916. My impression of the steward had not changed. Sensing my animosity, Sidorov kept his distance. At harvest time, somebody noticed no apples were served at dinner.

"Why is that?" Mother asked.

"There are none," the steward explained. "The trees you have here produce only every other year."

The next day we took a walk in the orchard. Sure enough, there were no apples.

Several days later I made a discovery. The lanky stable boy couldn't resist showing off a silver ruble the steward had given him.

"Was it a birthday present?"

"Trofim Petrovich gave it to me for picking apples," Ivanushka said with a sheepish grin.

I slipped him a coin to learn more.

"Come see," he said in a confidential tone, leading the way to a shed behind the stables.

"No doubt about it," I reported to Father. "The shed is full of pippins, the sour-sweet apples we like so much. Sidorov must sell them in the nearest town and pocket the money. You should fire him."

To my surprise, Father did not seem at all concerned. "So what?" he remarked calmly. "In other regards, he's a good man."

The matter seemed to end there. Yet, during the next few days, Father spent an inordinate amount of time checking the accounts. He discovered the steward had been stealing from the estate for over a year. Reluctantly he decided to let him go.

Father allowed Sidorov to keep the job until the end of the year instead of giving a week's notice. What a mistake that was. As soon as we had returned to the city, the steward got rid of everything he could. He found someone to buy the remaining fruit and vegetables. He sold the barnyard fowl, the pigs, the cows, the funny-looking goat we had nicknamed Grishka, even the grain stored in a bin, the lumber in the yard, some of our furniture, and a decrepit carriage you'd think no one would have wanted. Having thus enriched himself at our expense, the man vanished.

I felt furious. What irked me the most was that Father had vacillated when the situation demanded decisiveness. Dimly I recognized the same shortcoming in myself. I, too, avoided conflict. But it was much easier to add this incident to a long list of grievances and blame Father. I took the matter up with Nils.

"Doesn't he seem different from us? He shows absolutely no interest in our activities," I complained. When my brother didn't respond, I added, "What do you think?" He looked up from his newspaper and shrugged. "The very things we like he won't share."

"Like Beethoven?"

"Exactly. He listens to Delibes and Offenbach."

In conversation, Father sometimes mentioned sailing. He never failed to say how much he enjoyed the sport. From occasional remarks, we learned he owned a sailboat, which he kept at the Imperial Yacht Club. We gathered, too, that he considered himself quite a sailor, but neither Nils nor I had ever seen the boat. For years I thought Father couldn't be bothered to take us sailing. Now I realize the boat was in one compartment of his life, while family was in another. In his world, children stayed at home with the governess. They were not taken to the Imperial Yacht Club of St. Petersburg.

Still I wish things could have been different. Try as I might, I can only recall two occasions when he and I were alone together. Both are happy memories. I have already described the railroad accident. The second also happened early in my life. I must have been eight at the time. We were at a German spa called Vildbad. Father had run out of cigarettes and asked me to fetch some from the store. How proud I was to have been entrusted with this mission. I crossed the mountain stream that flowed past our hotel and followed the woodland path to the village at the bottom of the hill. I bought the cigarettes, ran back with them, and gave Father the change. He said, "You did that well," and kissed me on the cheek. Then we went for a walk in the woods together. I was in seventh heaven.

There were times when Father took Nils and me, sometimes Mother too, on excursions. I recall with special pleasure our visit aboard the tsar's yacht, *Standart*, at the pier in Yalta. The tsar was not on board, so we were able to explore. Father showed us his cabin. One of the officers brought me a delicious pastry. I was particularly impressed with the highly polished mahogany paneling in the dining salon. If I had been older, I might have noticed the sense of hushed efficiency that pervaded the yacht. "A floating palace," Nils remarked later.

We were both delighted with our visit. Such moments were rare, so rare that I held it against Father for not spending more time with me. I now see he had no choice. I was too young to grasp the dimensions of his world or the nature of problems at Court. He said little about them at home. Only occasionally did something happen that hinted at what those problems might be.

For instance, I remember a conversation late in 1916. Uncle Sasha's erstwhile companion had come to dinner. John Kirby had become an affluent businessman, a butter baron with dealings in Canada and Denmark. He offered to transfer abroad a substantial sum of money, perhaps a quarter of a million rubles: "Nobody will know it's yours."

"Thank you, but I can't do that," Father replied.

I could not understand why he would refuse such an offer. I knew his pioneering efforts in the renovation of St. Petersburg buildings had paid off. On his fiftieth birthday, four months after the start of World War I, he had become a millionaire. "Why not transfer money out of the country?" I asked after John Kirby had left.

"That would be unpatriotic in time of war."

To transfer money out of the country in wartime wasn't only unpatriotic. In Father's eyes, it would have been a sign of disloyalty. He felt a strong allegiance to the tsar although his relationship with the empress had already become strained, as I would learn later.

Everything began in the fall of 1914. The empress had heard about George's condition and, through an intermediary, suggested it might be a good idea for Father to meet Rasputin. Although aware of Aleksandra Feodorovna's faith in the healing powers of the *starets,* and of the possible consequences of a refusal, Father had declined. The risk of being tagged as someone who consorted with Rasputin was too great. This refusal had resulted in an immediate cooling of Father's relationship with the empress.

More problems arose unexpectedly in 1915. Injured in a train wreck, Anna Virubova, close friend and confidante of the empress, demanded that the *Konvoy* sergeant, who had rescued her, be promoted. When Father refused, Anna Virubova declared, "If that's the way it is, so be it. But just you wait and see. You'll have reason to remember me."

Father soon found out how vindictive Virubova could be. She seized the first opportunity to do him harm. In September 1916, the war with Germany had been underway for two years, and Father was with the tsar at General Headquarters in Mogilev. The empress was at Tsarskoye Selo. Virubova reported to her that Father was using tennis as a pretext for bringing the tsar together with the glamorous wife of a young officer. The empress, a jealous woman, believed every word:

> *Please don't let them present Mme. Soldatenko (her italics) to you – you remember I told you I had the conviction Grabbe wants to do it. And fancy that nasty man had the idiocy of telling Nini, his friend, that he hoped I will not be going now to Headquarters so as to get you acquainted with her & that she might become your mistress....*

Father did not learn that the tsar had tried to defend him until after the 1933 publication of the tsar's correspondence with the empress:

> *What you told me yesterday of Grabbe and what he told Nini (Voyeikov) greatly surprised me. I remember some time in the summer, Igor (Prince Igor Konstantinovitch, cousin of the tsar) spoke of arranging tennis here, expressing the hope that I would come and watch the play. I answered that he should mind his own business and not interfere with other people's. The same evening at tea I was left alone with Grabbe, and he told me how right I was to refuse to visit that place, which is frequented by Mme. Soldatenko and other ladies, as it would probably have given rise to all sorts of absurd gossip. So I do not know how to reconcile these two facts – I mean, what Grabbe told Nini and then me.[7]*

Despite this exchange of letters, the empress had apparently persuaded her husband to offer Father another assignment. To quote Father:

> *The tsar quite casually offered me the command of an army division. I thanked him but declined, saying I planned to retire soon. A few weeks later, the tsar again offered to appoint me, this time, Ataman of the Don, a post that had meanwhile become vacant. I again declined, suggesting in my place, my brother Mikhail. But this time I asked if the offer meant that the tsar was dissatisfied with me in any respect. This he denied, assuring me that he*

would take my suggestion and insisting that our relations had not changed. But I knew otherwise. I had been at Court too long not to know that anyone who incurred the disapproval of the empress did not stay around very long.

At this point, Father came to see that the relationship was no longer one of mutual trust. What sadness he must have felt at realizing the tsar could be influenced by Virubova's vicious slander. It must have been hard for the tsar, too, as Father was one of the few disinterested people around him. He was making the necessary preparations for retirement from the Army when the Revolution intervened.[8]

11

A GROUP OF us had gathered in our living room and were looking out the window. On Mother's left, Nils and I. To her right, Cossack Captain Makoukho, in command of the Petrograd contingent of the *Konvoy*. Several regimental officers waited nearby. Mother was leaning forward to get a better view. The captain, a big man, stood erect. He seemed more imperturbable than ever, his Oriental eyes fixed on the scene below. The frozen river shone in the sunlight. Fresh snow had fallen on its icy surface during the night. The Neva looked dazzlingly white and empty, like a frozen plain in some winter landscape. It was very cold that Monday morning, March 12, 1917.

"Any word from Aleksander Nikolayevich?" Captain Makoukho asked Mother.

"Not since last Wednesday. He must still be at General Headquarters with the tsar."

We kept our eyes on the Liteiny Bridge. On its farther side, something out of the ordinary was happening. A barricade had been set up in the middle of the bridge. On our side stood soldiers with fixed bayonets; on the other, a large crowd heaved and surged. I could see people waving banners. Soon the crowd pressed against the barricade.

"Will the barricade hold?" one of the officers said.

"The police had better stop this disturbance before it gets out of hand," Captain Makoukho replied.

The crowd continued to push forward. For a moment, we thought it would be contained. On our side of the river, a tank advanced toward the bridge. Then, in quick succession, two armored vehicles and more soldiers appeared. A detachment of mounted police rode briskly by, under our windows. Minutes passed. All of a sudden, the crowd broke through the barricade. A great mass of humanity swarmed across the bridge. It seemed to engulf the soldiers, the tank, the police, everything.

"Look at that!" gasped Nils, almost in a whisper.

A Cossack lieutenant entered the room. I knew this officer well and had nicknamed him Shamyl. We used to play tennis together at Peterhof. He was always impeccably dressed, had a powerful serve, and beat me regularly. Playing with him had improved my game. Now Shamyl's uniform was not quite as neat as I remembered. From the grim look on his face, I could tell he was upset.

"Units of the Volynsky Regiment have mutinied. They've rushed from their barracks, in defiance of their officers. A message just came through that they have joined the revolutionary crowds. The revolutionaries have invaded the detention prison there, on the opposite bank," Shamyl managed to say, trying to stay calm. "They've opened the cells, released prisoners. Stores are being looted."

As we took in this information, we kept our eyes on the scene below. By now the crowd was surging along the quay in front of the *Konvoy* barracks.

"We'll be able to see better from my room," Nils said. "Let's go."

I followed him down the hall, and we stationed ourselves near one of the windows.

The dense crowd continued to move past our building—soldiers and sailors, waving red flags and brandishing guns; university and gymnasium students in school uniforms, many wearing red armbands; nondescript civilians, clerks, and workers; and, here and there, inmates, still clad in prison clothes.

"What if some of them take potshots at us?"

Nils scoffed at this idea. "Why would they bother? They have bigger things on their mind."

"Where can they be going?"

"To the Duma, no doubt."

The Duma, Imperial Russia's legislative assembly, had become, of late, the scene of virulent criticism against the regime. It met in the Tauride Palace, a short distance away, and turned out to be the focal point of the Revolution.

Despite Nils's words, I lowered myself to the floor. With my back to the window, I held up a hand mirror and tried to use it as a periscope. This didn't work too well, so soon I stood up again, losing interest in the crowd. I felt like a spectator at some parade and had only a vague idea of the whys and wherefores of the uprising. The implications escaped me. In any case, I did not think it concerned me much. What did matter was that my holiday from school would probably be extended. That made me happy.

For the past few days, Mother had kept me home. "The streets are no longer safe," she had said.

True enough. Excited, unruly crowds filled the center of town. They marched around holding signs that read, *Peace, Bread, Land.* The police were barely able to contain the demonstrations.

Food shortages had developed in the capital. Flour had become scarce, creating a run on bakeries. People were going hungry. Hunger made them angry.

Thanks to Danila's foresight, our menu remained unchanged. He reported long lines of resentful men and women queuing up in the bitter cold to buy bread. Danila shook his head as he added, "Many workers are on strike. Revolutionary songs can be heard on the streets."

It was clear that feeling was running high not only against the tsar, but also against anyone who appeared to be well dressed.

Other serious incidents had already occurred. On the previous afternoon, when Nils had gone to the library on Nevsky Prospect, he had seen troops open fire on a crowd that refused to disperse. Within seconds, the street became deserted except for the people lying dead or wounded. Many had been passersby, like Nils. Soon after he returned home, one of his friends phoned to say Georgi Vuich, a boy two grades ahead of me at the Corps, had been set upon by rioters and thrown into a canal. He had drowned before anyone could come to his aid.

"The Corps uniform is what did it," Nils said. "That uniform spells privilege."

Apparently the school authorities agreed. We had received instructions to remove, from our epaulets, the tsar's gold monogram—NII. I avoided doing so as long as possible, not because of any special loyalty to the tsar, but for aesthetic reasons. Many of the other boys so identified with the monarchy that removing those epaulets seemed a form of betrayal.

The telephone rang throughout the day. Friends kept calling with conflicting reports. Some said troops loyal to the tsar were about to quell the rebellion. Others sounded full of gloom and spoke of their fear that the tsar would abdicate, plunging the country into chaos.

The sun went down and night came. Around eight o'clock, we heard insistent pounding on our door. Yegor opened it and several disheveled soldiers pushed their way in. With them came two young sailors whose navy caps were angled cockily on their heads.

"*Obysk!*"—"A search!" the leader shouted. "Where are your weapons?"

Without waiting for an answer, the intruders trooped into the living room, casting curious glances at the furnishings. Mother, Nils, and Yegor followed them into Father's study. I trailed behind, aware of the threat of violence. I kept my eye on the leader, a thin man with a livid scar. Two clips of machine gun bullets made an X on this chest.

"Aha, weapons!" exclaimed one of the sailors and lifted an ancient pistol from a display of antique arms.

"Put that back," the leader said. "It's of no use to us."

The men stood around for a few moments, then turned and left.

"What is the world coming to?" said Yegor as he closed the front door. "How do they dare?"

Only minutes after the soldiers raided our home, a shot rang out. Apparently their search of another apartment had met with resistance. Captain Makoukho reassured us that the leader probably had fired his gun as a warning. We might have been less fortunate. General G. E. Stackelberg, who lived on Millionnaya Street, was shot during a similar raid.

The first day of the Revolution finally drew to a close.

The following morning Captain Makoukho stopped by to report the upheaval had been relatively bloodless. He sounded discouraged. "The rest of the country has not yet taken part in the uprising and knows next to nothing of what is happening in Petrograd. The probable reason that you have still not heard from Aleksander Nikolayevich is that he must be in the Imperial train with the tsar. It left General Headquarters for Tsarskoye Selo. The tsar has given no indication that he might abdicate, but already a new government is forming. A Soviet of Workers Deputies has also been created. Both meet in the same building, the Tauride Palace."

THE TSAR abdicated in Pskov on March 15, 1917. Although Father was not present when Nicholas made this crucial decision, the two men were alone shortly afterward in the dining car where they chatted briefly over a glass of tea. As soon as Father got home, he recounted their conversation: "The tsar said in a matter-of-fact voice, 'Now that I am about to be freed of my responsibilities to the nation, perhaps I can fulfill my life's desire—to have a farm, somewhere in England. What do you think?' Only then—too late—was I being asked for my thoughts. 'What do I think?' I said. 'What will become of you, of us, of Russia, now that these questionable characters are in control? Your Majesty, this is a tragic step you have taken.'"

"How did he react?" Nils asked.

"Didn't say a word. His face showed no emotion, although he did seem hurt when he left the dining car."

None of us spoke, imagining the scene.

"I could have made a stir, forced my way past the guards, and allowed myself to be carried from the train by force. Everybody would have said, 'How admirable. How loyal. What devotion.' But I already knew I had been excluded from the tsar's entourage. I couldn't bring myself to make this futile gesture. Playing to the gallery at such an historic moment? No, I could not."

As I recall his wistful tone, I wonder whether he wasn't sorry that he hadn't done just that.[9]

"At least I was able to take care of my men," he added. "I initiated procedures to have them sent to the Caucasus and reassigned there as a group. My argument, that the *Konvoy* was closely identified with the tsar, proved persuasive. The Provisional Government is glad to see it go."

Father had arranged to have all the *Konvoy* contingents stationed in or near the capital—as many as three hundred men with families, horses, and personal belongings—board trains in the capital and at Tsarskoye Selo and return home, a task which must not have been easy in time of internal crisis and war. Then he presented himself to General Alekseyev, who was in command in Mogilev, and requested authorization to either retire or take a leave of absence. At first, the Chief of Staff refused, Father had reported, saying, "You have now come under my command." But General Alekseyev must have changed his mind, for the next day Father was able to return to Petrograd. He had immediately tendered his resignation to the Ministry of War and was retired from the army.

On the third day after the Revolution had begun, Nils and I ventured out of the apartment to reconnoiter. Outside, everything seemed peaceful, but, when we reached Liteiny Prospect, we were struck by the emptiness of this usually busy thoroughfare. The shops were closed, the streetcars were not running, and there were few pedestrians and no traffic. Only military cars, manned by soldiers and armed civilians, dashed about. A block further, we came upon the smoldering ruins of the Circuit Court. We looked for a newspaper, but couldn't find a kiosk or store that remained open. On our way home, we took a side street and passed what looked like a pile of logs; it turned out to be the bodies of dead policemen, stacked like firewood and partially covered with snow.

"Ugh!" I said, turning away.

"The crowd took it out on the police."

We hurried along in silence.

"I have to find out what's going on at the Tauride Palace," Nils said as we neared the *Konvoy* barracks. "That seems to be where things are happening."

We parted on the doorstep. I found Mother at home. She, too, had gone for a walk. I could immediately tell something had upset her.

"Imagine," she exclaimed as I tried to slip past. "I ran into Countess Sheremetiev and how do you suppose she greeted me? She said, 'Isn't it wonderful?' and I said, 'What's wonderful?' and she said, 'Why, the Revolution, of course!' and I said, 'Really, Countess. You're hardly the one to rejoice. It is precisely people like us who stand to lose everything.'"

I didn't pay much attention to Mother, preoccupied by what I myself had witnessed. I was beginning to realize the Revolution meant something different for everyone. While Countess Sheremetiev saw it as progress toward a better society, Mother could see only ominous signs for the future. For my valet, however, the Revolution seemed to hold the promise of a better day—Matvei planned to open a shoemaker's shop.

12

FATHER HAD arranged to have all the *Konvoy* contingents stationed in or near Petrograd—as many as three hundred men with families, horses, and personal belongings—board trains and return home, a task that must not have been easy in time of internal crisis and war.

Before the *Konvoy*'s departure, its officers gave a farewell party in our apartment. This party had curious repercussions for me. It so happened that my valet, an unexpectedly resourceful man, saw a way of turning the event to our mutual advantage.

Muscular and broad-shouldered, Matvei was a citified peasant who had lived long enough in the capital to learn its ways. As part of our morning routine, he would regale me with stories of his life, tall tales that invariably involved women. Garrulous and sometimes insolent, he had a strong element of the rogue in him. I enjoyed hearing about his conquests because the details were so unexpected. I would listen, fascinated, as he strutted around the room, boasting.

"Would you believe it?" he'd say. "In church Sunday, I guess it was a week ago, I met this girl from my home province, from Tambov. A pretty little thing, solidly build and ample where it matters. Well, as we walked along the avenue, chatting sort of friendly-like, suddenly she stopped. 'Here we are,' said she, pointing at a house across the street. 'That's where I live.' She led me up the backstairs of her master's apartment—the family was away somewhere—settled me in the pantry and treated me to wine, cheese, and freshly salted cucumbers. Mmm, delicious."

He rubbed his knee while savoring these pleasurable memories.

"You don't stand on ceremony in a case like that. Get 'er legs up and go to it." He paused again reflectively. "What a gal."

Matvei was also a great source of information on what went on in our household. On the morning after the officers' party, he woke me up at seven, as usual: "Time to get up, Pavel Aleksandrovitch." I watched him open the curtains and hang my clothes on a chair in front of the tile stove, which he had lit. From the look on his face, I knew he couldn't wait to tell me something. After I had sat up, he pulled on my socks, then, able to contain himself no longer, said in a lowered voice, "A lot of liquor was left in your Father's rooms last night. Nobody has removed it yet." He glanced at me to gauge my reaction and added, "I could get you a tidy sum for what's left in those half-empty bottles."

I stopped buttoning my shirt. "What did you say?"

"When your father's orderly cleans up later this morning, he'll take the vodka and he'll take the Cognac, and he'll sell it. Sure enough, that's what he'll do. He'll get fifty rubles for the vodka, I reckon. So, why let him make money when I can sell it for you, just as easily, with a ten-percent commission? That would leave you at least ninety rubles. You'd certainly have plenty of use for that."

"I guess so," I said uncertainly.

"It's about time you had some experience."

"What do you mean?"

"You know, women. And I can arrange that for you."

"Yes, of course."

I felt embarrassed and wanted to break off the conversation. Sex was never mentioned in our family, at least not in my presence. There were few even oblique references. Once, at dinner, I had heard Kolya make a joke about "woman as a receptacle"—a play on words. I wouldn't have noticed, except Mother hushed him up.

And then there was the time Kolya told a story about Sasha, unaware that I was listening. It seems Sasha had been asked if there were any difference between prostitutes in different parts of that world, and had answered, "Don't know really. Too much bother. Getting undressed, and then, well, you have to get dressed again." At that point everyone had laughed, and I had wondered what was so funny.

I did not learn anything about the relationship between men and women, or even where babies came from, until I entered Aleksandrovsky Kadetsky Korpus. Then a flood of information and misinformation poured over me. At home, only Matvei talked freely.

"You're fifteen. Not a kid anymore. I know a nice little gal here in town. You can stay a couple of hours, and it will only cost ten rubles, a bargain these days, with prices rising. You don't want to be like your brother Nils, now do you?"

"What's the matter with Nils?"

"He's afraid of women. If you ask me, I don't think he's had anything to do with them yet, and he's already nineteen."

"How do you know?"

"Time and again, I've tried to get him interested, but he won't make a move. Afraid, that's what he is."

"Really?"

"You don't want to be like your brother, now do you?"

"Uh...."

"Let me arrange a meeting with this wench."

"I have no money."

"Oh, but you do. Go into your father's study while everyone is asleep. Empty the open bottles into these buckets. Make sure you leave something in each bottle so as not to attract suspicion. Then, turn the buckets over to me. I'll do the rest. It's your father's orderly or you, so how about it?"

Armed with the two buckets, though still hesitant, I tiptoed into the study. The room was a shambles. Bottles, cigarettes, ashes, dirty plates were everywhere as if the occupants had been called away unexpectedly. Everything was quiet except for the pounding of my heart. I moved around the room, picking up bottles and emptying them as fast as possible. Then, with the vodka bucket in one hand and the Cognac bucket in the other, I hurried back to Matvei. He cast a quick look of approval at the contents.

"A good haul. More vodka that I expected."

The next morning, Matvei brought me one hundred rubles and I counted out his ten percent. I stuck twenty rubles in my pocket and hid the rest under the blotter on my desk. Then we were ready for our expedition. We took the streetcar up Liteiny Prospect, transferred, and got off near the railroad station. I followed my valet down a side street and into a poorly lit building.

"Wait here a minute," Matvei said as we reached the landing. He knocked on a door and it opened a crack. There was a brief discussion. Matvei motioned for me to approach. "I've arranged everything. Go inside and wait. She's agreed to make it a real bargain because it's the first time, only ten rubles. Don't forget to give her the money before you leave."

He hastened down the stairs while I stood there. Well, I had come this far. I might as well go all the way. Screwing up my courage, I went in and closed the door.

The small room was sparsely furnished. I took off my overcoat and hung it on a peg. I felt nervous, as if I had an appointment with a dentist. In fact, the place reminded me of a dentist's waiting room. Trying to look nonchalant, I picked a newspaper up from the table and started to read, but it was impossible to concentrate.

"Good morning," someone said. An attractive brunette stood on the threshold. Through her negligee I could see an ample figure and large breasts. She gave me a quick—but not unfriendly—look. "Nervous? Don't worry. It's going to be fine. Follow me."

The back room was even smaller. A huge bed was almost all it contained.

"Aren't you going to take off your clothes?" she said.

Awkwardly I began to untie my shoes. I removed my socks, then my shirt.

"I see you didn't bring anything to protect yourself."

I didn't know what she meant. "I guess not," I agreed.

"Well, you should have. My advice is never to have anything to do with a strange woman without protecting yourself."

I was silent. She reached into a drawer and handed me something.

"Here," she said. "Take it. And use it. Yes, use it."

Try as I might to remember what happened next, all that comes to mind is a merry-go-round with horses going up and down. Her voice I remember well. It was gentle and reassuring.

When I handed her a ten-ruble bank note, she smiled. "My name is Sonia. If you want to come back, I'll be glad to see you."

Although I never returned, I felt grateful. I have always liked the name Sonia.

WHEN I GOT home, I found Nils waiting behind the door. He grabbed my sleeve so I couldn't squeeze past.

"Guess what! Last night a battery across the river had its guns trained on this building. It took a lot of doing by Father's friend Tereshchenko— he's in the new government—to keep them from blowing up the barracks, and, all the while, we were sleeping peacefully."

While Nils was talking, I couldn't help but wonder whether he was really afraid of women, as Matvei claimed. My valet tended to exaggerate, and Nils would never tell. Still, only a short time earlier, when our conversation had touched on sex, he had made a face and said, "Disgusting!" Where could he have gotten that idea?

Nils blabbered on: "Kerensky is the man to watch. The others? Well, they can't cope. Mark my word. Oh, yes. Kerensky is the man."

That night, as I went to sleep, I thought over the day's events and again recalled what Matvei had said. Nils was my brother, yet what did I know about him? That he was brilliant and against the Revolution. Wasn't there more? He never discussed feelings. None of his school friends ever came over. Was that because Mother had managed to embarrass one of them once? It was more likely that he preferred solitude, studying a Wagner score or reading. He always had his head in a book, even on the street, as he walked along twirling his cane, oblivious to others. Temperamentally, we were different. Even in his music, Nils didn't express feelings. When I tried to tell a story, he tapped his foot with impatience. Perhaps I bored him. After all, he was four years older. Still, I was the first to experience a woman.

13

AS THE TURMOIL of the Revolution subsided and summer arrived, Father decided times were still too uncertain for us to bury ourselves in the country. Instead, with Grand Duke Georgi Mikhailovich, the tsar's uncle, we rented a villa in Finland, not far from Petrograd. The grand duke brought with him to Rettiaervi Villa his secretary, a personal valet, and an excellent cook for whose presence we were grateful. There was always caviar on the table, and I helped myself liberally, much to Mother's disapproval. She enjoined me to show more restraint: "Our share of the expenses does not include caviar."

Talk at dinner reflected everyone's concern about recent developments. Georgi Mikhailovich was torn between his desire to be with his family, in England, and loyalty to Russia. He felt it would be unseemly, even unpatriotic, to leave the country in time of crisis.[10] To allay his anxiety, he asked us to play three-handed bridge. Nils already knew the game and taught me.

WHEN WE RETURNED to our suburban villa later in the summer, the capital was ominously still. The Bolsheviks had tried to stage a coup, and Lenin was in town. Although I followed these events in the newspapers, I must admit I was more interested in having a good time. Every afternoon I played tennis with the golden-haired daughter of the banker who lived across the street. We even went to a costume ball together.

Meanwhile, Father's friends kept urging him to leave the capital. "Association with the tsar makes it risky for you to stay here," I heard one of them say. "Why not seek temporary refuge in some remote provincial town?"

At first Father was skeptical, but, once convinced, he acted quickly, buying tickets for Sochi, a semitropical resort on the Black Sea. Within a week we were on our way. The whole family didn't go. Nils, recently graduated from the Imperial Aleksander Lycée, was still at officers' training school, and planned to join us later; George remained in Petrograd under Yegor's supervision. Before our departure, Father rented our suburban villa to a candy manufacturer. As a deposit, we received eighty pounds of chocolate, an unusual arrangement dreamt up by Mother. Chocolate was becoming scarce, and she wanted to be sure to have enough for the entire trip.

And so, one evening in late August, Vlasyouk drove us to the railroad station where we boarded the fast train for the Caucasus. Our party also included Emilia, Fedyushkin, and Bullo, our French bulldog.

In those days Sochi was not widely known, nor was it easy to reach. To get to the resort, we had to change trains, sit up all night in an omnibus, and hire a boat for the last fifty miles. We were advised not to attempt this lap of our journey by car because bandits controlled the entire coastal highway.

When our motorboat reached Sochi, it docked at the Caucasian Riviera Hotel. Beyond the imposing white buildings we could see a distant chain of snowcapped mountains, the main range of the Caucasus. The town was located several miles inland. It had a few stores, a post office, a movie theater.

SIX MONTHS passed and there was still little evidence of the Revolution in Sochi. Most of the hotel guests spent their days enjoying the sunshine on the beach or lounging on their balconies. In bad weather, people stayed indoors and played cards. They also congregated in the game room where I met Seryozha Safonov, son of a rich Moscow merchant. As might be expected, Seryozha was always well supplied with money. He paid for our pool table and treated me to chocolate bars, which had become astronomically expensive. I relished his largess because Mother was niggardly. She even had special tongs for cutting her chocolate into small pieces.

Tall, blue-eyed Seryozha fascinated me. I had never met anyone quite like him. He parted his hair in the middle rather too carefully and wore flashy sports shirts, open at the neck. Watching him interact with older women, I half-believed the stories he told about his conquests.

Once Seryozha said, "Say, how do you view women? Do you look on them primarily as persons or as females?"

We were standing on the jetty in front of the hotel, and the question was rather unexpected. I wasn't sure what he was driving at. "It all depends," I said to gain time.

He didn't wait for me to come up with an answer. "I look on women as females. Women need to feel they are attractive. I tell them so. It sure pays off. Why, I could have a different woman every night if I wanted."

I knew he was boasting but thought I might learn something if I encouraged him to talk. "How would you do that?"

"I've got a system. Without a system, you're lost. It takes planning, scouting around."

"Did you say scouting?"

"I did. Take this hotel. I started with the blonde who handles reservations. I bought her candy and made a few compliments about her hair—buttered her up, in other words—until she let me see the hotel register."

"What good was that?"

"It's essential. The register gave me the names and room numbers of all the single women staying here. I copied them off, all those who might be divorced, widowed, or without husbands. Then I started my investigation on the third floor of the main building. I watched women come and go. In this way I picked out the ones I liked best and eliminated those with children, aunts, or other relatives in tow. That narrowed the possibilities."

"Go on," I said, incredulous.

"Having chosen a particular woman, I wait for her to come back from the beach, then knock on her door. When she opens it, I look embarrassed and say my sister Nadia had asked me to meet her there. I introduce myself and start a conversation. I look surprised because Nadia still hasn't arrived and say she must be on her way. 'May I wait for her a few minutes?' I ask. And by that time, I'm already inside, so I sit down and pay my hostess some compliment like, *You certainly have beautiful eyes.* A little obvious, but when it comes to compliments, women drink in whatever you dish out." He stopped to ponder this deep truth.

"What next, you probably wonder? Time to play my second trump card. In case you didn't know, women don't like to be dragged off to bed right off the bat. A little romancing is in order. I say that I have never met anyone so attractive, that she looks just like a rose. I tell her that, in fact,

I'd like to bring her some roses if she'll permit it. She laughs and says, 'You're a funny one.' Then I say, 'My sister doesn't seem to be coming after all,' get up and leave. The groundwork is laid."

"What then?"

"I wait a day or two and return with roses. The method is foolproof." There was a brief silence. "Of course you have to have a little capital. Not much, but something to invest, like any other enterprise, for the candy and flowers. Why not try? It works like a charm."

"I have no money."

"Get your hands on some."

"Not so easy. Where?"

Seryozha raised his eyebrows. His face tightened, making him look like a hunting dog on a hot spoor. "There you go," he said, draping one arm around my shoulder. "First I gather you have no woman, and now you tell me you have no money. No matter what you're after, things don't drop into your lap. You have to provoke them."

"How?"

"In your case, get hold of money. Persuade your parents to give you some."

"They say they don't have any."

"Nonsense. That's a way to hold you off. I saw your father paying the hotel clerk. His wallet was bulging with thousand-ruble notes while you're so broke you can't rent a pool table. He wouldn't even feel it if you were to relieve him of a few thousand."

"But how?"

With a curt nod, Seryozha walked away, and I concluded it was all talk. A week later, however, I ran into him again.

"I think I've solved your problem," he said.

"What problem?"

"I've found a way to get money out of your parents."

"You have? How?"

"Simple. Kidnap yourself and ask for a ransom"

"That's preposterous."

"Not in the least. It can be done, easily in fact."

Seryozha amazed me. All the things he could dream up!

His voice became that of a merchant making a sales pitch. "There was a kidnapping in the next town last month. You must have read about it in the paper. Why not here? Anyhow, I've already planned everything."

When he saw the disbelief on my face, he added, "No, really. I've got two friends, a pianist and a violinist. They share an apartment near the movie theater. We talked over your problem. In fact, I've arranged to take you there some evening. They agree to put you up, for a small fee, of course. You and I can write a note to your father, saying that you'll be released as soon as he delivers five thousand rubles to some tree stump. Meanwhile, you stay in hiding, and I'll keep you posted. Then we collect the money. One thousand for each of my friends, one thousand for me, two thousand for you. All that's required is a little daring."

"Much too impractical."

I thought that if I put the matter in these terms, Seryozha would give up, but he wasn't deterred. He thought a minute and said, "Maybe you think your father loves his money more than he loves you? Maybe you're afraid to put him to the test?"

"I'm not afraid. Let's do it."

Two days later, after dark, Seryozha led the way up a flight of stairs, on a street behind the movie house, and introduced me to his friends. We sat down around the kitchen table. Soon we had composed a note. The pianist printed it in red ink and signed in capital letters: The Mark of the Red Hoof. I spent the next few days in the musicians' apartment. I did not like either of them and must admit, I had begun to have second thoughts.

On the third day Seryozha came by and announced Father had done nothing. There had been some vague rumors about me at the hotel, but it appeared my parents had not told anybody I had disappeared, not even the police. This raised a problem. If he ignored the note and no money was left in the tree, what happened next? I asked Seryozha but he couldn't answer.

As I stood by the window, watching him disappear in the distance, suddenly I felt freed of his influence. What a fool I had been. My feeling of humiliation brought back the words of Vladimir Aleksan'ch. *Any wrong you do to others will hurt you, too.* At last I understood what he meant. Father must have realized what was going on. To make amends, I had to reappear somehow at the hotel without embarrassing anyone, my parents or myself. But how? Was there a way?

By the time Seryozha and the musicians returned, I had devised a plan. Words like *police* and *implicated* made them agree to help. So it happened that, after midnight, we all started out on a long walk. Our destination was a bench on a lonely path, which hugged the shoreline. As I had anticipated, no one was about at that hour. The musicians tied me to the bench. I asked them to tighten the rope around my ankles and put a handkerchief in my mouth. One said, "Hope you'll be all right." With that, they hurried down the path without a backward glance.

And then I was alone, facing myself. I knew sitting there all night wouldn't be fun. October nights in Sochi could be chilly. But that was the way it had to be. My family would look to me to find a way of saving face, and this had to be it.

I sat there waiting, grimly patient. Before me extended the sea, motionless and black. There was no moon. Waves lapped at the shore. Occasionally a seagull screeched, but otherwise there was no sound. An hour passed, then another. A breeze sprang up and gradually penetrated my clothing. The rope bit into my skin. I cursed myself. What had possessed me anyway? The money? Perhaps some impulse I didn't even understand? If anyone were to accept my story that the kidnappers had abandoned me there, I would need to be knocked out, incoherent enough to persuade people I had not engineered the whole thing myself.

Before dawn a man approached. From the way he lurched along unsteadily, I concluded he was on his way home from some party. As he drew nearer, I started making noises to attract his attention. He took one look, then veered away.

Another hour passed. In the sky I noticed the first light of dawn. My legs had begun to throb. The rope was probably interfering with my circulation. As the sun rose on the horizon, a man and a woman walked briskly in my direction, no doubt hotel employees on their way to work.

"Look over there," the woman exclaimed.

I made more noises in my throat, thinking this time surely I would be freed, but no. Instead of untying me, they whispered to each other and hurried off. Again I found myself alone. By then I felt quite numb and desperately cold. I comforted myself with the thought someone was bound to find me. And so they did. Two detectives drove up in a car. Apparently, the couple had gone to the police. The detectives took me to the police station and phoned my parents.

Father was silent on the way back to the hotel. As our taxi arrived at the entrance, he turned and said, "We received a letter from Prince Oldenburg. He's up north somewhere and invites us to stay in one of the apartments in his palace. We've decided to move. Nils has arrived from Petrograd. He and Mother have left already. The car for Gagri will pick us up at noon, so try and get some sleep."

He didn't scold or ask for details. In fact, for years no one in the family mentioned the kidnapping.

In time, however, I was reminded of the incident. Father's jealous younger brother Michael couldn't resist: "It's perfectly obvious he kidnapped himself."

Father never told me what Uncle Misha had said. Mother did.

14

"GAGRI SEEMS like an ideal place to sit things out," Father said as we took up residence. "The Revolution may never get here."

Judging from outward appearances, he was right. The town was too remote, its population of artisans and merchants too provincial to keep pace with political developments in the far-off capital. Even after the Bolshevik takeover in the cities, there had been no arrests, no searches. The Soviet was made up of local people who wouldn't think of bothering anybody.

One of the tsar's relatives discovered Gagri while exploring the coast. Prince Aleksander Petrovich Oldenburg had been so charmed by the village that he decided to turn it into a Russian Cannes, and ordered a large hotel built at the base of the highest mountain. Up the road, Prince Oldenburg had a palace constructed for his own use. We arrived at this palace in mid-November, 1917. Everything seemed peaceful. The weather was mild. We looked forward to enjoying a winter of sunshine. Although not entirely reassured about our situation, we hoped for the best.

Right before Christmas, relatives of the Oldenburgs, who were also seeking refuge from the Revolution, moved into the apartment above us. To celebrate the New Year 1918, Count Zarnekau and his wife gave a midnight supper in the banquet hall. The display of sabers and antique guns was decorated for the occasion with flowers. The long table, set for fifty, looked festive with ruby goblets, silver epergnes, and handsome English china. I marveled that our host had been able to procure legs of lamb, hams, and local delicacies.

During supper, each guest made a short speech, and then, following an old Caucasian custom, drained a hunting horn full of wine. We toasted the tsar, the empress, the tsarevich—at the time, captives of the Bolshvik regime—as well as the Russian army. I was almost sixteen and this was my first adult party. I was thoroughly enjoying the delicious food until I realized it would be my turn next. Fortunately, our host made sure the horn was only half full when he passed it to me. I toasted the New Year and what it would bring. Looking back, I am appalled to think that probably not one of the people present realized a complete break with the past had already occurred, making us all outcasts.

JANUARY PASSED quietly, except that a destroyer of the Russian Navy, commandeered by mutineers, anchored briefly near the town pier. Loaded with sugar stolen from an army depot further south, it was proceeding up the coast, selling the already scarce commodity along the way.

Then February came, and with it rumors of searches and arrests in the larger towns along the coast. By then, we had been in Gagri for almost three months, unaffected by events elsewhere, but Father feared that sooner or later the Revolution would catch up. As if to confirm his fears, we learned civil war had broken out in Southern Russia. We were completely cut off from our bank in Petrograd. At about that same time, mail service ceased and telegrams could no longer be sent to the capital.

To get news of George, Father sent his orderly by boat to Tuapse, the nearby railroad terminal. From there he was to travel by train to Petrograd. Fedyushkin departed and vanished. We never saw nor heard from him again.

All these events made us uneasy. And there were rumors that the Abkhazians were getting restless. This fierce people lived in the surrounding mountain villages. There was even talk that the Abkhazians might attack the Soviet intruders and push them out. When the only bank in town closed its doors, Father concluded Gagri had become a dangerous trap. "We have to get out of here, and fast."

"But how?" I asked.

"The coastal railroad, although only partially completed, has been dynamited," Father said, thinking out loud. "Bandits block the highway. The mountains are impassable. The only possible escape is by sea, but that route, too, seems unlikely. No passenger steamers have docked here all winter. Troopships and cargo vessels pass far out to sea. Of the small craft, none survived that recent gale. Only rowboats remain. Trying to escape in a rowboat would be foolhardy. Still we have to try something."

We all puzzled about what to do and talked it over together.

We were at breakfast one morning. Father had just started serving the honey. He had been able to locate a jug at the local market and had brought it home triumphantly. Honey was our substitute for butter. All of a sudden we heard shouts, rifle shots, and the sound of horses' hoofs. Father ran to the window and exclaimed, "Abkhazians!" Nils and I crowded behind him to get a better look. The scene was one of great confusion. People ran in all directions. About fifty riders galloped around the square. They wore fur hats and long Cossack tunics, with daggers in their belts.

Peering through his binoculars, Father called to Mother, "It's the Abkhazians, all right. What can they be up to?"

He turned from the window and said, as more shots rang out, "There's something I have to tell you. Last night I heard a rumor Bolshevik destroyers are nearby. A landing party is all they'll need to push these wild men back into the hills."

"Destroyers?" Mother said.

"Won't this place be their first target?" Nils asked.

"Absolutely. We have to leave the palace at once. There's a villa down the road. I'll go over there now and see whether we can rent rooms. Meanwhile, pack up our things."

We did as told. More and more, we had come to trust his ingenuity in getting us out of danger.

It was fortunate that Father succeeded in his errand. We moved into the villa that afternoon. Early the next morning, two destroyers appeared on the horizon, trailing clouds of black smoke. They approached Gagri and opened fire. From the nearby hillside, we watched Prince Oldenburg's palace, half expecting it to crumble before our eyes, but nothing happened. After an initial salvo, perhaps a warning, the destroyers lowered boats and put three landing parties to shore. There followed much shouting and gunfire near the square. The Abkhazians galloped off into the hills, and soon sailors occupied the palace.

That evening a group of them stopped at the villa in search of firearms. Father had anticipated their visit and removed from his service revolver a small but crucial inner part. When they left, he was jubilant at having outwitted them. The confiscated gun was a useless weapon.

In the morning the destroyers had disappeared. There was no indication that anything at all had happened, but, as we watched Father dole out the breakfast honey, we sensed the events of the previous day weighed on his mind. As it turned out, he was devising a plan.

Father pushed the honey jar to one side. "This has got to work. There's no other way." He looked at each of us solemnly. "I propose we watch the sea, watch systematically, each of us taking turns here on the balcony. In the meantime, we'll pack up again and be ready to leave. I'll go see that grocer Kalushkin about an exit visa. He knows how to arrange that kind of thing. Of course, I'll make it worth his while. Yes, and I'll have to tip some fishermen to ride in one of their boats. We'll get a handcart for the luggage. Then we'll wait. Sit on our suitcases, ready to go. And, when a steamer comes along...."

We waited three weeks. Smoke finally appeared on the horizon.

"A boat!" Nils screamed. "I see a boat."

Father grabbed the binoculars. He peered through them intently. "It's a tramp steamer. It may be heading in our direction."

"It may not stop here," I pointed out.

"Maybe, maybe not. In any case, we have to be ready."

As it turned out, the steamer anchored a quarter of a mile offshore. A launch was lowered. We watched as it headed toward the pier.

"This may be our opportunity. We have to act fast. Let's go."

We hastened down the road toward the beach, pulling the handcart with the luggage. The fishermen were waiting. We climbed into their boat. They rowed us to the ship. We clambered up the ship's ladder, a task that must have been difficult for Mother and Emilia. I carried Bullo in my arms. Behind us came the two fishermen with our suitcases. When Father had paid them off, they tipped their hats and disappeared down the ladder again.

Soon the crewmembers returned. Ten minutes later, the ship weighed anchor and we were under way. I stood on deck and watched Gagri disappear in the distance. We had lived there five months.

"God was with us," Father said. "We can all be thankful."

That was when we realized the ship was crowded. Everywhere we looked, people squatted on blankets or sat sprawled on suitcases and cardboard boxes. Many spoke a language that was strange to our ears. Father figured out these fellow passengers were Armenians, fleeing from farther south. Also on board huddled many soldiers, their uniforms in tatters.

Some wore red armbands.

"Probably deserters from the Turkish front," Father said.

"Please go find the purser," Mother said to Nils. "Ask if we can have a cabin."

Nils was soon back. He told us breathlessly, "There's no purser on board. Conditions are chaotic below deck. Everybody seems to be traveling without a ticket, and nobody has any idea where we are going."

A member of the crew passed, and Nils asked him our destination.

"See for yourself," the man growled, spitting over the rail. "If the coast lies to starboard, then we're heading north."

"Well, in that case, we might as well make ourselves comfortable and have something to eat—the chicken and hard-boiled eggs," Father said. "What else did we bring, Emilia?"

"Ham."

"Right. The ham. By all means, let's have the ham."

Father settled himself on one of the skylights. We followed his example. If we were heading in the general direction back to Petrograd, that was fine. By the time we got home, the Bolsheviks would surely have been overthrown.

The sun was setting. The sea was calm, the weather quite mild. I curled up near one of the ship's ventilators to stay warm, and fell asleep.

When I awoke, we were nearing Novorossiysk. Located on the Black Sea in the northwestern Caucasus, it had been the homeport of the Imperial Black Sea Fleet. Father was already up and had scouted around.

"I've found the stoker," he told me. "It seems there was a mutiny in the port not long ago. It spread through the entire fleet and many naval officers were dumped into the sea."

"How dreadful," said Mother, who had joined us at the railing.

"The town is now run by a high-handed gang of sailors. There are sentries all over. Anyone entering has his hands examined."

"What in the world for?" she interrupted.

"To prove he's a laborer. If so, his hands are calloused. If not ..." Father shrugged his shoulders.

"And you believed all this?"

"The stoker had no reason to mislead me."

"Does that mean we can't land here?"

Father didn't seem to have heard Mother's question. He was examining the harbor, shielding his eyes with one hand. I followed his gaze to the pier we were fast approaching. There, not more than a few hundred feet away from where our ship maneuvered to dock, I saw another steamer.

"It's about to depart." Father said in a lowered voice. "This may be our only chance to get out of here, our only chance."

When the gangplank was in place, the soldiers and refugees rushed to get off. We waited until the crowd had thinned. Then, at a signal from Father, we left the ship, clutching our suitcases. We hurried across the pier and stumbled up the gangplank of the larger steamer. Nobody challenged us or asked for papers. I was delayed because I had to stop to let Bullo do his business. As I rushed toward the ship, a sailor appeared on the bridge and shouted at somebody to hurry. Two other men stood ready to pull up the gangplank. Bullo and I made it back just in time. The engines started up, the whistle blew, and we were off. Where to? We had no idea.

So began another phase of our journey. We were more comfortable, since the ship was less crowded. When I awoke in the morning, the ship was rocking gently, apparently at anchor. The sun was rising and everything was still. Everyone on board seemed asleep. I pulled on my clothes and hurried up the companionway. On deck, Father stood scanning the sea. Due north, land was faintly visible.

"That must be the Crimea," he told me, as I joined him, narrowing his eyes.

"Why aren't we moving?"

"I guess whoever is in charge doesn't know how to pilot us through minefields."

We lay at anchor all that day and through the night. Early the next morning, out of a bank of fog, a ship appeared off our portside. A modern cargo vessel, it sailed at a steady clip, as if the captain knew what he was about. When the ship came closer, we heard excited voices from the bridge. The engines started up; we heaved anchor, and got behind the other ship. When it turned left, we turned left. When it veered right, we followed in its wake. In this strange fashion, we came to the small port of Kerch, the easternmost point of the Crimea, guarding the Sea of Azor.

"We're out of the trap," Father said as we prepared to disembark.

Mother took Bullo's leash and we picked up the suitcases.

Kerch seemed deserted. We trudged along the narrow street until we came to a small hotel. No amount of knocking produced any response. Nils peered in through a side window and saw a light, so we went around back and pounded on the door. Finally, a voice called out, "What do you want?"

Father talked to the innkeeper through the keyhole. It took considerable persuasion to convince him to open the door. When it swung open, a heavy man with small darting eyes appeared. He told us in a hoarse voice, "I'm alone here. Name's Gorbunov. My life's savings are invested in this hotel."

"Who's in charge of the town?"

"There are no authorities, no police," the man said. He kept shifting his weight from one foot to the other. "Gangs, including quite a few army deserters, are on the loose. You were lucky no one molested you as you walked up here. Real lucky."

"What about the Soviets?"

"They were in control for a time. Only yesterday, the Bolsheviks cleared out. They heard that the German Army was advancing. Its vanguard is supposedly only eighteen miles away. I closed the hotel in time to prevent looting. You can stay the night, but I have no food except black bread and cheese."

We accepted, grateful to Gorbunov for his generosity. I sat down next to Nils and ate as fast as I could. Then we went to bed, emotionally exhausted.

It didn't take the Germans long to restore order. In the morning, a proclamation appeared on every vacant wall, calling for the population to surrender all firearms: *After twenty-four hours, anybody caught with a gun will be shot.* That afternoon the military police arrived at the hotel and took down our names. In this way, we technically became prisoners of war.

"We have to act fast," Father said. "I'll go pay a call on the officer in command before anyone can restrict our movements."

None of us were surprised by this decision. He always looked to the human side of any situation, an approach that proved critical in our escape from Gagri, and beyond.

As soon as Father had returned, he reported what had happened at headquarters: "I introduced myself and asked to see the aide-de-camp of the commanding officer. I handed this young man my card. He looked it over with circumspection. Apparently impressed by my rank and title, he escorted me to his superior, Oberstleutnant Von Tannstein, commander of the advance forces occupying Kerch. 'Is there anything we can do to help you, Herr General?' the commanding officer inquired.

"'I plan to take my family to Riga,' I said. 'Since it will be necessary to travel behind German lines, I hope to obtain authorization for such a trip.'"

"During our conversation I mentioned that before the war I had been decorated with the Prussian Order of the Red Eagle. I also told him I had served as escort when the Crown Prince of Germany visited Russia. Up to that point the German colonel had been punctiliously polite, but cool. Now he turned amiable, and brought out a bottle of Cognac. 'Of course, Your Excellency,' he said. 'I'll have that pass issued immediately.'"

BEFORE WE LEFT for Riga, we went to see Mother's cousin, Sanya Troubetskoi, who owned a small estate fifteen miles away. The visit was of great importance because he lent Father five thousand rubles. Sanya came to fetch us in his car. When we reached the estate, he handed us a loaf of French bread and some freshly churned butter. I immediately sat down on a tree stump with Nils and had a feast. We hadn't seen white bread or butter in a long time. Nothing ever tasted so delicious.

A few days later we accompanied our host to the railroad station. He was off to visit a sick brother in Moscow. The last we saw of Sanya, he was waving from the window of a crowded train.

Soon we, too, would leave the Crimea. First we had to get from Kerch to Sevastopol, less than one hundred and fifty miles to the west as the crow flies. Unfortunately, there was no direct route. Along that stretch of coast lay several estates including the tsar's residence, Livadia. To preserve the natural beauty of the area and ensure privacy, no railroad had been built, so we had to make our way inland around the Crimean peninsula in rickety trains, jostled together on wooden seats. German soldiers crowded every car. The sandwiches we had brought seemed scanty fare for the eighteen-hour journey.

Finally we reached Sevastopol. The strain had begun to show. Father looked weary. Mother must have been tired, too. Nils had long since lapsed into silence. Even Emilia had turned grouchy. Bullo slept. As for me, I was ravenous and wondered not what the great port would look like, but what we would find to eat there.

Thanks to Father's foresight, we had been invited to spend the night at the home of a banker whose villa overlooked the harbor. Refreshed by a copious meal, I stood on the terrace at sunset to admire the view. Swinging peacefully at anchor, after spectacular action in the Mediterranean, was the famous cruiser *Goeben,* symbol of the German conquest.

Lieutenant Colonel Von Tannstein had graciously arranged for our passage to Odessa. Thus, the next day, we left as scheduled on a German troopship. When the ship reached the open sea, a school of dolphins caught up, and, to our delight, formed a playful escort. We watched them until dark.

"A good omen, these dolphins," Father said before turning in for the night.

The following morning, our ship reached Odessa. "What an impressive sight," said Mother. We followed her gaze to the cargo ships loading and unloading, the activity at the waterfront, the steps leading down to the harbor.

"This is where the *Potyomkin* crew mutinied," Nils reminded us.

As we disembarked, I wondered how much hidden support the Bolsheviks might still have in the port city.

TO PROCEED to Riga via Kiev and Warsaw, Father had to petition the German authorities in the Ukraine. It took three months to get the necessary papers. In the meantime, we rented an apartment in a residential part of town.

One day we paid a call on the Tolstoys at their suburban villa by the sea. Mrs. Tolstoy seemed anxious. She had not heard from her husband, still in Bolshevik-held territory to the north, or so she believed. Seeing Dalechka and Seryozha again brought back memories of the fun we had shared as children. But where was their glamour? It had faded. My two friends seemed subdued. No doubt their confidence had been shaken. Like our family and everyone else in the world we had known, they were groping for a new security.

Soon we were on our way again. In Kiev, we had to change trains, making it possible to see Uncle Fedya, who had served in the Duma. He brought a hamper of food, which Nils and I appropriated. I watched Fedya hug Mother as I bit into a sandwich.

"Manechka!"

"What's going to happen to Kolya and Sasha?" she asked, wiping away tears. "Can't you do something?"

"Cheer up, my dear. I've made arrangements to get them out of Bolshevik territory."[10]

We were in Kiev only a few hours before boarding the fast train for Warsaw. As we made our way closer to the Baltic, Emila's spirits picked up. She turned to me and confided, "I hope to take a holiday at Christmas to visit my home near Tallin. I haven't seen the family in years." I don't remember ever having heard her say so many words at once.

Since the German troop-line stretched from Riga to the Crimea, we were routed through Lvov. Exhausted, we reached Warsaw after thirty-six hours on the train. A cab took us to the nearest hotel where we were glad to find beds for the night. After one more day of travel, we reached our destination.

From Kerch to Sevastopol to Odessa to Kiev to Warsaw, we had made our way north behind enemy lines, all the way to Riga. It had taken nearly half a year to travel a distance ordinarily covered in a few days.

"Let's hope it won't be long before we're home again," said Mother.

15

WHEN WE reached the capital of Latvia on September 3, 1918, the German Army had occupied the city for a year, and order prevailed. The streets were swept. The trains ran on time. Few people anywhere realized Communism had come to Russia to stay. Newspaper articles on the subject were not accurate. They even reported the Treaty of Brest-Litovsk as a defeat for Russia and no wonder—the Communist regime had signed away to Germany vast tracts of land, including the Baltic states and Ukraine. In reality, the Treaty of Brest-Litovsk was a triumph for Lenin. It enabled him to take Russia out of the war and concentrate on the anti-Communist White Army, advancing both from Siberia and the south of Russia.

Lenin emerged victorious because he realized what the masses wanted and provided it: the soldiers yearned to go home; the peasants desired land. His single-mindedness amounted to genius, impelled as it was by emotional fervor. Lenin's own revolutionary dedication replaced religion. He thought the same would be true for others, so he dared to challenge the Christian Orthodox faith that people had held for centuries.

Since no one could foresee the course of events, we moved into a furnished apartment to await the fall of Communism. Yet, under the circumstances, we couldn't settle down to anything. The whole family was restless. Nils played Beethoven so continuously that Father started whistling snatches. Most of the time he read detective novels. Mother took walks with two Christian Science ladies whom she had met in the park. I tried to study German and algebra to qualify for the local school. When I wasn't studying, I went out to explore the narrow streets in the medieval part of town, or walked Bullo along the banks of the Dvina, watching the boats come up from the Gulf of Riga, nine miles away.

On November 11, World War I ended. With the Armistice, most of the German units guarding Riga were pulled back, leaving the city unprotected. At this juncture, a group of patriots, led by Karlis Ulmanis, proclaimed their country's independence and appealed to the Allies for protection. The Latvians hoped the British would respond, and, fortunately for us, they did. On Armistice Day, the British government extended provisional recognition to the Ulmanis group as representing an independent Latvia.

The following week we heard the Red Army had crossed the border with Estonia. Newspapers carried the rumor that troops were turning south toward Latvia. The Soviet regime apparently sought to ensure control of neighboring states. The Bolshevik invasion of Estonia made us apprehensive. Then, in December, the Red Army moved closer, and we realized we were in real danger. On New Year's Eve, our Russian neighbor knocked on the door. The weather, I remember, had turned colder, and there was snow.

"I'm afraid I bring bad news," General Verigin said. "The local Communists have drawn up a list[12] of undesirables to be liquidated as soon as the Red Army gets here. Your names are on it."

We looked at each other in horror.

"Have you heard anything else?" Father asked.

"Nearly forty thousand German soldiers remain in Riga. According to the terms of the Armistice, they're supposed to hold back the Red Army. Actually these troops are too demoralized to fight. Ulmanis has some Lettish regiments already attempting to stop the advance, but they seem deeply divided in their loyalties."

It was at that time, providentially, that several destroyers of the British Royal Navy steamed up the river and docked at the pier. With them was a 5000-ton minelayer, the *Princess Margaret,* converted from a Canadian Pacific liner. As we learned later, the British had also sent naval units to Tallin in support of the Estonians. They had come to Riga on a similar mission—to bolster Ulmanis.

No sooner had the British arrived than they sealed off part of the port with barbed wire, and stationed sentries at the gates. Several recruiting stations opened. It appeared Great Britain had decided to assist Ulmanis in his effort to enlist the citizenry for the defense of Riga. The city was alive with rumors. Why had the British come? Did they intend to fight? Could they prevent the Red Army from taking Riga?

As if in response to these questions, the British began training local youth. They marched the new recruits back and forth in plain view. They also took two guns off their ships, mounted them on trucks, and staged a parade led by a marching band. Behind the trucks came a company of marines, followed by several dozen recruits in military formation. This martial display was part of an attempt to raise the morale and reassure the population. The Red Army, only fifty miles away, was closing in fast.

At that point Father put on his navy blue serge suit and headed for the door.

"Where are you going, dressed like that?" I asked.

"To call on the senior officer in charge of the British ships," he said, pausing to straighten his striped red and blue tie. "After all, I did meet Admiral Beatty in 1914. It's a contact that may prove useful."

There followed a day of negotiations between Captain H. H. Smyth and Father, who had been joined by several other Russians. Smyth was asked to take on board those Russian families who would be in the greatest jeopardy if the Red Army entered town. He agreed, but said persons of other nationalities had to be included, too.

On January 2, Father, Mother, Emilia, Nils, and I, holding Bullo on leash, walked up the gangplank of the *Princess Margaret*. We were assigned two roomy cabins, notified whom to contact in case of emergency, and told where to assemble for meals. No sooner had we settled into our quarters than a sailor knocked at the door.

"Dreadfully sorry," he said. "I have orders to lock all passengers in their cabins. There's to be some action."

A few minutes later the ship shook as the British guns began to roar. Head down, Bullo took refuge in the closet. We assumed the shells were aimed at approaching units of the Red Army and felt horribly frustrated, unable to see what was going on. We didn't even know whether the Soviet troops would respond to the British guns. Could the Red Army be that close? Was it likely to be repulsed by a few shells? Would these sallies prove effective?

The bombardment lasted but a short time. Once the attack was over, the sailor unlocked the cabins. Then all the passengers were summoned to the dining salon, where Captain Smyth made a brief announcement: "I'm glad to report the shelling had the desired effect. It was directed at the barracks of two Lettish regiments, which had mutinied and threatened to join forces with the Red Army. The Ulmanis government has assured me no further revolt is to be expected in Riga, as long as we remain in port. Therefore, you have to leave my ship."

There was a general commotion at this news. Some people pleaded with him, arguing the Russians were not passengers in the ordinary sense, but refugees; the danger that the Red Army would seize the city was still very real.

They argued to no avail. The captain was adamant: "This ship is not a hotel."

With reluctance, we gathered our things together and disembarked. Where to go? Our apartment was no longer available. Fortunately, General Verigin could reclaim his, and invited us to join him on the fourth floor until we could make other arrangements. The building was within walking distance of the river.

AFTER SUPPER, Nils and I went out on the balcony to see if it was still snowing. The cold was intense and the night, dark. As we looked toward the river, we could see streaks of light crisscrossing the sky. At first we paid no attention, but, when the beams continued moving back and forth incessantly, it dawned upon us that they must come from floodlights on the British ships. But why were they lighting up the sky?

"They can't be looking for airplanes," said our host, who had joined us on the balcony. "The Reds can't have enough airplanes to risk even one. But, if not planes, then what?" He lit a cigarette. Suddenly he swung around. "Surely they wouldn't be signaling for us to come back on board unless, they were about to leave?"

We stood there for a moment, too appalled to speak. It had never occurred to us that the British ships might leave precipitously. But yes, it was a possibility. We sprang into action. Nils and I grabbed our coats and dashed out to investigate.

At the pier, Nils asked what was going on. One of the sailors said, "We're heading out. Get back on board as fast as you can."

We ran all the way to the general's apartment building. Mother had already gone to bed. We woke her up. As luck would have it, a cab drove down the slippery street. Father hailed it. The driver wanted an exorbitant sum to take us to the river. General Verigin handed him the money. Mother, Emilia, and Bullo got in. We piled our suitcases in the trunk. In another minute, the cab sped off. Father, General Verigin, Nils and I followed on foot, half-walking, half-running. The snow had started up again, and the flakes fell heavily, muffling all sound. We couldn't see more than half a block ahead.

When we reached the *Princess Margaret*, a sailor showed us to the same cabins we had occupied that morning. There were new faces among the passengers. Apparently not all the Russians had seen the searchlights, while other people had guessed their meaning. I noticed quite a few Letts, several Estonians, even a French family. We heard one of Estonians say the destroyers were leaving because of a report that the Bolshevik fleet had sailed out of Kronstadt to intercept the British in the Gulf of Riga.

The Frenchman said to his wife, "What will become of the young men the British recruited if they are left behind?"

The comment made me think of the Russians who had not seen the searchlights, and my heart went out to them.

It turned out there was an overriding reason for the withdrawal of the warships. Captain Smyth had been trying to get General Von Esdorff to rally his troops and stem the Bolshevik advance, but the Germans had no intention of abiding by the terms of the Armistice. Instead, they planned to evacuate Latvia, abandoning supplies and weapons. Thus, at the eleventh hour, as the Bolshevik army had come within twenty-five miles of Riga, it became clear the Germans did not intend to defend the city. Realizing that the naval units under his command would not succeed without help, Captain Smyth had no alternative but to order his forces to withdraw.

An hour before dawn on January 3, 1919, the British ships cast off from their moorings and headed down the river, single file. First came the *Valkyrie*, then the other destroyers, and finally our ship, the *Princess Margaret*. I stood at the railing and watched the city fade in the eerie winter light. Soon there were only snow-covered banks on either side, barren and desolate.

The moon was out, low in the west. From time to time I heard a rifle shot, which seemed to come from the right bank. We traveled the nine miles to the Gulf of Riga in complete silence, gliding, ghostlike, through the murky waters. Once in the open sea, we set our course to the northwest.

Two days later we reached Copenhagen. After the ship had entered the port, an announcement came over the loudspeaker that the Bolsheviks had taken Riga.

Father, General Verigin, and several others took up a collection among the passengers in order to present the crew with a token of our appreciation. Several Russians went ashore and bought a silver epergne. The following day, they organized a short ceremony. A Russian, who spoke English well, read the inscription on the silver bowl aloud: "Four hundred refugees of all nationalities, assembled in Riga, will always retain a grateful memory of their deliverance from the Bolsheviks in January, 1919, by the gallant captain of the HMS *Princess Margaret,* officers, and men."

We all let out a cheer: "Urra-a-a-h! Urra-a-a-h! Urra-a-a-h!"

And I am one of those refugees, I said to myself as I followed Father down the gangplank.

Manor house on our country estate, Vasilievskoye, near Smolensk, built in 1810, about 200 miles west of Moscow. (1902)

Troika at entrance to the estate, with Foma the head coachman. (1902)

The author, aged six months, with nurses. The wet nurse is wearing traditional Russian costume. The author's mother is on the verandah in the background. (1902)

The author, with governess and brother Nils, in Cannes. (1905)

Out for a walk at Vasilievskoye with French governess Mlle. Labouré.

Author and Nils return from walk on estate with French tutor Mr. Honorat.

Local peasant women, hired to do the haying. (1907)

Congregation at church near estate. (1908)

Peasant women after church service. Village simpleton is in the foreground, right. (1908)

Grabbe family on bridge at Vasilievskoye.

Author and Nils at Vasilievskoye. (1908)

Father, as a young officer, in his office, loading his camera. (1889)

Grabbe family with domestic staff at Vasilievskoye. (1904)

The tsarevich, with sisters Olga, left and Tatiana, right, on board the *Standart*. (The author never played with Alexis, although close in age.)

Father and the four Grand Duchesses, Anastasia, Maria, Olga, and Tatiana with Captain Chagine, skipper of the Imperial yacht, left, and Father, who is taking the picture. (1911)

Caucasian Riviera Hotel, Sochi, from a postcard.

Mother, wearing the pearl necklace sold after escape to Denmark.

Father with author and Nils in St. Petersburg. (1908)

Father, modeling one of his uniforms.

PART II

Danish Interlude

1

ON JANUARY 6, 1919, Father wrote in his diary:

> *After our harrowing escape from the Bolsheviks, thanks to the British fleet, we are now safe in Denmark, but with no means of support whatsoever.*

How well I remember that overcast day. We huddled together in a cold drizzle. Even our dog Bullo looked disgruntled. Father located a taxi with his usual efficiency.

"Hotel Central, *Raadhuspladsen*," he told the driver, hazarding the name of Copenhagen's famous square.

He muttered to himself as we drove along. We all knew what bothered him. There was no way we could afford a hotel. We had escaped from Russia with our lives and little else. All we possessed were a few personal effects, some clothing, and three hundred dollars in American currency. Fortunately, Mother had kept her double-strand pearl necklace, which might fetch a fair price.

Many people were about, some on foot, others on bicycles. I had never seen so many bicycles before. As we got out of the taxi, a bakery caught my eye, and I dashed over for a closer look. The display window was filled with Napoleons, chocolate eclairs, and cakes frosted with whipped cream. I admired the desserts for several minutes, not having tasted whipped cream for over a year and a half.

In the hotel lobby, a man with rosy cheeks and a blond moustache greeted us in Danish. I took particular notice of his neatly pressed black and white pinstriped trousers. My trousers were baggy at the knees. At first the hotel manager objected to our taking Bullo upstairs. He was quite firm about it.

"But we have just made a perilous journey across Russia. Our dog is a refugee from the Bolsheviki, as are we," Father said in German and slipped a bank note into the man's pocket.

A fellow passenger on the *Princess Margaret* had recommended Hotel Central as being old fashioned, but reasonable. The spacious room I shared with Nils had two single beds, an antique armoire, and a comfortable armchair where Bullo immediately settled. Nils and I went over to the window to admire the elegant square below. A large expanse of patterned tile decorated the center. The low sun emerged from behind a cloud. Pedestrians hurried in all directions. We could see people waiting on benches for streetcars or buying newspapers. Brightly colored posters covered the sides of the kiosks. Directly to our right rose the town hall, an imposing building with a clock tower. As we stood there, the bells began to chime and a low-pitched gong solemnly struck four.

"Hear that tune?" Nils said. "Danish composer Lange Müller wrote it with that belltower in mind. I read it in Baedeker."

The handsome buildings suggested stability and civilized living. After our escape, it seemed remarkable that such an orderly society existed anywhere. While we stood at the window, the sunlight gradually faded and street lamps came on. Shining puddles left by the rain reflected their light. Near one of the kiosks, a boy untied a bundle of newspapers. A streetcar emerged from Hans Christian Andersen Boulevard and noisily circled the square. Above the screech of wheels, I heard Nils say, as if breaking unpleasant news, "You know, Pavlik, you're going to have to learn Danish if you decide to stay here and go to school here."

I noticed my brother had chosen his words with care. If I decided to stay? And where would he be? Until that moment I had rather enjoyed the adventure of fleeing from place to place, dodging Bolsheviks, with Father always there to see us through, but here was Nils, reminding me that the Revolution was no joke, that I had to consider what to do next, that I needed to get on with my schooling. To Nils, an education was part of being civilized. In Riga, a few months earlier, I had been preparing to enter the gymnasium and had tried in vain to master algebra and trigonometry in German, a guttural language so unlike either Russian or French. Did I have to start all over again in yet another foreign tongue?

"You must return to school. It's important to get a university degree." Nils was looking at me intently now. "It doesn't have to be in Denmark. France, perhaps. But somewhere."

My brother was like a mother to me. How typical of him to worry about my future. Having earned a diploma from the Imperial Lycée in Petrograd, Nils was poised to become a diplomat, a lawyer, or a civil servant. His education hadn't been interrupted like mine. Set down in an alien environment, I felt even less able to cope than in Riga.

Sensing my mood, Nils tried to reassure me. "Come on, don't worry. We only just got here. All kinds of things can happen. Let's go have supper."

THE FOLLOWING DAY Father came straight to our room after calling on General Bezobrazov, an old acquaintance who had brought his
family to Denmark in 1918. "I explained the situation, and Vladimir
Mikhailovitch invited you to stay at his house for a while," he said with
obvious relief. "Our hotel bill keeps mounting. We should hold on to
every penny we can."

In no time we had boarded a streetcar for the suburb of Hellerup.
The general himself opened the door. We hesitated, expecting our host
to be different. Back in St. Petersburg, Father had often spoken of our
former neighbor as formidable, and the description had made an impression. During the recent war, Bezobrazov had commanded the Army Corps
composed of elite Guard regiments. "He's a man who fears nobody," Father had said. "Not even his superiors. Sends comments on decisions right
over their heads, he does, to the Supreme Commander, Grand Duke Nikolai Nikolaievitch himself." To Father, a disciplined military man, such
behavior seemed highly unorthodox, even rash.

Vladimir Mikhailovitch and his wife Nadezhda Vladimirovna, née
Countess Stenbock-Fermer, had three sons. The boys were all Corps des
Pages graduates. Other members of the family included a teenage daughter, Veta, and two sprightly younger children. Individualists one and all,
the Bezobrazovs were temperamental and opinionated. They were also understanding, impulsively generous, and very Russian.

For the first time in our lives Nils and I were living with strangers.
You might have thought privacy would have been at a premium with so
many people in one house, but that was not the case. Given a bedroom on
the first floor, we had meals with the family and soon felt quite at home.
What we all shared was a state of mind. Life proceeded as if everyone were
camping out, waiting to go back to Russia. We all believed Bolshevism
could not last. That we would soon return home seemed obvious.

Nils spent hours reading French and Russian newspapers for news of
the White Army. From time to time, he'd sit down at the piano. I missed
hearing him play Beethoven. Only Chopin seemed to express his mood
now. At other times, rather than socialize, my brother would curl up on
his bed and work on word puzzles in the Hachette almanac. As for me,
I busied myself with a collection of Tarzan books in French, which I had

found in a bookcase. I also played checkers with General Bezobrazov. And then there was Veta.

Veta showed me around, and soon we were taking long walks together. She was seventeen—exactly my age—blonde, stylishly slender. Sometimes chatty and gay, sometimes soulful and languorous, Veta had the most intriguing green eyes I had ever seen. When she looked at me in that special way of hers, I felt something inside me melt.

Veta had her own room under the eaves. Her most prized possession was a small, hand-cranked phonograph. On it we played jazz hits such as "Whispering" and "Alexander's Ragtime Band." I wanted to sit next to her on the bed, but was too shy.

One day, on the stairs, I took Veta in my arms. I kissed her, and she kissed me back. Here began a romance, which possessed me completely and from which it would take years to recover.

WHEN NILS announced three weeks later that he was leaving to join General Denikin's White Army in Southern Russia, I stared at him, aghast.

"You can't dissuade me. Mother and Father have tried and failed. My mind's made up. Father has offered to pay for my trip to France. After that, I can get to Southern Russia on my own. The French government will provide passage for émigré Russians. In any event, I plan to give piano recitals along the way, so I won't need to borrow any more money."

"But why enlist?"

"Because if I really believe Bolshevism is a menace, I should do something, not just sit here, fuming about it. Besides, my departure will relieve the situation a bit—for Father, I mean, trying to support us all. You know how little money we have. He's been out every day, looking for a buyer for Mother's pearls—someone willing to pay what they're worth."

Nils's decision came as a shock. I felt no inclination to fight Bolsheviks or anybody else for that matter. In any event, I couldn't imagine leaving Denmark—or Veta. Later I learned young émigrés who didn't volunteer garnered disdain from other Russians in Copenhagen. Pressure had much to do with Nils's decision.

So it came about that on a gloomy winter morning in early February, barely a month after our arrival, Father, Mother and I again stood at the end of Langelinie Pier and waved good-bye to my brother. Nils took off his cap and held it in the air. He was still waving as the freighter left the harbor. We returned to our respective lodgings, heavy-hearted.

Ironically, right after his departure, our circumstances improved.

"Good news!" Father told me over the phone the following day. "Luck, sheer luck. That's what it is."

"What is?"

"I'll tell you when you get here."

Grabbing my coat, I hurried to the hotel.

"What do you suppose?" Father tapped a cigarette against the table several times, waiting for me to take a seat. He relished a good story and knew how to tell one, but his audience had to be settled in before he would begin. "Yesterday the manager informed me that we would have to move unless we paid our bill. Then this morning, as I was coming across *Raadhuspladsen*, frustrated as usual with no prospects in view, I was about to enter the lobby when some impulse made me pause. Out of the corner of my eye, I spied, across the square, a man on horseback. On horseback? In this busy neighborhood? I turned around and could hardly believe my eyes. There, on a fine brown mare, sat King Christian himself. He rode along, greeting people. Closer and closer he came." Father paused to light the cigarette. Unaccountably he looked pleased.

"The King sat erect, but was casual in bearing. He wore a uniform, probably that of the Danish Horse Guards. Even at a distance I could tell the mare was a splendid animal. As the King passed the hotel, he glanced in my direction, recognized me, and reined in his horse. I had met him before and was well acquainted with the Danish queen. She's the grand-daughter of Grand Duke Mikhail Nikolaievitch, so I had known her as a young girl, when I was his aide-de-camp. The King wanted news of events in Russia and particularly the fate of the Imperial family. 'Is it really true,' he asked, 'that they were all murdered by the Bolsheviks in Ekaterinburg last summer?'"

Mother interrupted, "Isn't that horrible, Pavlik? Murdered! The empress and all those innocent young girls."

"I said that going through Odessa we had heard rumors, but, with everything in chaos, there was no way to tell whether they were true or not."

"Did the King mention Maria Feodorovna?" Mother asked.

"Still in the Crimea. He said they were worried about her. We talked quite a while, and he invited me to the palace. I noticed that the doorman had fetched the manager. They both stood there, gaping. After the King rode off, the manager approached and bowed, rubbing his hands. He put on his most ingratiating smile and said that since my circle of acquaintance was such as to include the King, he would consider it an honor if we would remain at the hotel. What do you think of that!" Father exclaimed, enjoying my look of amazement. Clearly he had recovered his high spirits.

While calling on King Christian and Queen Alexandra the following week, Father met a court official who introduced him to a prominent Danish banker. It wasn't long before Knud Jorgensen had admired Mother's necklace and announced he was prepared to pay handsomely to acquire the perfectly matched pearls. Father seized the opportunity to mention me, and Mr. Jorgensen wrote a letter of introduction to a business tycoon named Harold Plum. So here, unexpectedly, was a resolution to the question of what my future would be: not school as Nils had hoped, but a job. It was obvious I had to support myself until we were able to return to Petrograd.

2

THE OFFICE manager at the world headquarters of the Transatlantic Company led me to a large door. I entered a room with elaborately carved panels on the walls, reminiscent of a medieval banquet hall. At the far end, behind a baronial desk, sat a middle-aged man who was going bald.

"Glad you could come," Harold Plum said and held out a plump hand for me to shake. "Please sit down. You do speak English, don't you?" Plum reached for a silver box and lit a cigar. The pungent aroma reminded me of the excellent cigars the tsar's Minister of Court, Count Fredericks, would smoke when Mother visited his daughter.

The telephone rang. Plum picked up the receiver and spoke briskly in Danish. The matter resolved, he turned back to me. "Our company has a number of large investments in Russia. In time, you might be useful to us there. But first you would have to learn Danish and go through a training program."

His directness startled me. Since I didn't respond, he said, "Here's what I propose. I assume you speak English? My brother lives in Assens, eight hours away by train and ferry. For a year you'll be a member of his household and learn Danish. We'll pay you a small salary. During the summer, the family moves to Thorø. I own the whole island. You'll run the motorboat, transporting people back and forth. After a year, we'll bring you to Copenhagen and eventually send you to Russia, once the Bolsheviks are out, of course. Kai will be returning to Assens on Friday. You'll go with him. That is, if this plan of mine appeals to you." He smiled affably.

How to gauge the offer? I wasn't even sure I had understood everything he had said. Later I learned Plum belonged to a prosperous family from the island of Fünen. There, in the seaside town of Assens, he had built up a hardware and lumber business now managed by an older brother. Harold had left for Copenhagen where he joined a cousin in the butter business. Together they had perfected the canning process to facilitate export. Plum had greater ambitions, however. Early on, he had seen the possibility of investing profits in failing businesses and, to that end, had formed a holding company. Soon he owned over sixty diversified concerns in Europe and America, among them several fur-trapping and trading operations in Russia, a typewriter factory in the United States, a bottling plant in France. Thus was born the Transatlantic Company, whose assets were in the millions.

Had I known that the Danes considered Plum a financial genius, I would have been much too awed to utter a word, but I heard myself say, "Thank you Monsieur Plum. I will be prepared to leave on Friday."

Harold Plum rose. Again we shook hands. I walked the length of the room and out the huge door.

THREE DAYS later I met Kai Plum, on schedule, at Copenhagen's railroad station. Kai was extremely homely, but kind and unpretentious. We conversed in French as we boarded the morning train and settled in for the long ride. Neat farmland slid past the window, flat as in Russia, but cozier somehow. Farmers were out loading silvery milk cans onto trucks that were backed up to whitewashed barns. Kai tried, in his good-hearted way, to show friendliness, but I only half-listened to what he was saying.

In my daydream, I was back in Hellerup, playing checkers. "You've won!" General Bezobrazov exclaimed lustily. Then my mind shifted to another part of the villa. In his precise Russian, Nils read a newspaper report on a White Army advance: "The Bolsheviks are on the run...." Even further away in memory, I stood at mass in Count Sheremetiev's chapel, the icons strangely alive in the flickering candlelight as the choir began to sing "The Blessing of St. Georgi of Radenezh."

"Last stop!" the conductor shouted, rousing me from my reverie.

I think I could actually point on a map to where my life diverged from that of other émigré Russians, who more or less banded together after the Revolution. The line would go from the railroad station in Copenhagen, out to rural Denmark and that ferry at Korsör. I was about to become a member of a Danish community in which there were no Russians at all.

BY THE TIME we arrived in Assens, the late afternoon sun was setting. Kai's wife met the ferry. Malvina was a tall, attractive blond. She probably welcomed Harold Plum's suggestion that his protégé join her household, no doubt thinking a young Russian count would serve as a fine fourth at bridge, her favorite pastime.

Malvina pointed out the sights as we drove along. In those days, only five thousand people lived in the sleepy seaport. The sugar refinery smokestack was the most prominent landmark. At the pier, I counted three torpedo boats and several trawlers. The cobblestone road slanted up from the harbor. We passed a fish store, a grocery, a restaurant, a tailor's shop. Further along I noticed the office of *Assens Dagblad*, the local newspaper. Kai, Malvina, and their five-year-old daughter Else lived above a store.

Malvina led me up the stairs to a small bedroom with a pot-bellied stove. She threw a couple logs on the fire and opened another door to the exterior. "This way you can come and go as you like," she said and leaned for a moment on the doorframe. "Hope you'll be comfortable here. Supper at six. Anything you need, just ask. We're your Danish foster parents now."

I walked over to the window and looked down at the courtyard below where a dog sat scratching himself. Two men unloaded sacks from an old-fashioned cart. I felt grateful for this homey scene, so far removed from revolution.

HAROLD PLUM had sent me to Assens to learn Danish. At first I studied with a young man Kai had recommended. I made some headway, but not enough, so I tried a different method. What I did was translate, with the help of dictionaries, articles from a French daily and a Russian émigré newspaper. I cut out the articles and gave them to the Assens *Dagblad* editor. After he published them, I compared his version with my own.

My reading and writing were improving, but I had little opportunity to practice conversation since the Plums and I spoke French together. Kai and Malvina entertained several nights a week. At their bridge parties, I remained silent, listening to everyone chatter away in Danish. The most frequent visitor was First Lieutenant Count Moltke, commanding officer of one of the torpedo boats. Molke seemed bored in Assens. At the Plums, he was fussed over, served highballs, offered fine cigars. Malvina showed a special liking for him, and he enjoyed the attention.

Before long Count Moltke began inviting me aboard ship for bachelor bridge parties. One evening I agreed to accompany him on patrol beforehand. I peered into the gloom as we crisscrossed Lillebelt Sound at top speed. Visibility was limited. The moon, shining through the fog, gave the choppy sea an eerie look.

"Ten miles from here there's an internment camp for prisoners who are to be returned to Russia now the war is over," Moltke said. "Occasionally some manage to escape. Our orders are to make them turn back before they reach Danish soil."

"Aren't you afraid you'll ram into someone?"

He shrugged. From my pocket, I pulled a small flashlight to check my watch. It was almost midnight, time for our rendezvous with the second torpedo boat.

"I see something, dead ahead," Moltke said.

There, some distance off our bow, I spotted a dark blotch on the water. Could it be a trawler returning to Assens? Not at that hour. Russian prisoners trying to escape? I had accepted an invitation to play bridge, not to hunt down countrymen. Feeling it wouldn't be right to participate in keeping them out of the haven I had found, I reminded Moltke of our rendezvous. He glanced at me and altered course.

A few days later I saw several dozen prisoners, dressed in ragged uniforms. They were housed at the sugar refinery and clustered together singing. Some were not much older than me. Their songs brought back memories. Peasant women at Vasilievskoye had sung those same songs: songs of summer and the harvest and the wide open spaces of Russia. Stopping to listen, I could hardly tear myself away.

ÉMIGRÉ

IN LATE MAY, Kai proposed a trip to Copenhagen where his motorboat was in dry dock. While in the city, I dropped in at the Transatlantic Company to thank Harold Plum, who promptly invited me on a cruise. We drove out to Oresund in a funny-looking horseless carriage with a stick for steering. "This is a Milburn, imported from Toledo, Ohio," he said with pride. "Electric. Makes seventy miles on one charge. Noiseless, too." So it was, although we didn't go very fast.

His yacht was a sleek two-masted schooner that used to belong to the deposed king of Portugal, Manuel II. The other guests were already on board, busy discussing German inflation. As we set sail, I overheard Harold Plum say to one of the bankers, "He's the son of General Count Grabbe, military aide to the tsar." Not once did it occur to me that I probably never would have been included if I hadn't had a title.

I spent two more days in Copenhagen. Father had quite an amazing story to tell. He even started talking before I had removed my coat: "Imagine, Pavlik! We made a deal, a marvelous deal. I went, with several other Russians, to the second largest bank in Denmark, the *Landmansbanken*. We asked for enough credit to provide all the émigré Russians here with a yearly allowance. As collateral, we offered our combined holdings in Russia—the equivalent of some one hundred million dollars. The Danish bankers are so convinced Bolshevism cannot last that they agreed. Let's hope they're right."

That afternoon I made an important telephone call. Veta seemed cool, even distant. Apparently she had so many social engagements she couldn't find time to see me. I was horribly disappointed.

After dinner, I read several letters from Nils. Father's hands were shaking as he handed them across the table. Nils wrote he had worked as a teller in a Parisian bank before making his way from Marseilles to Constantinople by sea, and on to Novocherkassk on the Don. He was about to start Officers' Candidate School, prior to being sent to the Front.

A SURPRISE awaited me back in Assens. A young woman named Christina had arrived from Roskilde to be *unge Pige i Huset*, an arrangement customary in Denmark where girls would au pair in the households of

122

friends or acquaintances. She was fresh out of school and eager for a good time. From then on, while the others played bridge, we danced to jazz records at the far end of the living room.

In June, the household moved to Thorø where we settled into a half-timbered house with a thatched roof, in the style of an old peasant farm. Flowers rimmed the terrace, which offered a broad view of the sea. Early in July, Harold Plum arrived on his yacht with several guests in tow. The Treaty of Versailles had been signed on the 28th and everyone was in a festive mood. To commemorate the occasion, our host gave a dinner party at which we drank a toast to King Canute and Denmark's glorious past.

"There's to be a plebiscite next year in northern and central Schlieswig. The inhabitants will surely vote for reunification with Denmark," Harold Plum explained during the party. "You, too, have reason to celebrate, Paul. Support is being mobilized for General Yudenich in his push toward Petrograd. The Bolsheviks won't last much longer."

Welcome news. If true, the problem of my future would solve itself. I would soon be going home.

That weekend Harold Plum organized a picnic to a nearby island. I thought of a plausible excuse to stay home. While little Else went off to the beach with an aunt, Christina and I had the house to ourselves. I took her to my room where we made love. She confided later that she preferred kissing. At the time, I didn't understand the implications of this remark.

Harold Plum and his guests departed, and the household returned to its usual routine, but with a difference—I had become more daring. A discreet search revealed a discarded couch in the basement. One evening, when Christina and I thought everyone was intent on the bridge game, we slipped away. Malvina noticed our absence and called us back upstairs. She accepted my apology, but sent poor Christina back to Roskilde.

It wasn't long before the Plums decided to return home.

In Assens, a telegram awaited me: *General Yudenich captures Gatchina. Fall of Petrograd imminent. Congratulations. Harold Plum.* I read it several times and hurried to the post office to wire my parents. Father replied that my message had given him an idea. If Harold Plum was so sure Petrograd would fall, then perhaps his company might be interested in an option on our Mokhovaya Street apartment. The proposition appealed to Harold's brother Eric who paid Father a sizable sum. This advance, together with money from the sale of Mother's pearl necklace, made it possible for my parents to buy a share in a resort hotel in Germany. Part ownership provided room and board. Their only responsibility would be to help with bookkeeping. It was lucky Father acted fast because General Yudenich never did reach Petrograd. I was pleased to have had some part in their good fortune.

ALL SUMMER Mother and Father had been receiving letters from Nils, which they forwarded to me. When my brother completed officer training, he planned to join Father's former regiment, the Guard Cossacks, now reassembled in Southern Russia. Nils wrote that he had run into our cousin, Nicholas Leuchtenberg, working as an interpreter for the British Mission, at General Denikin's headquarters. Nicholas had urged Nils to take a similar job, but my brother had refused since his purpose there was *to fight Bolsheviks.*

The next letter, written September 9th, didn't reach Denmark until November. I have that letter here in front of me now, yellowed and frayed at the edges. In his neat Russian script, Nils had written that he was about to become an officer: *a step I am taking not wholly without misgivings.* He added:

> The officers of the regiment are all very fine people, but they are different from me. They are military men, professionals. Their interests run to wine, women, and horses; their conversation is mostly about uniforms and regimental trivia. I, on the other hand, am essentially a civilian, interested in literature, politics, music.
>
> Oh, how I miss my beloved Isolde! I left my miniature score of the opera at the Bezobrazovs. Please send it to me as soon as you can.
>
> And do not worry if you don't hear from me for a while. I am about to be sent to the Front.

Soon it was Christmas. I enjoyed spending the holiday as a member of the Plum household. The Christmas tree, the first I had seen since Mokhovaya Street, glistened with antique ornaments. We sang carols and exchanged gifts. At supper, while everyone was jabbering away in Danish, all of a sudden I realized I could follow the conversation.

On December 30th, I returned to Copenhagen where I found my

parents in a state of complete anxiety. It was known by then that General Denikin's army had been suffering reverses. Several months had passed without word from Nils. Father had sent letters to France, Turkey, and Southern Russia, in an attempt to locate someone who might have some news.

A few days later Father and Mother received a letter from a hospital in Rostov-on-the-Don. They read it together, standing by the window, and crossed themselves. Mother handed the letter to me. She managed to say through her tears, "Nils died last month."

A regimental wife, who worked at the hospital, had written:

He had contracted cholera. The army was retreating. He couldn't get much care until they brought him here. By then it was too late. We did all we could. I am very, very sorry to have to tell you this and send you and your husband my heartfelt sympathy.

Before I could react, Mother stiffened. "Where are your tears?" she cried. "Or perhaps you're happy now that you'll inherit all our property?"

Father looked at me, and I knew it was right not to answer.

3

IN JANUARY 1921, I started working for the Transatlantic Company in downtown Copenhagen. I spent my days filing letters from all over the world, a job so boring that I yearned for something different, something more exciting than being a clerk. First I sorted, then I filed, then I sorted some more. Harold Plum had assured me such menial tasks were preliminary to greater rewards, but I doubted I would be able to stand it that long. To make matters worse, my romance with Veta had fizzled. Since my return from Assens, she had treated me like a friend. Under these circumstances, it was hard to concentrate on anything.

Every hour, the office boy would deposit a new batch of carbon copies on my desk. A different color represented each subsidiary. One category—pale orange—provided some relief. Although each sheet was covered with figures, the author always signed his name with a flourish: *Axel Larsen, Office Manager, Estonian Trading Company.* A lively imagination is behind these dull digits, I said to myself. Soon I looked forward to reading the orange onionskins. Apparently, the Estonian Trading Company had been having problems with the Bolsheviks. From the tone, I could tell things weren't going well. *The Communists are recalcitrant,* Axel Larsen reported about an issue related to the eastern border.

Estonia had only recently declared its independence. Within months, the Red Army had invaded the country. The Estonians were able to turn back the Red Army's advances, thanks to the support of the British fleet. War had been averted, but the threat of invasion remained.

After a while Larsen's letters gave me an idea, a possible solution to my boredom. At my first opportunity, I went to see our office manager, a tall man with a sharp voice, a sharp nose, and an authoritative air.

"Mr. Berner, I'd like an appointment with Mr. Plum."

"What for?"

"I'd like the company to send me to Reval. I think I could help Estonian Trading make contact with the Russians."

"What makes you think it needs such help?"

"The idea occurred to me after reading some letters."

There was a silence while Berner looked reflectively out the window. Since I was known to be Harold Plum's protégé, the office manager probably decided he had better let the great man deal with me himself.

"So you want us to send you to Reval," Harold Plum said a few days later. "Tell me about it."

I repeated my request and concluded, "At the very least, I can study the situation and report back." Since Harold Plum said nothing, I added, "As a Russian, I may have a better understanding of how to deal with other Russians."

Harold Plum frowned, unimpressed by the intuitive approach. "I doubt you know enough about the business, but you certainly have initiative. That's to be encouraged, so we'll send you to Reval for three months, pay your expenses and salary. When you get back, give me a report."

I shall always remember Father's reaction the evening I related my good news: "Now that we are collecting a monthly allowance from *Landmandsbanken* for each member of the family, you might like to have your share three months in advance. Chances are you could use the additional money during your trip."

I smiled back at him, grateful for his thoughtfulness. I knew he regretted that circumstances had deprived me of the carefree times I might have enjoyed in Russia.

TWO DAYS LATER my journey began. I settled comfortably into the first-class compartment of a sleeper car, which was to be ferried across Oresund to Malmo, where it would become part of the Stockholm Express. I was in an ebullient mood, off on an adventure all my own. From Stockholm, I traveled by steamer to Reval. My Danish crowns, exchanged for inflated Estonian marks, made me feel rich. A cab whisked me from the dock to the offices of the Estonian Trading Company, located in three rooms of a private residence. Axel Larsen himself opened the door. He was short and distinctively plain in appearance, but a mischievous twinkle came into his eye, and I knew we would become friends.

"Housing here is tight," he explained. "I tried to get the widow who owns this place to rent you a room, but she's afraid of strangers. If you'd like to stay with me, you're most welcome. I have an apartment on the other side of town. By the way, what are you here for?"

Until that moment, it hadn't occurred to me that, in his eyes, any report would reflect on his performance. "I'm supposed to write a report for Harold Plum."

"A report, eh? No matter. I'll be glad to have some company. The town is provincial, but there are compensations—nightclubs, women."

So began a very special period in my life, however brief. Axel Larsen introduced me to his neighbors, Russian émigrés from Moscow. His Danish friends accepted me as one of their own. We'd march, arm in arm, through the streets singing songs. Usually, we met at an outdoor cabaret, which ran continuous performances late into the night and served horrible cocktails: raw alcohol sweetened with fruit syrup.

With my days with the Russians and my nights with the Danes, time passed pleasantly, and I forgot about the report for Harold Plum. It wasn't that I was irresponsible, but rather that I had succumbed to the illusion of living a carefree life. Two months passed. Then Berner wrote to remind me of my deadline. I shared the letter with Axel Larsen.

"Tell you what," he said. "I'm due to return to Copenhagen on holiday. The first passenger flight ever from Reval to Berlin has been scheduled, and I plan to be on it. Why not come along? On the way back, we'll dream up something to tell Plum."

THAT WEEK I made the acquaintance of Prince Isheyev, a small man about my father's age. We met at the café where I played pool. He approached seemingly out of the blue and complimented me on my game. Although his serge suit was neatly pressed, it had a visible sheen.

"Isheyev," I repeated, unfamiliar with the name.

As if reading my thoughts, the stranger leaned forward and whispered in my ear, "Your suspicions are correct. I made it up. You'll understand why once you hear the whole story, but not here, not now."

We saw each other at the café a couple more times. One afternoon the prince moved his chair closer and said in a lowered voice, "I have known your father and your uncle for a number of years. Yes, indeed. They served our country well. And I trust your integrity as a member of such a distinguished family."

I put down my beer glass. What was he talking about?

In a solemn tone, Isheyev continued, "Providence has made it possible for you to do our country a great service."

I raised my eyebrows. "Our country? You mean, Russia?"

He cast a glance around the room and refused to say another word. We went outside and hiked up to a remote spot on the seacoast. Above us loomed the remnants of a castle. It was in this Gothic setting that Isheyev revealed his secret.

"You've heard of the Knights of Malta, right?"

"Vaguely," I said, trying to recall what I had read in history books. "Isn't it a religious order?"

"They possessed an early icon of the Virgin Mary—the Madonna of Philermo—believed to have miraculous powers, and a sacred relic: the Hand of St. John the Baptist, in a gold reliquary. In early Christian times, the Knights were hospitalers in Jerusalem, and St. John the Baptist was their patron saint."

What did all this have to do with Russia? The prince was making me curious. Noticing my interest, he relaxed visibly. Naïve dedication shone in his blue eyes as he lit a cigarette.

"When Bonaparte drove the Knights from the island of Malta, they traveled to Russia. They entrusted the relics to Tsar Paul I and made him Grand Master of the Order. He was delighted and gave them the Vorontzov Palace as headquarters. That's the building where you went to school."

"Do you suppose that's why the Maltese Cross became our insignia?"

"Most likely."

Isheyev smoothed down his beard, deep in thought.

"After a while, the relics were moved to the Winter Palace. Part of the time, they were kept at Gatchina. They were there in 1919 when General Yudenich captured the palace from the Bolsheviks. After the White Army was forced to retreat, a patriot rescued the sacred objects. He bundled them up in burlap and walked them to Estonia. In Estonia, they were hidden in an Orthodox convent. That's where they are now."

As I listened, I kept on wondering why Isheyev was sharing this incredible story.

"The treasures are not safe here. The Bolsheviks, the Estonian Government, and, more importantly, the Vatican and the Orthodox Church outside Russia—even the Knights of Malta themselves—are looking for these precious objects for their own purposes, political or otherwise. The precious stones alone are worth a fortune. Sooner or later somebody will find out where they're hidden. That's why we have to act fast."

Isheyev paused, then said with visible emotion, "You're in a unique position to take these treasures to a place of safety and preserve them for the time when a tsar will again rule our country. Their importance lies in the fact that they establish the legitimacy of the Crown in the eyes of the devout."

"How in the world would I do that?"

"The Dane with whom you're staying. He's a friend of the Consul. With a little effort, I bet you could get him to persuade the Consul to seal the relics as a diplomatic pouch and send them with you, as courier, to Denmark. That way the treasure could pass through Sweden without being opened."

"Persuade the Consul? Not so simple."

"Not simple, but possible. I'm sure the dowager empress, Maria Feodorovna, would be most appreciative. She's back in Denmark now."

Ah, yes. The dowager empress of Russia, born a Danish princess. It dawned on me that I might not need to return to Copenhagen empty-handed were I to cooperate. I accepted Isheyev's proposal.

I MET THE prince at the appointed time in a sparsely settled part of town. He led me to a car and told the driver, a man whose face I could not see, to proceed according to plan. I drew back as Isheyev pulled a blindfold from his pocket. I hadn't expected such elaborate measures. Evidently the stakes were high.

The car soon left the cobblestones and turned onto a country road. After about half an hour, the car stopped. The prince led me up eighteen slippery stone steps. I felt the wooden planks of a circular staircase beneath my feet and heard Isheyev knock on a door. I stepped across a threshold, and at last the prince removed the blindfold. We stood in a narrow room with a vaulted ceiling, facing two women dressed in somber clothing. One of them held a candelabrum, which cast eerie shadows on the stone wall. As my eyes grew accustomed to the dark, I realized the women were nuns.

"I hope we have not kept you waiting," said the prince. "Pavlik Alexandrovitch, meet the Mother Superior."

I bowed.

"Welcome and may God protect you."

A younger nun waited beside an oak refectory table. On the table there was something covered with a piece of white linen.

"Are these the relics?"

"They are."

Isheyev and the Mother Superior exchanged glances. At her nod, the younger nun lifted the cloth. The prince crossed himself. I took a step forward to get a better look.

One of the objects was a rather large icon of the Virgin Mary, adorned with jewels that sparkled in the candlelight. As I examined it, I saw that the image of the Virgin had darkened with age, but the expression, grave and unearthly, could still be discerned. Pearls, emeralds, and rubies embellished her vestments, overlaid with silver. From a gold collar hung a necklace. The gems were spectacular Ceylon sapphires of a delicate shade of violet. I recognized them because Mother had a Ceylon sapphire mounted on a pendant.

The second object was even more remarkable: an embossed casket of solid gold with a lid of plate glass. Along the rim of the reliquary were encrusted six indigo-blue sapphires and two diamonds the size of marbles. Through the glass, I could see the skeletal remains of a hand, held firmly in place on a piece of frayed red velvet—a right hand with several fingers missing. Incredulous, I gasped and drew back from the table. There really was a withered hand in the casket.

For a few moments no one spoke. Everything was so bizarre. As we stood there in the damp chamber, illuminated only by candles, I felt the sudden urge for fresh air.

"When the time comes to re-establish the monarchy, these relics will be important," the prince mused, almost as if talking to himself. "Who has them, I mean."

I placed a hand on my stomach, feeling more and more nauseated by the minute. "Shall we go?"

"Not yet. A prayer service has been arranged to ask God to grant you safe passage."

The nuns led us down a flight of stairs. We paused in front of a wooden door, covered with carvings. The younger nun pushed it open. We followed her through this side entrance and found ourselves near the altar where several women knelt in prayer. I had always pictured nuns as rather plain, but most of these women seemed quite pretty. There was something incredibly appealing at having them pray for my safety.

Two hours later I was back on the darkened street outside Larsen's apartment. The sound of Isheyev's automobile gradually receded in the distance. I had, in my possession, an odd-shaped package, wrapped in burlap and bound with heavy cord, looking exactly the way it did when spirited out of Gatchina. I tiptoed into my room and closed the door. I sank, with relief, onto the bed.

THE NEXT MORNING Larsen stuck his head in the room. "Not up yet?" he said in a cheery voice. "That's what happens when you go gallivanting around all night. Where were you?"

I hesitated as the improbable events at the convent came flooding back. Quickly I reached under the bed. The bundle was still there, hard to my touch. For a moment, I had thought it might have all been a dream.

Over a cup of coffee, I told Larsen the whole story. He listened until I broke the news ever so gently of the role he was to play. He refused.

"If you want to get involved in shady affairs, that's your business. My line is trade, not international intrigue. No. I don't want any part of it."

"But...."

"Absolutely not. I don't want wild men chasing after me. I enjoy life way too much."

All morning Larsen sulked and we argued. Finally I hit upon the right approach. "You're involved whether you like it or not. At this very moment men in black raincoats, with hats pulled down over their eyes, may be roaming the countryside in search of the relics. Before long, the trail will be traced to our doorstep unless we act fast."

"Oh, all right already. I'll take the Consul out for a drink, and we shall see what we shall see."

For the next thirty-six hours I tried to contain my excitement by reading *The Adventures of Arsene Lupin*. Finally Larsen returned, looking rather haggard. "What a day! First I went to the Consul's office. I took him to lunch. I picked him up again around five. After supper we went to the Black Cat and found some girls. Then we drove out to the country."

"And?"

"A quick shave and a bath are what I need." Larsen winked.

"Come on, joking aside."

"It's done, but it took a lot of persuasion. Sending a thing like that is rather irregular. He agreed to cooperate after I reminded him that Russia's dowager empress is a Danish princess. But he vetoed having you as courier because you're not a Danish citizen. We solved that one, too. I decided to do it myself. I'll go on holiday now. There's a boat leaving for Stockholm the day after tomorrow. On the way here, I stopped by the steamship office and booked our passage."

I DON'T REMEMBER much about the crossing. We were careful not to let the package out of our sight. I put it under our table at dinner and touched it with my foot from time to time.

As we entered the port of Stockholm, some health inspectors came on board. Any ship from Eastern Europe, so recently in a war zone, had to be inspected, which, specifically, meant searching passengers for lice. I felt embarrassed by the presence of nurses during this exam, but the package got through customs with its seal intact.

The following day, in Copenhagen, we drove through the fog to the Ministry of Foreign Affairs. Larsen signed an official document, and I handed over our booty.[13] Three days passed. On the fourth, I received a phone call. I didn't recognize the voice of the woman speaking to me in Russian. She introduced herself as lady-in-waiting to the dowager empress of Russia.

"Her Imperial Majesty has asked me to express her gratitude for rescuing the sacred objects. She would like to know if there's anything she could do to express her appreciation."

What to answer? I drew in breath as an idea came into my head. "Please tell Her Majesty how happy I am that Providence has enabled me to serve Russia this way. In point of fact, I was acting as an agent for my company and, if I may be so bold as to suggest...."

"Yes?"

"It is the directors of the Transatlantic Company who are responsible. If Her Majesty wishes to express thanks...but, I hesitate."

"No, no. Do go on."

"It might not be inappropriate if Her Majesty were to invite Harold and Eric Plum to tea."

Around the middle of the afternoon, a sudden hush came over the office. I looked up to see the Plum brothers striding down the aisle past the rows of desks, dressed in cutaways and adorned with all their ribbons, off to their appointment with the dowager empress. Two days later, Berner called me in to say that I had been given a raise. There was no further mention of the Estonian Trading Company or of any report.

4

I WAS GLAD to be back in Copenhagen because it meant seeing Veta Bezobrazov again. During my year in Assens, Veta had become very popular with the diplomatic set. If I dropped by and she had already gone out, I'd stay for a game of checkers with her father. Vladimir Mikhailovitch probably thought I might marry his daughter some day, although I felt so unqualified as a serious suitor that I never brought up the subject. Once in a while Veta hadn't been invited to a party, and we would spend the evening together, playing jazz records in her bedroom, the way we did when I was a house guest in 1919. The difference was now she kept her distance. If I tried to take her in my arms, she would break away, saying, "You're a friend, Pavlik, a dear friend. Like a brother."

I didn't feel like a brother, but had to act like one if I wanted to see her at all. It was with reluctance that I would listen to her latest account of how attentive the new French military attaché to Denmark had been or what a good time she had had on some sunset cruise on the Oresund. In her special way, Veta needed to feel she could turn to me, another Russian of the same milieu, for comfort and advice. After a while, she would get bored with the Danish crowd, and I intended to be around when that day came. In the meantime, I could admire her from afar.

One night Veta phoned to invite me to a party. "I'm meeting some friends for cocktails at the Hotel d'Angleterre. Saturday at five. Want to join us? Meera will be there, and a few other friends, including Elena, a beautiful divorcée who speaks Russian like a native."

"Did you say she's Russian?"

"Not sure. She might be from the Caucuses. Dark good looks, elegant, sophisticated. Wait 'til you meet her."

Did I detect a teasing note in Veta's voice? What was she up to? I would have to wait all week to find out.

A welcome distraction came with the arrival of the Moscow Art Theater for five sold-out performances. I was offered a temporary job as interpreter and took a leave of absence from work. During the day I accompanied the players around town. In the evening, I sat in the audience. As I watched Chekhov's *Three Sisters*, I forgot the Revolution and imagined myself back in Russia. The play by Gorki also made a profound impression: *Lower Depths* is about a bunch of vagabonds and derelicts who meet in a flophouse to discuss life. I had seen ragged peasants in the countryside and beggars in the city, but the world Gorki described shocked me. After the Moscow Art Theater, it was hard to return to reality.

While I was in Estonia, the Transatlantic Company had gone bankrupt. German inflation had eroded the empire of Harold Plum who, for some time, had been over-extending his credit. A subsidiary, United Export, survived, and Berner had arranged my transfer. Now I spent my days transcribing invoices. I typed as fast as I could, but never fast enough. The constant clatter of typewriters added to the stress. At noon, I would stop long enough to eat a marzipan bar. In the evening, I was so exhausted I had to lie down for an hour before supper. And all the while I kept wondering whether United Export might not also fail.

Something else worried me. I had rented a room in a boarding house, run by a Russian couple, and it was not a cheerful place. Conversation at supper reflected the past. Listening to the other émigrés, I realized the Revolution had brought their lives to a standstill and had impaired their ability to cope. My life, too, had been interrupted; my self-confidence, undercut. Most of the boarders assumed the new regime would collapse, but there were signs they might be wrong. What if the Bolsheviks remained in power? Father and Mother had barely enough money to get by, and my job situation certainly held no promise. Of late, I had been going to night school to learn bookkeeping and stenography. However, the prospect of a future as a clerk lay like lead upon my spirit. I attended the courses for three weeks and quit. Such a life was not for me. Vague stirrings spoke of broader vistas, stimulating acquaintances, challenging creative work.

I COULD HEAR music coming from the lounge as I entered the Hotel d'Angleterre lobby for Veta's party. She was dancing with her current beau. Couples sat at small tables around the dance floor. I stood and watched for a moment. When Veta saw me, she led her partner back to their table. Our mutual friend Meera Boldayeva sat beside a stranger. Veta introduced us. "This is Elena," she said with an impish smile. "Do sit down here between us."

Elena Böhme had that special allure which older women sometimes possess and girls cannot yet command. Her evening dress, cut rather low, showed off a stunning figure. She wore tiny amethyst earrings set in gold and a small hat, perched at a stylish angle. I realized she was older than the rest of us, but couldn't guess her age. Elena looked straight at me without taking her eyes from mine, as if she were sizing me up. When I looked away, she asked whether I was a friend of Veta's, and something similar to an electric current passed between us.

We chatted in Russian about this and that—current movies, impressions of Copenhagen, a restaurant on the Stroget where strawberries and cream were served year-round. We were drinking champagne cocktails. I waited until the others had become involved in conversation to ask what I wanted to know: "Do you live here?"

"I do. Right in this very hotel."

Veta took a sip of a second cocktail and, leaning toward me, said with a mischievous grin, "If a woman's strap slips from her shoulder, it's a sign she likes the man next to her."

Sure enough, Elena's strap had slipped from her shoulder. Pleasantly flattered, I suggested we dance. The orchestra began to play a foxtrot. As we moved around the dance floor, Elena pressed closer to me. Her perfume was intoxicating.

With sudden daring, I said, "When do we meet again?"

To my surprise, Elena answered without hesitation, "Tomorrow, if you like, at five. Wait for me in the lobby."

When the party broke up, Veta went off with her escort, Elena took the elevator to her room, and I walked Meera back to her hotel. Meera and I had become close friends. She knew all about my feelings for Veta by now. I had also told her father, who greeted us as we entered the lobby.

"So, how did the party go?"

With one eyebrow raised, Meera said, "We met this glamorous older woman, and she seemed rather interested in you-know-who."

"You're imagining things!" I protested and turned away, hoping they wouldn't notice I was blushing.

Artemi Konstantinovitch adjusted his spectacles and jumped to his feet. "Let me walk you across the square. I've located a little apartment a block away and would appreciate your opinion."

I HAD GOTTEN into the habit of meeting Artemi Konstantinovitch, also known as A. K., twice a week for supper at a cozy restaurant on a side street near the Royal Opera House. Before the Revolution, he had been a civilian aide-de-camp to Grand Duke Nikolai Nikolayevich and his wife Grand Duchess Anastasia of Montenegro, and was famous for having introduced Rasputin to the empress. A. K. wrote poetry and lived on the same allowance as the other émigrés in Copenhagen. Homesick for Russia, he encouraged me to tell him about my childhood.

"We took a cruise on the Baltic. The waves crashed against the ship's hull and made it tremble like…."

He smiled, urging me on. "You need a figure of speech. Go on. Don't be afraid. Like what?"

"A wounded animal."

Nobody had ever mentioned figures of speech to me before, much less encouraged their use.

I knew the Russian colony disapproved of Artemi Konstantinovitch because he went out with much younger women. My parents considered him a libertine. I didn't care about his sexual habits and was curious to know his method for picking up women. A. K. was happy to share: "I wait outside the *Magasin du Nord* at closing time. I choose a girl who appeals to me, introduce myself, then take her to my apartment."

This sounded altogether too easy. "But how do you establish contact?"

"Nothing could be more simple. Women welcome attention. I might begin with, *From the moment I first set eyes on you....*"

I wondered whether self-confidence was the explanation. Did the girls sense his experience? Were they flattered by the attention of an older man of Russian nobility?

"In my youth, when I met someone attractive, I hesitated, agonized." He paused to stroke his gray beard. "Now I know that if a man pursues a woman in a determined way, there's a good chance she won't turn him down. Each woman is different. You must read them first."

"Read them?

"My daughter Meera, she's predominantly indigo. And your Veta, she's emerald green. The women in her family all have a streak of wildness. They usually calm down once married," he added with a chuckle.

"She insists on treating me like a brother."

"That won't do. You'll have to make her perceive of you as a man."

"But how?"

"Make her jealous. Why not pay attention to somebody else? Anyone attractive would work, provided Veta thinks she's got style."

"Where would I find such a woman?"

His face lit up. "Why, it's as clear as the eye of a crayfish. That woman you met Friday night. Meera says Veta thinks she's quite special. Elena. Why don't you pay attention to this Elena?"

I NEEDED no persuasion. Indeed, ever since the cocktail party, I had been seeing Elena almost every day. I'd tell the receptionist to call her room, then retreat to a corner of the lobby. Hidden behind the potted palms, I'd wait, sometimes up to an hour, trying to look as if a business colleague were on the way. Eventually Elena would appear, voluptuous as ever. She'd saunter over to me with her usual poise, offering no explanation for her tardiness.

For our first date, Elena chose a restaurant on the far side of town and insisted on sharing the bill. It was not only her company I enjoyed, but the opportunity to see myself as the escort of a beautiful woman of the world. Soon I had told her all about myself, even my concern about my job situation, but still she chose to reveal nothing of her own past, not even why she happened to be in Denmark.

One evening as we were leaving for dinner, a corpulent gentleman strode up to us. Elena introduced him as Klaus Krute. I shook his clammy hand and stood back while they joked together. Elena stepped to one side, calling out to the concierge, "Pardon me. My friend here would like a bottle of Chateau Lafitte, 1910. Could you please send someone to fetch a bottle from the wine cellar?"

I watched as Krute briefly put his arm around Elena. The familiarity of his manner was jarring. I puzzled over their relationship as we walked outside.

In the taxi, Elena gave me a swift glance of encouragement. That was all I needed. I took her in my arms and kissed her. She invited me to visit her in her suburban apartment the following day.

ELENA'S COTTAGE was located half a mile from the Charlottenlund railway station. Her second-floor suite couldn't have been more secluded, but a new problem presented itself: every time I dropped by, I found Elena with Karen, a teenage neighbor who idolized her. Once Karen had left, I thought I had Elena to myself, but the wire-haired fox terrier, sleeping at her feet, bared his teeth whenever I tried to take her in my arms.

She reached down and patted her pet on the head. "This is Shpitz. He has been with me since last month. Isn't he darling? Just look at that sweet expression."

Baffled, I paid another visit to A. K., who was busy moving into his new apartment. He put down the box of books in his arms to wipe his brow. "Well, now. Seems this Elena—and I'd say she's a shade of mauve—Elena is trying to recapture her youth. She's intrigued by your glamour as a titled nobleman and wants to fall in love, but can't unless you show her you're a man."

"That teenager Karen is always in the way."

"Wait until she's not around."

"And there's this dog."

"Lock him up in the bathroom."

"And then?"

"Act with resolution."

The following day, as luck would have it, Karen was out walking Shpitz. When I sat down in the overstuffed armchair, Elena appeared dressed in a yellow peignoir, trimmed in black lace. She wore a velvet ribbon in her hair and feathery red mules on her feet. Before I could utter a word, she had slipped into my lap. Remembering A. K.'s advice, I carried her into the bedroom.

Later Elena ruffled my hair and said with an endearing smile, "You know, you can compliment yourself." I didn't understand exactly what she meant, but recognized from her tone that she had enjoyed herself.

As I was leaving, Elena asked me to take a few more days off from work. "Can't we spend more time together? At the end of the month I have to return to town."

"Why? Isn't this place ideal?"

"Forgive me. I can't explain. Next Saturday, I have to be back at the hotel."

THAT ENTIRE WEEK I told my colleagues I was sick and stayed in the suburbs with Elena. We went on long walks and discovered quaint little teahouses, where we ate pastries. After her move back to town, I launched a determined search for lodgings near the Hotel d'Angleterre. Finally I located a studio, but by then it was already too late. Elena announced she was leaving Denmark.

On a cold night, I accompanied her to the station. The sky was full of stars. We had almost reached her sleeping car when she put her hand on my arm. Even now I think I could recognize the perfume she wore that night.

"I do so wish you would come to Germany with me," she said softly. "Won't you change your mind?"

My heart was pounding. "I can't," I said hoarsely. "I didn't bring any money."

"I'll lend you some."

"I have no visa."

"You don't need one. At least come as far as Gedsen. I have a compartment. Oh, please."

A hissing sound drowned out her next words as the engineer tested the brakes. Then the whistle blew. Elena hurried up the steps and turned to face me. The whistle blew again. In her traveling clothes she seemed more desirable than ever. The conductor closed the door.

What held me back? The precipitous nature of the invitation? I would have been obliged to get off at the border and find a train back to Copenhagen. The situation awakened memories. So recently had we been trapped in Riga… *the Red Army closing in. The Latvian Communists putting us on their most-wanted list. The German authorities allowing only German soldiers to board the trains. Father's saying, "By sled? We can't escape by sled. Too much snow. The only port open to us, Libava, is over a hundred miles away."*

Nervously I lit a cigarette. There had been so much uncertainty in my life. I simply couldn't take any more. The railroad cars began to slide past, accelerating into the night, and Elena was gone from me.[14] That was when I remembered my original plan to make Veta jealous. I took Meera out for a drink and hinted at my affair, in the hope it would get back to Veta. Meera watched me with a puzzled expression on her face.

"You are aware, of course, that Elena is a demimondaine, notorious in European society?"

"A courtesan?"

"Why, yes. Everybody knows, including Veta. I heard a rumor that Elena's the mistress of the owner of the Hotel d'Angleterre."

"Oh?"

"And what's more, she's considered *déclassée*, not accepted by society. Other people may look askance, but I don't hold her personal life against her. She has a good heart, and what legs."

Elena had given me confidence in myself. If that was what Veta had in mind in bringing us together, she had succeeded. In Elena's presence, I had become a man of the world. Yet in spite of this affair, I was still in love with Veta.

5

"I HAVE A problem," Veta said one evening while we were listening to jazz in her room. "I need money. Where do you suppose I can get some?"

"Money? How much?"

"Quite a bit. The stores refuse to give me any more credit."

"Whew, that *is* a problem!"

Actually, I didn't have the slightest idea where to get hold of any money. I knew Veta needed the right clothes for the parties she attended. She prided herself on being well dressed, and I admired her for her stylishness. Veta sat there, wide-eyed, presenting me with an insoluble dilemma. I had started a new job as secretary to Klaus Krute, Elena's wine merchant friend, but he was not likely to give me an advance. There was a silence. Veta was looking up at me in that provocative way of hers.

"If I had any money, I'd gladly give it to you, but, as you know, I have none."

THAT EVENING I sat at the dinner table in my parents' apartment, only half-listening to the conversation. They were discussing their imminent departure for Berlin and how much cheaper life would be in Germany. I heard Mother say that the hotel they had bought into was ready to receive them, then my mind shifted back to Veta's problem with credit. All of a sudden, Mother leaned over and tweaked my sleeve.

"Wake up! What's the matter with you? Haven't you been listening? As I said, Emilia has decided to return to Estonia. I'll be sorry to part with her. We certainly have been through a lot together. Fortunately, we've found a Russian lady, someone who likes dogs."

"To take Bullo," Father added as I stood up.

"I'm glad for Bullo. I have to leave. I promised Veta...."

"Wait!" Father said. "There's something else. A package arrived from your godmother. She's in England with her daughters."

"Is she?" I pushed in the chair to reiterate my intention to leave.

I had met my godmother, Grand Duchess Maria Georgievna, daughter of the King of Greece, only once and remembered her as rather stately and austere. I knew her husband better since we had shared a villa in Finland during the summer of 1917.

"Maria Georgievna writes how glad she is to hear we're safe in Denmark and goes on to say that she's taking this opportunity to send something to her godchild. That means you."

"She has never given you a present," Father said as Mother produced a rectangular white box, which she had been holding on her lap.

"And what did she send?" I asked with growing interest.

"Maria Georgievna says it's something for your future wife. A bracelet."

"Oh?"

"You'll have to write her a nice letter. A thank-you note."

I watched Mother unhook the clasp on the box.

"Let me see that again," Father said, leaning forward. "Yes, it's Fabergé, without a doubt."

I could hardly believe my eyes. On the white velvet lining lay an emerald bracelet of perfectly matched gems, linked together in gold. I drew in a breath. Reaching for the bracelet, I blurted out, "I'll give it to Veta."

Mother covered the box protectively. "Maria Georgievna said it's for your future wife, and I don't think you're going to marry Veta."

"And why not?" I growled.

"Because you have no money. If I know Veta, she's not going to marry someone who would take her to live in a boarding house."

Mother was a realist, but sometimes spoke with no regard for the feelings of others. Her statement infuriated me. "I won't be living in a boarding house forever," I shouted, choked with emotion. "And I don't care what my godmother said."

"You should," she retorted, raising her voice.

Intent on laying claim to the bracelet, I tried to grab the box. Mother refused to let go. We both pulled until she lost her balance and reached for the edge of the tablecloth. Plates clattered to the floor. I continued to pull until she was bending over the table. Finally, I yanked her hair and wrested the box away. It all happened so fast that Father had no time to intervene. He jumped up and seized me by the shoulder. I wrenched myself free. A brief scuffle followed, during which we aimed blows at each other. At the first opportunity, I made for the door, the bracelet safe in my coat pocket.

I found Veta at her desk, writing a letter. I placed the box on the blotter as she laid down her fountain pen.

"Here. This is for you."

Veta looked up. "For me? What is it?"

I lifted the lid. The emeralds, set off against the white velvet, sparkled temptingly, splendid as the jewels Tsar Saltan gave his bride in Pushkin's famous fairy tale.

"It's for you. It should solve your problem."

"Fabergé! How could I accept?"

"It's mine and I want you to have it. It was a gift from my godmother, and I'm giving it to you. You can sell it. Those jewels should bring a lot of money. Enough to help you out."

"Oh, Pavlik, you're wonderful!" I watched her unhook the bracelet and slip it onto her wrist.

She moved her arm so the emeralds sparkled in the lamplight. There was nothing more to say, so I smiled at her and left. Slowly I walked back to the streetcar stop, relieved that I had a room at the boarding house and didn't have to confront my parents.

THAT FALL MEERA and I continued to go out with Veta who was dating Hans Bruun, heir to a butter fortune. We all knew that, in time, this personable young man would probably take over the family business. Hans had a smart little Vauxhall. The four of us would squeeze into his roadster, laughing and joking. Hans wore expensive clothes and always paid for our tickets, evidence of plenty that I found disheartening.

One evening, in a festive mood, after a motion picture starring Douglas Fairbanks, we all agreed to Meera's suggestion that we stop in at the Tivoli Gardens. Veta had recently turned twenty, so in a way we were celebrating her birthday. We watched fireworks and took the roller coaster a few times. Around ten p.m., Hans drove us home. First he dropped off Meera, then he stopped the car on *Kongens Nytorv,* near my boarding house.

I was about to get out when Veta spoke. "Wait a second. I need to ask you something."

I settled back into my seat as she switched into Russian. "Tonight, Hans proposed. Should I accept?"

Involuntarily, I raised a hand to cover my mouth. "Why ask me?" I stammered.

"I'd appreciate your advice."

I should have said, *Tell him you're sorry, but you're going to marry me,* but the words wouldn't come. I had nothing to offer and could barely support myself. It hadn't occurred to me that Veta might have been willing to wait, if it meant marrying a Russian of her own background.

"Well, well," I said, finding it hard to control my voice. I looked away. A light fog had settled over the city. Across the square, the Royal Opera House stood out as stolid as ever. "It's a personal matter, something you have to decide for yourself."

Veta thanked me. We said goodnight and she was gone.

The following day, I found a message to call her.

"I wanted you to be the first to know," she said in an excited voice. "I've accepted the proposal. Will you be one of my best men?" I wanted to refuse. The very notion of being best man at the wedding of the woman I loved was insanity. But how to avoid it? "Pavlik? Are you still there?"

I took a deep breath and told her she could count on me.

THE WEDDING took place several months later in the Lutheran church in Gentofte. The service was followed by a ceremony in the Russian Orthodox Church on Bredgade, attended by the entire Russian colony. Flowers filled the nave. Veta entered, tense but smiling. Luminous in her tulle wedding gown, she seemed more beautiful than ever. My heart was beating so fast that I hardly dared look at her.

In a Russian wedding, the bride and groom each has several best men who take turns holding crowns over the heads of the couple to be married. Toward the end of the service, there's a procession around the altar. First comes the priest swinging the censer, then the bride and groom, each followed by a best man. I held the crown over Veta's head as she and Hans circled the altar.

After the service, the Bruun family gave an elaborate dinner party for forty people at Nimbs, one of Copenhagen's finest restaurants. The meal was followed by a reception. Around ten, we all escorted the newlyweds to the railroad station, and they left on their honeymoon.

I scarcely noticed the cold as I walked back to the boarding house in the moonlight. I paused at Sortedams So, the artificial lake that runs through Copenhagen. There, on the surface of the water, dozens of wild ducks caught my eye. Every year, with the approach of winter, ducks, flying south, came to this spot to rest before taking flight again. All at once, I heard the swish of wings. Several mallards had risen from the lake and flown away. I could barely see them in the moonlight. As they vanished, I thought, maybe that's what I should do. Leave. Travel as far away as Australia. Such a trip might clear my head.

The next morning I went to work a changed man. After a while Klaus Krute stalked out of his office. I still remember the way he looked that day: thick lips, baby face, pig-like features. Krute thrust under my nose a letter he had dictated and demanded, "What do you think of this letter of mine?"

"It's tiresome. Much too long and whiny."

"How's that? What did you say?"

"I said I think it's tiresome, this continual whining of yours. To Haig & Haig one day, to the Armagnac people the next. Nagging them about your commission."

"Is that so? See here!" he shouted. "I could fire you."

I had forced myself into action. Instead of feeling apprehensive about losing my job, a devil-may-care attitude had come over me. What Krute thought no longer mattered.

During lunch hour, I hurried to the British Consulate and applied for a visa for Australia. I had been well received by the British and, in fact, had recently attended a full-dress ball as a guest of the Ambassador. However, my optimism was premature. The embassy turned down my application. An official said he was sorry, but Britain couldn't allow any more Russians into Australia lest communists slip though. Soon after that, I was introduced to the American Vice Consul who suggested his country and said he could get me in on the quota. The United States. Why not? It made no difference where I went, since I would eventually return to Russia.

I wrote my parents about my plan, and they answered promptly. Mother said she had a friend in New Jersey—a fellow Christian Scientist, Dorothy Kates—who would be glad to serve as my sponsor. Father thought America seemed like a good idea and offered to finance the trip with money left over from the *Landmandsbanken* loan—there was enough to pay my ticket, as well as an additional three hundred dollars for expenses. Delighted, I booked passage on a Scandinavian-American liner.

Artemi Konstantinovitch also approved: "You'll make a fortune, and when you come back, Veta will be divorced and you can marry her. Then you'll show her a thing or two. Girls like Veta—and Veta's a shade of green—are difficult until the man comes along who can handle them."

THE FOLLOWING WEEK I went to visit my parents in Germany. Runaway inflation made this trip possible—a few Danish crowns exchanged for marks increased my purchasing power twenty-fold. Once across the border, I transferred to first class and enjoyed a delicious dinner with wine and liqueur. I took advantage of my temporary affluence to stay at one of the best hotels in Berlin. When I exchanged a few crowns at a near-by bank, the teller handed me seven thick packets of one-thousand-mark bills, only two of which fit in my pocket. I was unloading the paper money when my parents knocked on the hotel door. Father shook his head at the bank notes, almost worthless now.

"What inflation has done to this country. How people are suffering. Their salaries and pensions no longer stretch."

Something in his voice startled me. Never before had I heard him speak with such feeling about the suffering of strangers. He had changed in other ways, too. Father had put on weight, but still stood tall. At six feet one, he remained the famous Russian general, identifiable at a glance. Now that I was about to leave Europe, I looked at him with different eyes. I felt a kind of pride, however grudging. The Revolution hadn't beaten him down. At age fifty-nine, he had dared to embark on a new path in life.

My parents began talking at once.

"People here have to part with their jewels and take whatever they can get," Mother said. "Their furniture, too." She sounded like a reporter trying to make sense of a bizarre new situation.

Father was still speaking and I only caught the end of his sentence: "…at the Treaty of Versailles and the reparations forced on the country," he said. "That's what's ruining the German economy. I hate to think…."

Mother finished her thought. "But they brought it upon themselves."

Soon we were off to the *Müggelverder*, a favorite spot for conventions and weekend outings of local businessmen. According to Father, at the height of the season, as many as three hundred Berliners would spend the weekend at this quintessentially German hotel, located on a lake. Access led across a narrow birch bridge, which reminded me of Vasilievskoye. We passed a bar where people were singing and clicking steins. Father nodded to the bartender as we walked toward the lobby. Their suite was on the second floor. The living room had a view of the Müggelsee. Further away stood some tall linden trees. I told my parents I thought they had chosen well.

THAT EVENING, after supper and a bottle of *Rudesheimer*, I got up the courage to ask about sweet-faced George. Ever since our escape, we had all been worrying about his fate in Russia's new proletarian society. No one, in fact, knew his exact whereabouts. My parents told me they had received disquieting news from Emma Fredericks, who had taken shelter in our Petrograd apartment with her father after their home had been ransacked. Emma had heard Yegor had left Bogorodskoye and taken George along.

"For a price," Father said with a grimace, "it's possible to get people into Finland. That border is the hardest for the Bolsheviks to patrol with all those marshy lakes, forests, and weather freezing so much of the time."

"But who will find George?"

"Your old tutor. I've succeeded in contacting him through his brother, the well-known opera tenor."

"Koukoulya?"

"Kryzhanovsky's promised to do what he can. I have a hunch he's been looking for a way out. Thank goodness we put some money aside. When he finds George, we'll rent a room in a sanitarium somewhere."

I wondered how my parents could possibly envisage the expense, but didn't ask.

"Yes, a sanitarium," Mother said. "I guess it's the only option. Your father's right." Her eyes had a faraway look as if remembering George when he was a small baby—her firstborn.

Father reached under the table to knock on wood. "Let's hope for the best." Adroitly he changed the subject. "What will you do in America?"

"You don't even know the language," added Mother who had been raised by a governess from England and spoke fluent English.

"Nor do you have any skills or experience to help you find a job."

"Look up the First Reader in the Christian Science Church. She'll introduce you to people."

My parents' anxiety came through in their voices. Father was right: I had no job prospects or marketable skills. I could not acknowledge this reality even to myself. It was simply too grim to face. Yet, I had to do something to survive until we could all return to Russia.

That evening Father gave me a present, an exquisite silver cigarette case. Over the years he had saved his epaulets. He had given them to Fabergé to be melted down after a final promotion as general. Gratefully I accepted the gift.

We went on talking late into the night. Several times I was on the verge of describing my Estonian adventure, but took my vow of secrecy seriously. I felt mixed emotions when we parted. I didn't know that I would not see my parents again for fourteen years.

Back in Copenhagen, another good-bye awaited me. Veta and Hans, who had settled into a villa on the Oresund, invited me to dinner. I didn't want to go, but Veta insisted. She couldn't see me off the next day, due to a sprained ankle. As soon as Hans left the room to make drinks, Veta switched into Russian, leaning in to explain the injury. I didn't want to hear the story, but she told it anyway.

"Hans was chasing me around the bed. I tripped and fell…."

Was she implying her marriage had been a mistake?

I LEFT DENMARK on February 14, 1923, which happened to be my twenty-first birthday. The sky was overcast as it had been when we arrived in Copenhagen four years earlier. Axel Larsen came to see me off, as did a few other friends, including Artemi Konstantinovitch Boldayev. We exchanged hugs and handshakes. I mounted the gangplank. The ship's whistle gave three loud blasts. A few minutes later, the steamer moved gingerly away from the pier, toward the open sea. I stood at the stern and waved good-bye. Would I ever see any of these friends again? Axel Larsen? A. K.? Would I ever see Veta?

Author in Corps des Pages uniform. (1916)

Tsar Nicholas II in the dining car of the Imperial train with Father (first on left), Alexis, and members of staff, en route to the front lines. (1915)

Tsar Nicholas II at Mogilev, followed by Alexis and Father. (1916)

Princess Margaret, the British minelayer on which the Grabbe family escaped from Riga. (Photo: Imperial War Museum, London)

The epergne presented by refugees to Captain H. H. Smyth of *Princess Margaret*.

The author with his parents and their French bulldog, Bullo, in Copenhagen. (1920)

Veta Bezobrazov, author's teenage sweetheart in Denmark.

King Christian X of Denmark, whose morning ride changed the Grabbe family's fortunes.

Nils, author's older brother, a talented musician, shortly before his death from cholera while serving in the White Army. (1920)

Author on Thorø, near Assens, Denmark. (1919)

Elena Böhme with her dog Shpitz. (1921)

Author's father saw this photo of himself, taken in 1916, as a bad omen because his sword is crossed with the dagger given to him by the tsar.

Jeweled cover, which encased the Madonna of Philermo when author rescued the icon in 1921.

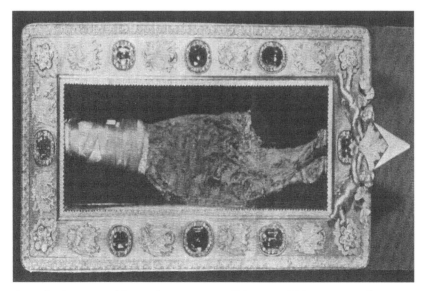

Sacred relic rescued by author in 1921. "The Hand That Baptized Christ" disappeared in World War II.

Crossing the Atlantic on the SS. *Oscar II*. Left to right, Olof Brahe, the author, Lars Kleberg, and Jan Hanum. (1923)

PART III

Coming to America

1

IN DENMARK, a friend had told me I might not like America. "You're a European," he had said. "The United States is not just another country. It's a whole other world." This warning began to make sense on board the *S. S. Oscar II,* a seaworthy old steamer, making ten-day voyages between Copenhagen and New York City. I shared a cabin with a Danish immigrant returning to New England after vacation.

"*Er de Dansk?*"

I looked up and saw a man with bright blue eyes.

"No, Russian," I said in Danish. "Émigré Russian. My name is Paul Grabbe. What's yours?"

"Grabbe," he repeated. "Uh-oh. Better change that. Much too hard to pronounce." He was looking down at me from the upper berth, an earnest expression on his round face.

"Change my name?"

"Lots of immigrants do."

Did everyone change their name? How strange. Here was somebody undermining my fragile sense of identity, even before I had set foot on American soil. We both fell silent. Then I said, "Perhaps immigrants change their name, but I'm not an immigrant. I'll be going back to Russia one of these days."

"How will you feel when folks call you Grab or maybe Grabby? Because that's what they'll do for sure if you keep a name like that."

Since I didn't know whether to take him seriously, I changed the subject. "You haven't told me your name."

"Hjalmar Christiansen, but I don't go by that anymore. In business, a name's important. That's why I shortened mine."

He handed me his card. I read, *H. V. Chris, House-painter, New Haven, Connecticut; Satisfaction Guaranteed.*

"I had nothing when I arrived ten years ago. But I've worked hard and now I'm in charge of four employees." He made a gesture as if to say, *the sky's the limit.*

After Chris had left, I thought, what do I know about the United States? I'd seen a few Fairbanks pictures and read books in translation: *The Adventures of Tom Sawyer, Uncle Tom's Cabin.* In geography class at the Corps des Pages, we had learned about the Western Hemisphere, but America had seemed far away at the time. Now the country had become more than a mere shape on a map. Soon I would be landing in New York, and what was I going to do once I arrived with no job prospects, a smattering of English, and only three hundred dollars in my wallet?

THE FOLLOWING morning we docked in Oslo. I twirled my leather-cased bamboo cane while an immigration inspector examined my papers. I felt impatient to go ashore. Other passengers streamed past.

"These aren't valid," the Norwegian said finally.

"But I got them from the Russian Consul General in Copenhagen."

"Which government would that be?"

"Russia's Provisional Government."

"Doesn't exist anymore."

"The American Consul didn't object. See? Here's my visa." I produced a card that read *Declaration of Alien About to Enter the United States.* It bore my photograph.

"That means nothing to us. We have to watch out for communists."

"How could he be a communist if he has a visa to enter the United States?" said a man with a Swedish accent.

I turned to face a stranger wearing a double-breasted overcoat, a green felt hat with a feather, and spats. He held out his hand for me to shake. "Lars Kleberg, journalist and fellow passenger."

"Thanks for trying to help me out," I called as Lars strode off down the pier.

It took so long to check my visa that I never did visit Oslo.

By evening we were heading into the North Sea. A gusty wind arose, and the ship began to roll. In no time at all I felt seasick. I couldn't leave my berth for hours. By then we had passed the Shetland Islands.

Passengers mingled informally on the *S. S. Oscar II*, a one-class ship. I met up with Lars again and he introduced me to his friends, Olof, a recent engineering school graduate, and Jan, a Dane heading to Cornell for postgraduate work. A member of the crew agreed to photograph us as we stood, arm-in-arm, with a lifeboat as a backdrop. In this picture, the three Scandinavians appear composed, each secure in the knowledge that he has a homeland. I lacked this feeling and could not yet grasp the reality of my new circumstances. The terrifying fact was that I belonged nowhere.

Fourteen days out of Copenhagen, we celebrated our last night together. At supper time, my cabin mate received an invitation to sit at the Captain's table. The Captain gave a little speech and wished us all the best. Then he singled out Hjalmar. "Before we part company, I need to congratulate this fellow on his accomplishments. Chris, you're a splendid example of the way America extends opportunity to newcomers. Take a bow."

My cabin mate stood up and everyone clapped.

I mused over the incident. In Europe, people received recognition for significant deeds, not business success. But maybe customs in America were different. No doubt I'd understand better once I had spent some time in the New World.

The following morning I awoke early and watched the *S. S. Oscar II* nose its way through the Narrows into Upper New York Bay. It was going to be a sunny day. Fellow passengers had joined me on deck to admire the Statue of Liberty. There she was, close off our port side, her outstretched arm holding the torch, symbol of hope. Manhattan came into view. In my mind's eye, I was imagining the vast continent that stretched beyond the metropolis. That was when it struck me that I knew next to nothing about America and would be obliged to fend for myself—a daunting prospect.

A NOISY CROWD milled about on the huge Hoboken pier. Two lines had formed under letters of the alphabet. Customs officials stood at tables, opening and closing luggage. I found the appropriate line and settled in to wait my turn.

An inspector reached for my cane. "Whatcha got there?"

"It's a walking stick."

He tried to slide the cane out of its case and failed. Frustrated, the man scribbled something on a slip of paper. "If this here cane's okay, you can pick it up in a few days. Your receipt."

"I want it back, now."

The emotion I felt was out of proportion to the incident, but I was attached to that cane. I hadn't heard of Prohibition, so it didn't dawn on me that anyone might think I could be smuggling liquor into the country.

"Oh, here you are," someone said.

I swung around to face the plump little woman at my elbow, Dorothy Kates, whose sponsorship had made it possible for me to enter the country without going to Ellis Island, and a young man who seemed to be her son.

"Welcome to America! You look just like your photograph. John, have a word with the inspector, would you please?"

In no time John had retrieved my cane and we were off on a ferryboat.

"I've booked a room at the Chelsea, an inexpensive hotel on West 23rd. It's famous. Mark Twain stayed there, as did O. Henry," she said as her car streaked out of the 23rd Street slip. "We'll wait while you check in, then go have lunch. I've reserved a table at one of our best restaurants."

Mrs. Kates talked non-stop. I was too overwhelmed by first impressions to take in much of her conversation with John. I felt grateful they had come all the way from East Orange, New Jersey, to welcome me, and I certainly did appreciate the delicious three-course meal at the Astor Hotel. After dessert, John handed me his business card.

Early the next day, I bought the *New York Times* and searched the classified. None of the jobs seemed to fit my profile. Since John had said to contact him if I ran into any problems, I got out his card and walked over to his office on Fifth Avenue.

"I need help with these ads. I've found wanted, accountant; wanted, mechanic; wanted, salesman…."

"I bet you'd make a crackerjack salesman," John interrupted. "With a little training, of course. Why not answer some of the ads for salesmen?"

"Okay." I had learned the expression on board ship. Now was no time to quibble, although I couldn't conceive of myself being able to sell anything. Approaching strangers with merchandise? *Nyet.* I was not cut out for such work.

Two days later I returned to John's office. The interviews had come to naught.

"I've been thinking this over," he said with a quizzical look on his face. "Maybe you should get to know the country first? I sell neckties to major outlets in the Deep South. How about driving through my sales territory? Maybe we could find you an heiress, say in New Orleans where I have some friends? What do you think of that idea?"

An heiress? The prospect didn't appeal to me at all. What I wanted to do was go west and explore the country. I had bought a map of the United States at the drugstore with that goal in mind.

"I think I would like to visit Turtle Lake instead."

"Turtle Lake? Where in the world is that?"

"North Dakota."

"In March? Good Lord. It's probably freezing in your Turtle Lake. Fifty-nine degrees below zero. Why go there?"

I didn't dare to admit turtles suggested balmy weather and palm trees. Instead I said, "I am obliged to start somewhere."

"In that case, choose a place with a decent climate."

"Would you be so kind as to suggest such a place?"

John scratched his head. "How about Colorado Springs? Picturesque, not too cold."

"Where's this Colorado Spring?"

"Out west, in the Rocky Mountains."

"Do I have to inform the police prior to departure?"

"What for?"

"In some countries it's a requirement for foreigners. Even in Denmark I had to present myself at the police station on a regular basis to have my residence permit renewed."

"Is that so? Well, here you don't have to do anything of the kind. It's a free country. People go wherever they please."

DURING THE NEXT few days I roamed up and down the streets of Lower Manhattan. As I explored the financial district, I sensed excitement in the air. The Woolworth Building was the first skyscraper I had ever seen at close range. I found I could order a meal or ask for directions and usually understood the gist of what people said. Having listened to Mother converse with her friends from England had stood me in good stead.

On my way up Fifth Avenue I counted a dozen Rolls Royces. It was a shock seeing a Renault limousine exactly like the one we had owned in Petersburg. I remembered the pleased expression on Father's face the day he hired a chauffeur. We had all trooped outside to admire the shiny new car while Vlasyouk stood there, cap in hand, bowing. Sometimes, in my early teens, Vlasyouk would drive me to school. I'd enjoyed a certain sense of superiority as I watched the pedestrians trudge past while we sped along in style. Now, on the sidewalks of New York, it was my turn to be the pedestrian.

Every once in a while I paused to gape at window displays. I bought a flashlight, a fountain pen, a roll of canvas, and splurged on a thirty-eight-dollar wardrobe trunk. Fancy luggage seemed a symbol of affluence that had been quite inaccessible to me in Copenhagen.

I MET JOHN for lunch at an Italian restaurant near Washington Square. On the sidewalk stood an elderly organ grinder, playing a tune while a red-jacketed monkey perched on his shoulder, tin cup extended. My companion dropped a coin in the cup. The monkey tipped his cap.

"What's the name of that music?" I asked.

"Yes, We Have No Bananas."

"If he has no bananas, why does he say yes?"

John tried to explain. "The song is about an immigrant pushcart vendor. He has sold all his bananas, but knows that you do best in this country if you always look to the positive side of things. That's why he answers by the affirmative."

I nodded, but didn't understand. Even if someone had been there to interpret this vibrant country, I couldn't possibly have made sense of it all. I had entered the United States in the early 1920s, a decade known as the jazz age, now legendary for bootleggers, gangsters and flappers, dancing the Charleston. George Gershwin and F. Scott Fitzgerald rose to fame. Lindberg flew to Paris. It was an era marked by the early days of airmail and radio, consumer credit, the euphoria of prosperity that people thought would never end, and, finally, by the stock market crash, which ushered in the Great Depression and brought the United States to its knees. I would come to know this dynamic, complex civilization intimately over the next half century. As I prepared to leave for Colorado, however, I had no inkling of what lay ahead.

TWO DAYS LATER, John and his mother drove me to Grand Central Station. I knew at once that I was in a very special place. Sunlight streamed in through clerestory windows. The blue and white vaulted ceiling conveyed a feeling of serenity.

"When they built Grand Central, architects looked on a railroad terminus with the awe appropriate to a cathedral," Mrs. Kates explained. "Railroads span the continent now. Not like the Trans-Siberian—not as many miles of tracks—but inspiring the same kind of pride in a major achievement."

The conductor called out, "All aboard for Albany, Utica, Chicago, and points west!"

I walked down the ramp and turned to face John and Dorothy Kates who were waving good-bye. I felt a mixture of exhilaration and misgiving. Most people do not get the opportunity to embark on such an adventure. At the time, I didn't think of myself as an immigrant in need of a job. I was heading west to see the broad expanses of land portrayed in motion pictures. I imagined wagon trains, bands of outlaws pursued by sheriffs, keen-eyed Indians peering out from behind boulders, and, of course, the hero riding off into the sunset.

There weren't many passengers in the coach, but I could tell I wouldn't be the only one to sit up all night. Across the aisle a couple huddled with a child, and, toward the front, sat a wizened old man who used a cane as he hobbled off to the restroom. Near Albany, snow began to fall. Soon slush was seeping under the door. My mood of bravado slipped away. There was no turning back—nowhere, in fact, to turn back to. I had begun my journey to another life.

2

TRAVEL BY COACH is exhausting. By the time the Rocky Mountain Special reached Colorado Springs, it was all I could do to stagger half a block to the Antlers Hotel. Behind the hotel rose Pike's Peak, startlingly close in the clear mountain air. Before taking a nap, I felt under the pillow to make sure my last fifty dollars was safe. When I awoke, sunshine streamed through the window. Good heavens! It was morning. I had slept around the clock.

Impatient to get started, I threw on some clothes and went down to breakfast. Back in my room twenty minutes later, I unrolled the piece of canvas I'd purchased in New York and drew a map of Russia. Satisfied with my handiwork, I rolled up the canvas, reached for my cane, and set off to explore.

In 1923, Colorado Springs still had a small-town feel. Briskly I walked down to the building that housed the local newspaper. I had to climb a rickety staircase and squeeze past a pile of cartons to reach the office. The balding man at the typewriter went right on with his work. He had a toothpick in his mouth. I picked up a copy of the *Colorado Springs Gazette* and began reading. After a while the man acknowledged me.

"What can I do for you, son?"

I cleared my throat. "My name is Paul Grabbe, just arrived from Denmark." I handed him my Danish calling card on which was written *Count Paul Grabbe*. He examined it, but made no comment, so I went right on talking and talked as fast as my limited command of English would allow: "I come west to see this part of the country. I plan to give a lecture on Russia where I grew up. I thought you maybe can help arrange it." I paused to unroll the canvas. "I brought along the map I will use. My lecture is to be called Russia: the Known Past, Uncertain Present, and Problematic Future."

The man held out his hand. "Name's Joe Arnold. Call me Joe. Hope I can help you out." I watched him type something on a piece of paper. "When you get downstairs, turn right. You'll be facing the post office. Jim Brown's the postmaster. Give him this."

At the bottom of the stairs, I opened the unsealed envelope. The note was to the point: *A strange bird blew into my office today. He says he wants to lecture on Russia. What he needs is a job. Anything you can do would be appreciated.*

At the post office, clerks were busy sorting mail. A tall man with a friendly smile seemed in charge. I handed him the note.

"Guess you need a job, huh?" he said after reading it.

"Guess so."

"Across the street from the *Gazette*, you'll see a sign: Kenmore Employment Agency. Ask for Magruder. He'll fix you up. Meantime, I'll give him a ring. Tell him Jim Brown sent you." The warmth of his voice was reassuring. "You from the Old Country?"

"I'm a Russian émigré."

"Are you now? Had to leave when the Bolsheviks came to power?"

"My family was on the black list."

"Really? Tell me about it."

For the next twenty minutes, I described our escape. Jim listened attentively, interrupting from time to time to ask questions.

At the employment agency I waited until the man behind the counter had hung up the phone.

"Please, I'd like to speak to Mr. Magruder."

"That would be me," the man said, looking askance at my bamboo cane. "And what would it be that you might want?"

"I am in search of a job."

"What we do here is match people to jobs and we don't have any jobs you match."

"Mr. Brown suggested I—"

"Good day," he said and turned away.

Well, there was nothing to do but go back to the postmaster.

"The line was busy. Hold on. I'm sure I can get him now." Mr. Brown must have reached Magruder because he lowered his voice, tapping a pencil on the desk. "But he's really okay." He hung up the phone and smiled. "We have you all fixed up. There's an opening at the Cragmor Sanitarium, a few miles north of here. They're looking for a waiter. Bus leaves at four."

Once outside, I laughed out loud at the idea of becoming a waiter. I walked along Pike's Peak Avenue, twirling my cane. Two teenage girls exchanged glances as I tossed the cane into the air and caught it again. Was I right to take the job? Back in Copenhagen, I had once turned down a similar opportunity, although guests at the Hotel d'Angleterre were known to be generous with tips. Had I become a waiter in a class society, even my Danish friends would have disapproved. But perhaps it was all right here. America was a different world where class wasn't acknowledged.

I checked out of the hotel and hurried back to the employment agency. A small bus, plainly marked *Cragmor Sanitarium,* stood out front, empty except for a pretty girl seated several rows back. I settled down opposite her. Almost immediately the bus got under way. Soon we had left the town behind. The girl moved across the aisle to join me. Her hair was vivid auburn, her cheeks flushed. "Are you the new waiter?"

"Y-e-e-s." I was trying to be non-committal. Father had taught me never to confide in strangers. *In the world of diplomacy as well as in the ranks of the military, you must be reticent,* he had advised.

"I'm Cathy, one of the waitresses," the girl said. "Guess we'll be working together."

"I am pleased to meet with you."

"Daddy Curran's our boss. He treats us real good. You're not from these parts are you? You talk kind of funny."

"I'm from Russia. What kind of a place is this Cragmor Sanitarium?"

169

"Oh, it's one of the best in the country. The air is so good here, you know. People come from all over to get cured of TB."

"What's TB?"

"Tuberculosis. Some get well, some die. We never hear about it though. Undertakers remove the bodies during the night." She said in a wistful voice, "I don't want to die."

"Why should you die?"

Cathy didn't answer, looking out the window. After a short time she asked, "Don't you have TB?"

"Not that I know of."

"Well, I do. Everyone at Cragmor does: nurses, doctors, kitchen help—not only patients. The people with money are the patients. The rest of us are the hired help."

The bus circled a stone bluff and stopped beside a large, three-story structure, as dismal as an army barracks with nary a tree or shrub in sight. Outside stood a middle-aged man of crisp appearance. To me he seemed the epitome of the urbane, self-possessed butler.

"You must be Paul," the man said, extending his hand for me to shake. "Stanley Curran. Welcome."

"How do you do?"

"You've waited on tables before?"

From inside the building somebody shouted, "Telephone, long distance."

"Be right back," Mr. Curran said and hurried away.

Had I ever waited on tables? Of course not, although I had observed what an experienced butler was called upon to do. Even as a young boy, I often ate meals with the grown-ups and well remembered Yegor, always immaculate in his cutaway, moving noiselessly about our dining room, assisted by Matvei, both in white cotton gloves, removing the soup plates, pouring wine, bringing in the entrée. Wine was poured from a person's right, dishes removed from the left. Plates were never stacked. Mother said only common people allowed anything like that. Also, butlers had to know when to be on hand and when their presence wasn't desired. They had to avoid bumping into anything, especially the narrow side-table laden with *zakouskis* such as caviar and smoked salmon, large French sardines, and *paté de Perigord*, served with any one of several kinds of vodka, poured from crystal decanters lined up on the buffet.

Once, I had managed to sneak into the dining room before my parents received important guests. I had just picked up a slice of ham with my fingers when my eyes met those of my aunt's husband who was watching me with amusement from the doorway. I had always found the Duke of Leuchtenberg intimidating, not only because he was related to the tsar, but also because Nikolai Nikolayevich was powerfully built, resembling, in my imagination, one of those knights errant in some Russian folk tale. And now this huge man was waving his finger and saying, "Not with your fingers, Pavlik."

I stabbed the ham with a fork, but felt too abashed to eat it. As I dashed toward the children's quarters, I caught a glimpse of Yegor at the door, carrying a large sturgeon on a silver tray. He wore a distinct look of disapproval. Strange how I had never asked myself why Yegor should be waiting on me, not me on Yegor.

Stanley Curran reappeared at my side. "If you don't have experience, you can learn," he said. "We're one big family here. We work hard and get along, and that's the way I like it. Let me show you to your room."

He led the way along a gravel path to some bungalows and a two-story building. At the entrance, he made a gesture that seemed to take in half the world. "What a view! I never get tired of it."

Before us, in the distance, stretched the Rampart Range of the Rocky Mountains, starkly clear in the sunset. I made a mental note to buy a camera with my first paycheck in order to take pictures, the way Father had done in Russia.

Curran ran the pantry, ordered the food, and supervised the dining room. Although he could be abrupt, I found him a good sort. Fortunately, he overlooked my early blunders and let me eat as many grapefruit as I pleased. So started my first job in America, an auspicious beginning.

My duties consisted of setting tables, serving meals, and clearing dishes seven days a week, breakfast, lunch, and dinner. There were two sittings at each meal: first, a round of thirty nurses; later, about three dozen patients. Cragmor's eleven doctors came as their schedules allowed and ate at a reserved table.

My pay was modest, $1.25 a day. Free time was minimal, two hours in the morning, three in the afternoon. We finished work at around eight p.m. Every other week we had one afternoon and evening off. That such a schedule was too strenuous for employees with TB was evident from the fact that some couldn't take it, and quit.

From the beginning, Fritz, the headwaiter, gave me invaluable help. "You have to be aggressive with the kitchen staff or they'll give you a hard time," he said. I especially appreciated his advice on handling patients: "The trick is to hold down the pressure. You'll feel it from all sides. The first rule is don't become rattled. If you do, don't let it show. The customers get anxious if they sense you're not in control, and can be difficult."

What Fritz taught me turned out to be useful not only at Cragmor, but on future jobs as well.

I had expected waiting on tables to be a cinch, a simple matter of carrying trays, but there was more to it than that. The nurses often arrived together, and each expected to be served at once. Several patients fussed over their food. A theatrical producer from New York was especially cantankerous. First, George Porterfield wanted this, then he wanted that. He was always sending me back to the kitchen on some errand. Remembering Fritz's advice, I tried to remain calm no matter what happened.

After a few weeks I got into the swing of things. Dressed in black trousers and a neat, white jacket, I would rush from table to table, doing my best to help everyone out. As soon as I went into the pantry, however, my manner would change. Taking my cue from Cathy, I'd shout at the short-order chef, "Two bacon an' over." Even though the words came out with a Russian accent, the louder I shouted, the quicker the order came.

As my confidence grew, I introduced innovations. I brought people coffee before they had placed orders and made a point of asking how patients liked their meat. Such attention to detail should have garnered extra tips, but did not. The reason soon became all too clear. On my second day of work, an article had appeared in the *Colorado Springs Gazette*. The headline read, "Russian Count Takes Dive into Cold World to Make His Own Way."

Something new under the sun at last. Enter Count Paul Grabbe of the Russian nobility, a visitor in a strange land...here sans cash, sans very many clothes, and sans everything, in fact, except a desire to get a job. And why?

I had come to Colorado, Joe Arnold explained, because I considered it typical of the nation's heartland. Readers were told I planned to lecture on Russia. The article ended with, *he is learning to work as others learn to swim—by turning himself adrift without money or food into the busy sea of existence.*

While I felt grateful to Joe for his help with my job search, what he

172

said in the article made me uneasy. In Europe, my title was accepted as part of my name. Here it tagged me as a curiosity. I had begun to realize Americans feel ambivalent about titles and accord them glamour only with reluctance. In Europe, if your family has distinction, status carries over from one country to another. With it comes deference. In the United States, you are nobody until you demonstrate ability and are able to put it to good use, preferably by making money.

The effect of Joe's article was immediately apparent. Patients stole curious glances as I moved around the dining room. Clearly, they were disconcerted at being unable to categorize me. From then on, everyone withheld tips except sophisticated George Porterfield.

ONE ASPECT of Cragmor was particularly trying. At night I could hear coughing, an eerie reminder that death was close by. The sound sometimes kept me awake, even with the window closed. To escape the oppressive atmosphere, I went exploring in my spare time.

Armed with my new Kodak, I struggled through underbrush and over boulders to a ridge offering a view of the Rockies. Ever since Stanley Curran had pointed out the Rampart Range, I had wanted to capture those spectacular mountains on film. There it was, that snow-capped barrier, rising from the plain, forbiddingly beautiful in the afternoon light. A cow grazed near a ramshackle barn. Around me not a soul, not a sound. I often returned to this remote spot for the opportunity to be alone. Here I felt less of a stranger.

Eventually I made friends with some of the patients.

"Call me Olive," said one young woman, confined to her room. She held me with her eyes as I removed the breakfast tray. "Soon I'll be well enough to visit Paris. You must have been there, what with that accent of yours."

Olive was quite appealing in her pale pink bed jacket, propped up with pillows. She kept talking about what she would do when she got well. As I left, she asked for some French lessons. I came back with La Fontaine's *Fables*, but found her euphoria depressing. By then I knew she would not survive. Once Olive had a fit of coughing. She held a lacy handkerchief to her mouth, then lay down, visibly exhausted. I went to comfort her, but drew back at the sight of blood. I didn't dare call a doctor since it was against regulations for me to be there in the first place.

Fortunately, at that juncture, a new adventure took my mind away from the sanitarium. On my afternoon off, as I was walking down Pike's Peak Avenue, a sign for the Christian Science Reading Room caught my eye. Mother's suggestion popped into my head: *In a strange city, look up the First Reader in the Christian Science Church.* That's just what I'll do, I said to myself.

I approached the woman at the desk, cleared my throat and declared, "I'd like to speak to your First Reader."

"Mrs. Caldwell isn't here just now."

"In that case, may I have her address?"

"We're not allowed to give out addresses, but I suppose it's okay if I let you have her phone number."

"That's so very kind of you."

She was now looking me over and picking up the phone.

"I'd be glad to call her if you like. Hello? Mrs. Caldwell? There's a young man here, hankering to talk to you. No, I don't know what he wants. Let me put him on."

With some hesitancy, Mrs. Caldwell asked me to stop by for tea, an invitation I immediately accepted.

A MAID IN a black uniform opened the door and led the way to a sun parlor where two women rose from a couch. The older one held out a hand, then introduced me to her daughter. Helen Jones and I looked at each other. I liked her right away. Her appraising glance suggested the feeling might be mutual.

Later Helen offered to give me a lift home. I followed her outside in high spirits. Here was an attractive American woman who seemed to want to spend time with me.

"You in a hurry to get some place?"

"Not really. I am at Cragmor Sanitarium and have the rest of the day off."

She drew in a breath. "You're a patient at Cragmor?"

"No, I work there." Seeing the horrified look on her face, I added quickly, "And I don't have TB."

"Shall we take a spin through our municipal park? It's called the

Garden of the Gods. Afterwards, if you'd like, we can go back to my place for a bite to eat."

We drove west toward some reddish hills outlined against a backdrop of blue mountains. After a while we came to an area strewn with huge boulders, eroded into strange shapes. They were scattered about, as if the gods had tossed them around like pebbles.

"This one is called Red Rock," Helen said as we passed a cliff overhanging the highway. "Look up there. People call that The Kissing Camels, and this one here used to be called The Seal Making Love to a Nun—a publicity man's idea. The townspeople got furious and changed the name."

I strained to see the rock with such an odd appellation. Soon we turned into a driveway off Cheyenne Road. Through the trees, I made out a bungalow set back several hundred feet. As we entered, a little girl appeared. Helen introduced us. There was something wistful about the eight-year-old.

"I'm Lolly," she said politely. "How do you do?"

The living room, lined with bookcases, had a cathedral ceiling. Gingerly, I sat down on the leather couch in front of a massive cobblestone fireplace.

"How about a drink?" Helen said. "I've obtained some really good bourbon."

"What is bourbon?"

"Corn whiskey. I found myself a great bootlegger."

"Bootlegger?"

"We have to go outside the law to get liquor these days. Merck's a bit crude but knows his way around and always delivers on time. Or, perhaps you'd prefer wine? Back in Pittsburgh, I developed a taste for wine with meals."

During dinner, Helen told me she had recently separated from her husband, a steel executive. She was interested in photography and had turned the pantry into a darkroom where she experimented with different types of paper. By the time she drove me back to Cragmor, we had already made plans for a darkroom lesson. I could hardly wait.

The world seemed much brighter after spending the day with Helen. Cathy even commented on my high spirits.

"Had some good news, have you?" she remarked as I strode by, whistling.

I had been at Cragmor a few weeks when I discovered a typewriter in the front office and obtained permission to use it. For the next three months, I stayed busy in my off-hours, typing my lecture.

One day Dr. Foster, Cragmor's director, stopped in for a chat. I well remember his animated eyes and quick, resilient gait. He couldn't learn enough about the situation in Russia and was particularly curious about Lenin's role and why people didn't see where he was taking the country. I explained as best I could. The friendly doctor bolstered my ego by asking questions about my homeland. In many ways, my life there still seemed more real than at Cragmor.

Dr. Foster and I got into the habit of meeting on the terrace. We would walk back and forth, engrossed in conversation. My English must have been approximate, but he didn't seem to care. There were so many things he wanted to know.

"Ever meet the tsar?"

"No, nor his family. The empress discouraged social contact between her children and those of any members of the aristocracy, except my Leuchtenberg cousins, who were related to the Romanovs. Besides, I was too young."

"But your father knew him, right?"

"He knew the whole family. During the Great War, as Commander of the *Konvoy*, he traveled everywhere with the tsar. In fact, he even had his own compartment on the Imperial train. Father was on that train, only a few cars away, when the tsar abdicated."

"You don't say! Did the tsar ever consult him?"

"Alas, no. The tsar liked to socialize, go hiking, play dominoes in the evening, but had a fixed rule never to discuss affairs of state with his suite, only with the official concerned."

Once Dr. Foster seemed satisfied with my answers, I, in turn, asked about tuberculosis. I found out that, in those days, doctors used a variety of treatments to cope with the deadly disease, but that a cure had yet to be discovered.

ON MY NEXT afternoon off, I was the first to climb on the bus for Colorado Springs. Helen and I were supposed to rendezvous outside the *Gazette* office. As the bus turned into Pike's Peak Avenue, I looked about eagerly. Yes, there was her Dodge. We headed for the mountains. The sun, already warm, suggested summer.

"You drive, don't you?" Helen asked as the road began to wind upward.

"I learned in Denmark. It's flat there."

"Here, take the wheel. I'll teach you."

Helen stopped the car so we could exchange seats. As she climbed over my knees, I felt her warmth. I drove on up the mountain until we reached a plateau. Ahead of us, I spied a row of adobe dwellings, carved into the side of a cliff. We left our picnic basket on a large, flat stone and entered a room, empty except for a stone table near the wall.

"Some American Indians were cliff dwellers. This is a ceremonial chamber where rituals were performed."

We stood there, awed by contact with the past. Slits above the table let in a faint light. Impulsively I took Helen in my arms and kissed her. In that dramatic setting, we made love for the first time.

Later, over supper, I asked, "Where are the Indians now?"

"Most live on reservations. When European settlers first came, this country had a large population of Indians. At first, relations were friendly, but, as more settlers arrived, they started crowding the Indians out, even breaking peace treaties. The Indians resisted being pushed off their lands. In their eyes, the White Man was destroying their culture. They resorted to war."

"Yes, I've read Fenimore Cooper's *The Last of the Mohicans* in translation."

"His portrayal of Indians as bloodthirsty savages is very biased. In the conquest of the American West, savagery was mutual, only the Indians were defending their rights."

From that day on I chafed at having so little time to spend with Helen whose mental abilities stimulated my mind in a way I had never before experienced. A natural-born teacher, she went out of her way to help me learn about America. Our fortuitous meeting, so soon after my arrival in the United States, made a big difference in my life. When I admitted ignorance about her country's history, Helen produced a copy of the Declaration of Independence. She also pointed out passages in de Tocqueville and talked about pioneer days. She even took me to a rodeo.

"In the old West, a rodeo was part of the roundup where the cowboys could show off their skills."

To me, it seemed the height of folly for a man to straddle a careening steer and do his best to hang on only to be thrown off, but I didn't let on.

"What a strange profession!" I commented on our way back to her bungalow.

"What do you want to do with your life?" she asked suddenly.

"I dream of becoming a writer." I had never shared this secret with anyone before and surprised myself when I heard the words pop out of my mouth. "Last week I put a deposit on the Harvard Classics and signed up for a screenwriting course with Hollywood's Palmer Institute of Authorship. Ever heard of it?"

Helen shook her head slowly. There was a wry expression on her face. "What?"

"I don't go for packaged knowledge. At least it will improve your English."

My first assignment was to write a scenario about the adventures of a lively, young Russian émigré who strikes it rich in Hong Kong. I did research in Helen's marvelous library. One evening, while I was there, her bootlegger friend, a broad-shouldered, swarthy fellow named Merck, stopped by. His manner was somewhat familiar, but Helen didn't seem to mind. She lent me a number of books. I read avidly about clairvoyance and the astral world, reincarnation and the law of Karma. Helen's interest in East Indian philosophy carried over to Oriental lore about making love.

"Hindus know a lot about making love," she said. "They know, for instance, the importance of prolonging it."

Her remark startled me. I had no inkling my lovemaking was less than satisfactory. I wished she could have been more explicit, but in 1923, the topic of sex was taboo.

DR. FOSTER had arranged for me to have periodic check-ups in the infirmary. On one such occasion, I met Dr. Monnet, a research fellow from France. We chatted in French while he warmed up his stethoscope.

"So, when did you catch TB?"

"Oh, I don't have TB."

Dr. Monnet looked baffled. "Then what are you doing here? Didn't anyone tell you how infectious this disease is? You're taking a needless risk."

His words made sense. I had heard about Cripple Creek, a gold-mining town on the other side of Pike's Peak. The idea of going there attracted me even if it meant leaving Helen for a while.

Right after the check-up, I set off for the main office to announce my decision. Stanley Curran started speaking as soon as he saw me.

"Fritz is leaving us next week. Want his job?"

There was some gratification in the offer, but I had no intention of accepting. Not for a moment had I thought of myself as a waiter. My real self had merely stood aside while part of me played the part. As I wondered how to refuse gracefully, I recalled a conversation with Father the day I had told him I didn't want to pursue a military career.

"But why?" he had said. "When you graduate, you can join any of the crack regiments of the Imperial Guard and have enough money to enjoy life, to travel."

"Life as an officer would be too limited."

Father couldn't understand. Although he distracted himself with the renovation of old houses, he had enjoyed his position at Court. He spent hours with his tailor, being fitted for uniforms: the scarlet one for parades; the blue one for formal wear; that elegant field uniform, sepia; the green one for daily use. He even had a uniform made of deep purple tweed. How could I say I didn't want any of it? If I told Curran that I wasn't looking for a better job, but rather for something more, perhaps an opportunity to use my mind and express my abilities creatively, he probably wouldn't have understood either.

"I appreciate your thinking of me," I said. "I like working here, but have to move on. I plan to go to Cripple Creek and see what it's like to be a miner."

MY DEPARTURE became quite the occasion. Dr. Foster invited me to his table at dinner. After the meal, I faced an audience of a dozen patients, three nurses, and several doctors. Stanley Curran had hung my map on a mobile room divider and reviewed my script, which gave me confidence. I turned to the map and made a sweeping gesture, as if to suggest the immensity of the country and the scope of my topic.

"Ladies and gentlemen," I began. "Russia is not a subject one could draw conclusions about in a few minutes."

Reading over that speech sixty-five years later, I feel embarrassed by my naiveté. Even though I had seen impoverished peasants in the countryside and read Gorky's *Lower Depths*, I was still able to maintain the illusion that such conditions, while deplorable, were the exception:

> *Before the Revolution, life went on normally in Russia. The country was progressing and rapidly catching up with other nations. Everybody had enough to live on, and, if somebody hadn't enough to eat – which was seldom the case – to borrow from a neighbor was easy enough. Everybody criticized the nobility for their life of extravagant luxury and their ways of spending a fortune in a day's time, but really, I don't see why people shouldn't spend their money, when they have some, and live as they like.*

Finally I reached the end. The audience clapped. I appreciated their applause. Not only had I managed to say something in the English language, I had defended the Russia I knew.

The next morning I carried my suitcase toward the bus stop, in front of the main building. I felt sad to be leaving. Everyone had been so kind. My first job experience had represented more than simply waiting on tables.

Cathy came outside to say good-bye. Beaming, she held my hand in both of hers and said, "Oh, Paul. I had such good news today. The doctor says I'm better. He says I can date again, even go dancing. Isn't that wonderful?"

Stanley Curran also shook my hand and gave me the morning paper as a going-away present. I opened it as soon as the bus got under way. To my surprise, the *Gazette* had run a story about my impending move. The headline read *Leaven of Democracy Working as Count Takes Step Forward.*

3

MY EXPEDITION to Cripple Creek began on a cloudless July day with Helen at the wheel of her Dodge. The scenery was spectacular. As we drove out of Ute Pass, on the other side of Pike's Peak, and neared the timberline, the air became more rarefied, and the pines, lashed by winter winds, assumed strange shapes. Ahead of us, clearly outlined in the distance, rose the jagged peaks of the Sangre de Cristo Range.

Around noon we looked down from the crest of a hill on an area with no vegetation at all. A feeling of desolation dominated the landscape. Huge piles of mine tailings covered the surrounding hills. Forlorn dwellings hugged the valley below.

"That's Cripple Creek," Helen said as we started down. "It sits right in the crater of an extinct volcano."

In Cripple Creek itself, nothing stirred. The place was like a ghost town. No people, no animals, not even a clothesline with laundry out to dry. It was hard to believe that only twenty-five years earlier this had been a thriving community of 20,000 with dance halls, churches, gambling casinos, and all the feverish activity of a mining camp. Millions in gold were taken out of the ground. By the turn of the century, after most of the high-grade ore had been extracted, Cripple Creek fell into hard times, and the inhabitants drifted away.

As we drove along Main Street, I kept looking for someone who might direct us to a working mine. At last Helen spotted an old geezer on the stoop of a ramshackle hut and stopped the car. He sat motionless, eyes half-closed. We thought he was asleep until we noticed smoke rising from his pipe.

"Probably a prospector from Gold Rush days." Helen raised her voice: "Hey there! Could you please direct us to an active mine?"

The man removed his pipe and spat out of the corner of his mouth. "I hear there's work at the Cresson," he said in a scratchy voice. "That's over Victor way. Between Squaw Mountain and Raven Hills."

"We'll find it. Is there a good place to stay in Victor?"

"Nope."

"How about here?"

"Not much here neither. McCabe's widow takes in boarders, if you ain't too fussy. On Second Street. She's got a sign out front: Gibbs House, Restaurant."

Gibbs House was a two-story brick building. It didn't take long to rent a room.

"All set," I told Helen and we drove on. "One dollar a day, including room and board. Couldn't do much better than that."

Before long we approached a sign: an arrow indicated the Cresson Mine.

"Where do you want me to pick you up?"

"In five weeks, at Elkton – that's the railroad stop nearest Cripple Creek—around noon on Sunday, August 26."

"Okay," Helen said with a smile. "You've got yourself a date." She pulled a book from under the seat. "Here's a little present. Don't want you to get bored." She handed me R. S. Wordworth's *Psychology*. "Good luck."

I started up the dirt road. All around me rose barren hills pock-marked here and there with abandoned mine shafts. The door to the Cresson office was wide open, so I walked in. As my eyes adjusted to the dark, I made out a man at the far end. He seemed to be studying a list of names, tacked to a wall.

"Good afternoon," I said. "I'm looking for a job."

"Okay, Duke." The man checked something on a schedule as if he had been expecting me. "You're on the night shift, shoveling ore. Hours are five p.m. to eight a.m. The pay is $4.50 a day and it's damn hard work. There's a 45-minute break for supper. Where you staying, Duke?"

I hadn't expected to be hired so easily, with no questions asked, and what made him think my name was Duke?

Before I could answer, the man reached for a plaid jacket, glancing at his watch. "I'm going to Cripple Creek. Want a lift? When the boys head out for the night shift, you can come back with them on the Midland Terminal. That's the railroad. Runs a special train for the miners. Only you better wear rougher clothes. Got any?"

"I brought a pair of overalls."

"That'll do. And bring a sandwich for supper. By the way, name's Mac, short for MacDougall. Welcome to these parts. Hope you'll like it here. Some of the miners are from the Old Country, too."

Mac was in his mid-thirties. The raw-boned, lanky Scot had red hair, like me. His lack of guile showed in his face. Although the night-shift foreman spoke with a burr, I had no difficulty understanding what he said, and we chatted amicably as his Model-T bounced down the hill.

THAT SAME EVENING I went to work with pick and shovel. What stays in my memory about that first night is my feeling of apprehension at being lowered into the mine. There were about thirty of us crammed into the skip, a two-layer platform elevator with waist-high metal sides that carried men and ore to and from the working levels.

No one spoke as we waited for the descent. Water from the cable dripped onto my neck, one cold drop at a time. We were packed in so tight I couldn't move. The burly fellow next to me had a flask on a leather strap, hung over his shoulder. It looked so moldy I couldn't imagine any-one drinking water that way.

All of a sudden the skip started. I held my breath. We descended into total darkness. My stomach tightened as we traveled one thousand four hundred feet down. The skip dropped faster than any elevator, then stopped with a jerk. The first thing we did was take off our jackets because it was warmer than above ground. Then each man lit his carbide lamp. We stood in the hoist station for that level, a fairly large space lit by two electric bulbs. The miners separated into groups of three or four. I was assigned to the same group as the man with the moldy flask. His muscles indicated he was no newcomer. We set out, bending over as we proceeded along a low passageway. I couldn't see underfoot and stumbled a couple times.

"Better keep close. It's easy to get lost," the man ahead of me said.

The flickering light from the lamps cast strange shadows as we trudged along. First we turned right, then left, then right again. Sometimes we stepped over wagon tracks. Other tunnels branched off from ours. Later I would learn that the whole hillside was honeycombed with passageways, most of them long since abandoned. As we made our way in the shifting light, I began to understand the importance of sticking together.

After we had walked for about ten minutes, the passage broadened into a space the size of a small room where we could stand up straight. Two men attached pneumatic drills to a hose that brought compressed air from the surface. Without a pause to rest, each miner began to drill a hole in the wall. The drills made loud, explosive sounds, murder on the ears. Trying to disregard the noise, I picked up a shovel and started to pitch ore into a nearby wagon. The ore looked like unpromising lumps of gray rubble. The bigger pieces had to be picked up with both hands. When I stopped to catch my breath, I noticed that the miners' bodies were shaking violently from the vibration of the drills.

An hour went by, then another. I was breathing hard and straining to keep up. How my muscles ached. My mouth felt parched. Soon I could barely lift the shovel. The man with the moldy flask offered me a drink. Whatever I had thought earlier was forgotten. I gulped the water gratefully.

At nine p.m. came our break, but not the opportunity for fresh air. Everybody gathered around the hoist station, sitting on the ground to eat. The miners didn't talk much during supper. Each had a lunch box and a thermos. To save strength, some took naps. The man who had shared his flask sat down beside me.

I tried to start a conversation, introducing myself: "Paul Grabbe,

Russian émigré."

"Samo Chalupka's the name," he said, filling the cap of the thermos with coffee. "I'm from the Old Country, too. Came here as a kid. Bratislava. Know where that is?"

"Slovakia?"

"That's right, Duke. Slovakia, on the Danube."

Samo explained the main job of the night shift was to drill holes and fill them with dynamite. At 2:00 a.m., shortly after the miners had left, the fuses were lit, producing an explosion. The rubble settled during the night. The day shift loaded the ore into wagons and pushed them to the skip. Once the ore was hauled to the surface, it went to a processing plant. The night shift shoveled up whatever the day shift hadn't finished.

After the break, I tripped over what looked like a pile of Roman candles stacked against the wall.

"What are these?" I asked Samo.

"Sticks of dynamite."

"Couldn't they explode?"

My question brought a smirk to his face.

That first day I stayed as far away from the dynamite as possible. The final hours were pure torture. Samo and the others pretended not to notice. Their compassion helped. At quitting time, a foreman appeared with a yardstick. He pushed it into each of the holes to gauge their depth. After the holes had been checked, the miners filled them with dynamite. Then everybody assembled at the hoist station. Mac checked off names to make sure no one had been left behind. We all climbed into the skip and were hoisted to the surface. Not ten minutes later we could hear an ominous rumble deep below ground.

Next we trouped into Mac's office where he went through the motions of frisking each man. This frisking was a carry-over from the old days when miners were known to smuggle out chunks of rich ore. After this ritual, we walked down the gulch to Elkton where the train took us back to Cripple Creek. It was nearly 3 a.m. by the time I reached Gibbs House. I threw myself onto the bed, too grimy to crawl between the sheets, too exhausted to undress.

Days went by, then weeks. Soon I found I wasn't quite as tired any more. I also got used to the darkness, the cramped quarters, the noise, even the fine gray dust that was hard to wash off in the morning. After a while

I would even sit down to rest from time to time on the pile of dynamite.

DURING MY MINING days, I received news of my brother George's fate. Father wrote he had succeeded in locating my former tutor. Russia was torn by civil war. Eager to get out of the country, Koukoulya had agreed to look for my brother. A gardener at Bogorodskoye told him Yegor had left George stranded in the manor house. It seems our butler had absconded with the family silver. Further inquiries revealed George had taken shelter in a nearby village. At the time, the village simpleton enjoyed a special status in Russia, for such a person was regarded as closer to God than ordinary mortals. George had been able to wander from village to village. Everywhere he was given food and shelter. Eventually Koukoulya caught up with him and brought him back to Petrograd. Father arranged to have them both smuggled across the Russian border. Everything had gone according to plan. Father found a sanitarium in the French Alps for George, and Koukoulya joined his brother in Paris.[15]

After receiving this news, I wrote to add my thanks and to say how glad I was to know he was alive and well: *Remember the motion pictures we enjoyed together, about outlaws and Indians, and wild goings-on in the American West? Well, dear Koukoulya, believe it or not, here I am in Colorado, right in the middle of the West. Only I don't shoot from the hip or hold up stagecoaches. I shovel ore in a gold mine for four dollars and fifty cents a day.*

WHEN I WASN'T at work, I explored Cripple Creek with my camera. The inhabitants were camera-shy so there wasn't much to photograph. I did manage a few shots of their homes, mere shanties, which offered even less protection from the elements than a peasant's *izba*.

The miners were simple, straightforward men. Many were immigrants from Eastern Europe. Their talk was interspersed with oaths and frequent references to sex. I wondered why they swore so much and in such good-humored fashion until I realized swearing was a substitute for a vocabulary they did not possess. At first they kept an eye on me. Would I share a sandwich, lend a hand, participate in an emergency? They planned practical jokes and observed my reaction, in a kind of initiation to find out whether I could be trusted to face danger as part of the group. Gradually they lost interest and accepted me, if not as one of their own, then, at least, as part of the landscape. Strange as it may seem, time flew by. August 26 was fast approaching.

It so happened that on my last night an incident occurred that demonstrated how dangerous mining can be. We had gathered at the hoist station and stood around waiting.

Mac asked in a tense voice, "Where are those two lads we took on yesterday? Anybody see them?"

Without a moment's hesitation, a dozen miners fanned out in all directions. The rest of us climbed into the skip and rose to the surface. By then only a few minutes remained before the dynamite was due to explode. All I could think of was what might happen to Samo and the others, in imminent danger. The skip finally reappeared. Everyone cheered at the boys' rescue. Soon, from below ground, came the familiar muffled rumble of the explosion.

When I went to the Cresson office to be paid off, Mac pushed a stool in my direction and offered me a cigarette.

"Hey," he said. "You can't leave without my giving you some history. In the 1890s, there were quite a few gold mines operating in this area. One was the Cresson, within a few miles of the famous Independence Mine. Everyone said the Cresson was a dud. Then along came the Harbeck brothers, two insurance salesmen from Chicago. Well, they got involved in a gambling spree and woke up the next morning owning this mine. Nobody thought the property was worth a damn, but somehow those Harbecks had caught gold fever. They gave up their business, sold shares to people they knew in Chicago, and sank everything into the Cresson. What they found was low-grade ore, difficult to ship out. We're located at the top of a narrow gully. The Midland Terminal Railroad wouldn't run a spur up here. A punk mine, people said, a six-hundred-foot hole and eighty thousand in debt.

"At this point a young fellow named Dick Roefels turned up. He had been trained as an engineer back in Pennsylvania. The Harbecks were looking for a manager, and somebody recommended him. Roefels turned out to be a miracle worker. He introduced new ways to speed up mining and worked out a safety device to stop the skip from running out of control. He even developed an overhead conveyor to transport the ore down Eclipse Gully, right into Elkton. The Cresson began to pay for itself in a

186

modest way. Still, no one could have expected what happened next. It was every gold miner's dream." Mac slapped his thigh, enjoying the suspense he had created.

"One day late in November of 1914, Roefels was down on the twelfth level for a routine inspection and came upon a cave, what miners call a *vug*. He stepped through the opening and lit a magnesium flare. What he saw took his breath away: the walls were lined with jewels, sylvanite and calaverite, shining with flecks of pure gold.

"Roefels didn't lose his head, oh no. He had a steel door installed to close off the vug and placed three men with revolvers out front. Forty feet high, it was. Came to be known as Aladdin's Cave. In the first four weeks alone, it brought in over a million. And that was just the beginning. The Harbecks could start paying handsome dividends to the shareholders in Chicago. Not many vugs like that in all the history of mining.

"And, you know, after they discovered that gold, they knew there must be more, deeper down. And, there was. All the way to the eighteenth. Up to now the Cresson has brought in more than twenty million." He paused reflectively. "Let's see. It's just nine years since Roefels discovered Aladdin's Cave, five since they took out the last of the treasure."

"I got here too late."

"Yup," he said, laughing. "Me, too. There's only low-grade ore left now, but thank the Lord it will keep us going for a while."

I couldn't help asking before we parted, "Mac, why does everyone call me Duke?"

"It's that article the *Gazette* ran, saying you were Russian nobility. The miners had never heard of counts, but they heard of dukes: the Duke of Windsor, Duke Ellington. They figured you must be a duke, too."

AFTER BREAKFAST on August 26th, I packed my suitcase and paid my bill. I walked down Bennet Avenue, past several men sitting in the sun, and stopped to say good-bye. A few of them, including Samo, accompanied me to the station. One even insisted on carrying my suitcase. By the time we reached the platform, I was at the head of a little procession.

The train consisted of a wooden railroad car, drawn by a steam engine. There were only two other passengers on board, tourists I took to be English spinsters. They looked at us sideways as if we were part of the local color and not to be missed.

To my surprise, I felt sorry to leave. People who face physical danger together develop a strong sense of solidarity. In Cripple Creek, for the first time in my life, I had shared this feeling. Not since the Corps des Pages had I been part of a group. Having found solidarity, it was hard to tear myself away. Yet I needed to get on with my life.

The miners gathered round as I made a farewell speech: "Samo, Joe, Josh, I'm sorry to say goodbye. I can't tell you how much it has meant to spend time with you here in Cripple Creek. You all mean a lot to me. If ever there is a revolution in this country, I know where to go to find friends."

Josh stepped forward and shook my hand. "So long, Duke. Good luck!"

The engine gave a toot. The men lifted their caps into the air. I waved back.

Samo called out, "Goodbye to you, Duke of the Bolsheviki."

In no time at all the train had reached Elkton. As I descended the steps, I spied Helen's Dodge parked some hundred yards away. The engine gave another toot, and the train started up again. As it rattled past, the English ladies peered, wide-eyed, in our direction.

I told Helen about my experiences as we headed for Colorado Springs. After a while I realized she was only half-listening. She filled in the ensuing silence with the latest news: "Harding has died under strange circumstances. The newspapers are full of rumors of oil leases and all kinds of corrupt goings-on in Washington. There's even talk of indicting Cabinet members."

It was my turn to be mildly interested. At the time I knew nothing about President Harding. How to make a living after the Revolution had crowded out all other concerns. I couldn't even keep track of current events.

The closer we got to Colorado Springs, the more conscious I became of Helen's mood. Something was different. Perhaps her husband had returned and she didn't know how to break the news? She pulled up outside my rooming house, but didn't turn to face me. I asked if I could stop by. She gave her head a quick nod, eyes downcast.

In the morning, the mailman delivered a letter. It was crudely printed in red ink and read as follows:

We give you notice to get out of town. We have watched you and the likes of you are not welcome here. Get out before we tar and feather you. K.K.K

At first I couldn't understand the message. What did *tar and feather* mean and who was K.K.K.? The tone, however, made the meaning all too clear. I hurried over to Helen's bungalow, but no one was there. After a while, Lolly showed up on foot.

"When will your mother be home?" I asked.

Lolly shrugged. Together we ate peanut butter sandwiches. I decided to go for a walk. It was dusk by the time I returned. Helen's car stood in the driveway. The August night was warm, and the windows were open. I could hear voices. I moved a bit closer and immediately recognized her companion: the bootlegger!

Instinctively I crouched behind some shrubbery, still too far away to hear more than snippets of conversation. Merck reached out and touched Helen's cheek, making the intimacy of their relationship obvious. I clenched and unclenched my fists, finding it hard to breathe. How could she be interested in someone so limited? I watched him pick up a bottle, refill glasses. He must have told a joke, because I heard laughter. Minutes passed. Then the couple disappeared into the bedroom. Blood rushed to my head. I wanted to storm the house and confront my rival, but he was bigger and powerfully built. Wild with jealousy, I stood there, feeling helpless. After several minutes of indecision, I turned away and walked aimlessly along Cheyenne Road. That night I lay in bed, unable to sleep.

In the morning I returned to the bungalow. Helen sat in the kitchen, drinking coffee. She looked startled to see me. I took the crumpled note out of my pocket and smoothed it out on the table.

"Look what came in the mail yesterday," I said.

"How awful, the Ku Klux Klan!"

She glanced toward the bedroom and seemed to be about to say something when the door opened. Merck took one glance at me and stalked outside.

"Wait! Let me drive you into town," Helen called, grabbing her purse.

Dumbfounded, I stood there and watched her run after him. I paced for a while, then sat down and tried to compose myself, drumming fingers on the table. Soon Lolly came home.

"Hi, Mr. Grabbe. I spent the night at Libby's. Mommy's promised to take me to the mountains for a picnic. Maybe you can come, too. Want to color with me?"

I sat beside Lolly without uttering a word. She handed me some crayons. From time to time we exchanged smiles.

Helen returned a half-hour later and invited me along on their picnic. Our route took us past Red Rock. As we approached the timberline, she parked near a huge boulder. I hardly touched the elaborate lunch of fried chicken and deviled eggs, waiting until Lolly was out of earshot to speak: "This place looks familiar. We've been here before."

Lightly Helen laid her hand on my arm and whispered, "I'm so sorry." She was about to elaborate when her daughter came running back.

"Mommy, Mommy!" Lolly cried, all out of breath. "I heard a chickadee. Over in those trees. Come see. I want you to hear it, too."

As Helen disappeared into the woods, I had a feeling of irretrievable loss. I hugged my knees, staring at the ground. I thought back to the last time we had been there together, and it occurred to me that she must prefer Merck's lovemaking to mine.

"Lolly insists she heard a mountain chickadee, but it was probably a finch," Helen said as she resumed her seat. "Chickadees are rare here at this season. It must have been a straggler that overstayed his time."

"Overstayed his time," I repeated under my breath.

Denver was the closest city to Colorado Springs. I had just enough money for a bus fare. I told Helen I was leaving and she offered to drive me. The following day, I watched her Dodge weave through traffic and disappear in the afternoon haze. As I trudged into the lobby, I realized who had written the note: Merck! Helen must have realized, too. That explained why she had driven me so expediently to Denver: to avoid an encounter with the Ku Klux Klan.

4

A DOUBLE ROOM at the Denver YMCA cost five dollars a week. At that rate, I could last without a job for a while. The clerk handed me a key. I located Room 37 at the end of a hallway. Through the open door I could see a skinny man stretched out on a bed. He held a magazine in his left hand to catch the last rays of the setting sun. Articles of clothing lay scattered on the floor. He didn't look up at my knock. Slowly I put my suitcase down, feeling like an intruder.

"May I come in? My name is Paul Grabbe, from Russia. I'm an émigré. The clerk downstairs said we could share this room. Do you mind?"

"Not in the least. Name's Danforth Barney. Make yourself at home."

As I stepped across the threshold, Dan sat up, brandishing the magazine. "It's marvelous."

"What is?"

"Mencken sounding off."

"Who's Mencken?"

"Don't tell me you've never heard of H. L. Mencken! Why, he's the country's number one debunker. Goes after what he calls the *booboisie*. Shows them up for the bigoted fools they are. Here, for example, he quotes a minister from Arkansas who has no use for grand opera. Just listen to this." In a mocking tone, Dan began to read:

> *The Reverend Dr. Culpepper, pastor of the Grand Avenue Methodist Church, in discussing National Music Week at the request of the local Music Club, scored the members for devoting their time to the study of grand opera, which, he said, "No one can understand, and, if they did, it would do them no good."*

"Do you have anything else he has written?"

"Sure thing."

With his thumb, Dan indicated a pile of magazines. He thrust feet into some shoes and reached for a jacket. "Say, how about we grab a bite to eat? There's a good place—the Mountain Dew—right around the corner. Their apple dumplings cost only fifteen cents apiece. I fill up on them every day."

"Do you have a job?" I asked in the lobby.

"Next week, at about this time, I'll be selling refrigerators, of all things. Hate the whole idea. I'm not a salesman. Never will be. It's my mom's idea. She's got a new friend who's in the business and agreed to hire me."

Something had discouraged Dan, no doubt his father's recent suicide, and at twenty he was trying to make sense of life. Like me, he was at loose ends. Mencken provided an immediate bond. The writer criticized the Puritanical narrowness and crass materialism of a society in which neither of us felt at ease.

The next day I bought a copy of the *Denver Post*. Again I didn't fit any of the classified ads. I searched the paper for days, but to no avail. Then, one morning, an ad caught my eye: *Room, board, and $5 weekly for student willing to work hard helping at meals in boarding house.* Without wasting any time, I set off for the address indicated.

A frumpy woman was putting up her hair when she threw open the door. Hairpins jutted from her mouth. "Bertha Crump," she growled. "Come about the job?"

"I saw the ad," I said uncertainly.

"You'll do. Get your things and be back by five."

That afternoon I went to work washing and drying endless stacks of dishes. The light in the kitchen wasn't strong enough to tell whether the plates were clean, and I had to keep a folded newspaper handy to swat cockroaches. To make matters worse, it turned out Mrs. Crump's boarders all had tuberculosis. After my experience at Cragmor, I knew it was pure folly to stay, but, at twenty-one, one doesn't weigh odds. Besides, I needed to eat. Deliverance came in an unexpected way. On a Sunday morning, I was hanging up dishtowels when Mrs. Crump appeared behind me.

"Can you see through those windows?" She dragged her pointer finger across the pane, covered with a greasy film. "Well, I can't either. Make sure they sparkle before you leave."

Why, the old hag! I muttered under my breath as she hobbled up the backstairs. *That ad didn't mention any windows. Imagine horning in on my free time like that.* Reluctantly I set to work. For the first time in my life, I was discovering what it felt like to be exploited.

Ten minutes later Mrs. Crump came stomping back into the kitchen. "What's this?" she demanded with venom in her voice, thrusting, under my nose, one of Helen's pamphlets, *The Healing Power of Positive Thinking*. In her other hand, she held R. S. Woodworth's *Psychology*, which she tossed to the floor at my feet. "I bet you plan to work some of that mental stuff on my roomers. I'd lose them all, one by one, if I put up with the likes of you. Psychology? I'll show you where that leads. You're fired."

I packed my suitcase and returned to the Y, grateful to be able to move back in with Dan.

"That nasty old bitch," he snorted after I had described her behavior. "Of all things, to be mistaken for a healer." Dan must have found the incident funny because he laughed until he noticed the disgruntled expression on my face. "Oh, I'm sorry. Hey, you must be short of cash. I've just been paid. Here, take this."

Gratefully I accepted the loan of twenty dollars. "Dan, what can you tell me about the Ku Klux Klan?"

"They're a secret society, small-time yokels who ride around in white robes, wearing masks and hoods. They gather at night and burn crosses. Why do you want to know about that scum?"

"Why do such things?"

"To scare people. They want to force their screwy ideas on everybody. They're Bible thumpers, ultra-nationalists, anti-alien, anti-everything progressive. For a while nobody paid them any mind, but lately they've been growing in number, and they're dangerous."

"What does *tar and feather* mean?"

"Sometimes they get violent. Drag people from their homes. Beat them up. Even dip them in tar and feathers."

"I didn't know anything so wild still existed in America."

"Heard about the Frontier? It's still here. What makes you so interested in the Klan?"

I removed Merck's note from my pocket and unfolded it again.

"Doggone! You stay away from the Klan. They're a vicious lot."

In the morning, I resumed my job-hunting routine. The experience with Mrs. Crump made me wary of ads that offered room and board. Yet, when Dan's loan ran out, reducing me to a diet of one apple dumpling per day, it was precisely such an ad that I answered. This time I was more fortunate. The address led me to Clarkson Street in a quiet, once fashionable neighborhood. The place was now a boarding house run by one Frances Leatherman, a buxom, middle-aged lady who started talking as soon as she had let me in the door. I sat there politely on a stool in her kitchen for about twenty minutes, wondering whether I would get the job. I heard all about her beloved husband, Wilbur, who had mysteriously disappeared, and the grocery store they ran together.

"I have the best people staying here. My nine roomers are all schoolteachers with steady employment. And I set a good table."

That sounded promising. But what was the job description?

"Running a place like this takes a lot of work if you're going to do it right," Mrs. Leatherman said. "I do the cooking and have two college boys to help in the kitchen."

My heart sank. Did that mean the job was already filled?

Abruptly she made up her mind: "Where are your things? You can have the attic room, the one with pink wallpaper."

My duties consisted of setting tables for the evening meal and running the vacuum cleaner once a week, but, actually, I had been hired for a different purpose altogether. Mrs. Leatherman had a need to unburden her soul. What's more, when she noticed Professor Woodward's *Psychology* on my bedside table, she became convinced I must be in touch with the occult and could call on magical power to bring her husband back.

Every day after breakfast, and sometimes after supper, Mrs. Leatherman would make her way to my attic room, sit down with her red hands clasped in her lap, and expound on theories of what might have happened to Wilbur. I would look as attentive as possible as the stream of words poured over me, nodding from time to time to indicate sympathy.

"Such a good man," she kept repeating. Every now and then she'd ask, "When do you reckon he'll be back?"

"Well, I don't know," I'd reply.

She'd look pleadingly at me and say, "By Christmas?"

The whole situation made me uncomfortable, as if I were there under false pretenses. I liked my landlady and didn't want to mislead her. This is only temporary, I told myself. The situation in Russia can't last forever.

In order to diminish the frequency of Mrs. Leatherman's visits, I persuaded her to allow Dan Barney to move in with me. He promptly set up a radio and installed his antenna. Every night he'd twist the cat's whisker on the galena crystal and pick up signals. Sometimes we'd listen to jazz from as far away as California.

After a few weeks, Dan decided to move to San Francisco, where it was possible to find work on a tramp steamer. At Thanksgiving, he invited me home and introduced me to his mother. With the holiday came a foot of snow, which gave Denver a festive look. I watched Vivian Barney place a large turkey, sizzling brown, on the dining-room table. Her friend served up slices of turkey breast, followed by dark meat.

"Have more cranberries," he said, passing the dish. "Got cranberries in Russia?"

"Yes. Turkey, too, before the Revolution."

"Revolution? Must have been tough on your family. You're lucky to be out. Yes, siree. And to have gotten yourself to this country."

"Dan was my first American friend," I said. "I hate to see him move away."

"Apply for citizenship yet?"

I usually answered such questions by saying I was only a visitor and planned to return as soon as conditions would permit, but this time my little speech didn't go right. Something—perhaps the look on the man's face—made me realize what I was saying wasn't true. Up to that point I had always dismissed the thought that the communist regime could last. Now the possibility that it might well outlive me struck with great force, as if someone had shouted, *You fool! Stop kidding yourself. You'll never go back. Never.* I excused myself and went outside. Distraught, I wandered aimlessly through the snowy streets. I felt as if lights inside me were being extinguished, one after the other. I couldn't delude myself any longer. I would never see Russia again.

In the morning I felt even worse, with that sinking feeling people get in the wake of tragedy. I took a bus downtown and bought a black necktie, as in a ritual of mourning. I also special-ordered black-rimmed Christmas cards. Once back in my room, I stretched out on the narrow bed. I lay there, staring at the wallpaper, my limbs heavy, thoughts drifting. Familiar sounds reached me from the outside world. There was a dull throbbing inside my head. I had lost the will to live.

Memories of Vasilevskoye returned: the excitement of climbing a tree near the river, casting my line, feeling a sudden tug. I remembered long walks with Koukoulya in the snow along the Neva. Several knocks at the door broke into this reverie.

"I've made chicken soup," Mrs. Leatherman said. "You better have some."

"Thanks," I mumbled.

I wasn't hungry. All I wanted was to be left alone. In my mind I was reliving my 1920 trip to the Russian border, the year I traveled to Estonia. I stepped from the train in Narva and immediately recognized the sights and sounds characteristic of a provincial town: words written in Cyrillic on every storefront, on bare walls, on dilapidated signposts; buxom women in colorful scarves behind their vegetable stalls; horse-drawn *droshkies*, plodding along. Everyone was speaking Russian. I paused in front of a store window to listen to passers-by.

"Are we far from the border?" I asked a stranger.

He pointed at a nearby hill. "On the other side, there's a strip of land several versts wide. We call it No Man's Land." He smiled sardonically, as if glad to have the opportunity to share his emotion. "Separates our country from the land of the Bolsheviki."

I climbed the hill and sat down on a fallen tree trunk. The day was overcast. Marshland extended to the east. In the distance, I could make out a wooded area, the border with Russia. Even as I strained to see through the mist, my mind raced beyond those woods, one hundred miles east to Petrograd, my birthplace. For quite some time I sat there and simply gazed straight ahead, motionless and silent.

Later I returned to the station where a railroad car sat on a siding. "Is that part of the train for Reval?" I asked the stationmaster.

"No. It's the private car of Maxim Litvinov, Commissar for Foreign Affairs. He has to wait for a locomotive to take him to Moscow."

It didn't seem fair. He could go back to Russia, but I couldn't. In his eyes, I would be *an enemy of the people.*

As I reflect on my intense distress that day, I realize the loss of one's country can be one of life's greatest sorrows. Exile, I've learned, is not emigration. It's not something you choose voluntarily, like a different place to live. It means being expelled from your homeland to live elsewhere. From that moment on, one must accept the world of a stranger and struggle to understand a foreign culture.

I lay on the bed in that Denver boarding house and tried to imagine what it would mean to live out my life in America. I thought back to the time I had learned to skate as a small child. Even with the help of a governess, I was barely able to keep my feet from sliding out from under me. When she let go, I was left standing rigid on the ice. I didn't dare to move and felt utterly wretched. Losing one's country was like that feeling, only worse. What was gone was the essential support which only one's native land can provide—the reassurance of familiar faces, the comfort of places one knows by heart, the knowledge of being in one's element.

I'm not sure how many days I lay there feeling sorry for myself. It's fortunate a powerful instinct recalls us all to life, and so it was with me. After a while I gathered enough strength to turn away from the wall. As I did so, a spider caught my eye. Industriously, it spun its web above the window frame. That spider didn't necessarily want to spin a web, but there it was, making the best of the situation. So it would be for me. I could live without going back to Russia. With this realization would come the willingness to face the world and make myself a part of it.

Once my acute nostalgia had passed, I talked to Dan's mother about my situation. Vivian Barney suggested I take advantage of my knowledge of French and contact the *Alliance Française*. The head of the local chapter received me warmly. After we had chatted a while in French, Marie de Mare suggested I escort her to a party at the Thompson mansion on Logan Street that very evening.

Not since Europe had I seen so many elegant people in one place. The hall was decorated with lilies. We each took a glass of champagne from the buffet table. Marie whispered, "See that tall blonde in the green dress, over by the potted palm? That's Jean Cranmer, Denver's leading patron of the arts. Her family made its fortune with a silver mine. Let's go talk to her before she decides to leave." I followed Marie across the room, intercepting some hors d'oeuvres as a waiter carried them past.

"Jean, I'd like to introduce Count Paul Grabbe, a Russian refugee from Bolshevism. I thought you'd enjoy knowing each other."

I bent to kiss Jean Cranmer's hand. It smelled of perfume. In her emerald dress and black hat, she looked soignée and at ease with wealth. Intelligence shone in her eyes. The three of us talked for a few minutes, then she left for another engagement.

THANKS TO Marie de Mare, Jean hired me to tutor her children. Early in January, we traveled to Santa Barbara, California, where we stayed at the exclusive Miramar Hotel. My salary was one hundred dollars a month, with all expenses paid. I liked the children, but found the social situation demoralizing: other people my age were off playing tennis while I had to work. I hadn't minded being a waiter or a miner, but, as a tutor, I had to function in a role I saw as inferior to those around me, people whom I considered equals.

Another difficulty related to my new boss. It turned out Mrs. Cranmer was in search of an escort. After dinner, determined to improve my English, I would disappear into my room instead of accompanying her to some party. I was discovering Joseph Conrad, who set out to write books in a language that was not his mother tongue. The heroes survived cataclysmic situations despite the odds. I could identify.

As I read *Lord Jim*, I realized I was reacting to Conrad's use of language. English came alive as never before. The impact was such that I felt compelled to write. Without wasting any time, I sat down beside the window and attempted to describe the sunset. Those paragraphs were my initial literary effort in English.

With my first paycheck, I purchased a portable typewriter.

5

THE CRANMERS dropped me off in San Francisco. I had kept Dan Barney's new address, so the first thing I did was look him up. As luck would have it, my old friend was home and greeted me with his usual languid smile. Dan was shipping out to Singapore that week and offered to sublet the apartment he shared with Noble Johnson, who worked long hours at a local cemetery. The moment I met my future roommate, I realized we had nothing in common. Noble led the way to the bathroom window and raised the shade. "This apartment offers a special bonus. The neighbor has a lover. They never turn out the lights." He started snickering: "Free show!"

Fortunately, Noble left early in the morning. I had started writing a screenplay and, after his departure, I'd type away all day on a first draft. After three weeks, I ran out of money. Noble suggested a job at Cypress Lawn and offered to introduce me to the funeral director. So began my life among the dead.

CYPRESS LAWN occupied a tract of land on both sides of a highway running south from San Francisco. In 1924, a dozen gardeners worked to keep the place as trim as any of the best front lawns in the city's more affluent suburbs. The idea was to make visitors feel as if they would repose not merely in peace, but in a permanent state of material wellbeing should they to choose the cemetery as a final resting place.

The stucco building at the main entrance served as the business office. Noble took a footpath that led up the hill to an aboveground burial place called the Catacombs. A Chinese pagoda, supported on Romanesque arches, conjoined a Greek temple in a mish-mash of architectural styles that startled the eye. Ferns, strategically placed around the sealed crypts, softened the effect of all that white marble.

"Apparently burying a relative in the Catacombs has its appeal," Noble said as we walked back out into the sunlight. "Mourners appreciate being able to come at any time of day and linger in a pleasant, heated area, protected from rain. For these privileges, they're willing to pay more."

A wiry man hurried up the hill toward us.

Noble did the introductions: "Everett Davis meet Paul Grabbe, Russian émigré."

Davis grasped my hand and shook it heartily. I felt disconcerted by his exuberance.

"You want to look a fucking dead man in the face, do you? That what you're here for? Got the guts? Think you can hoist a casket?" After examining my clothes, my shoes, my face, he took a step back and shook his head. "A guy like you with all these stiffs? Holy Mother of God, you chose the wrong place, you young whippersnapper you. What brings you to these parts anyhow?"

"Paul needs a job," Noble said before I could respond.

"Hell, don't we all? Okay. You'll be making one hundred forty-five dollars a month. Go to the office and sign up. Tell them Davis sent you."

Davis was quite a character. I immediately began jotting down his more felicitous verbal sallies. When I found myself alone, I would practice my favorites, learning some by heart. Gradually, I incorporated the slang into my own speech. The change made me feel more at ease.

MY EIGHT co-workers were a motley bunch. There was Noble Johnson, of course, and Vlas Sanichek from Bohemia. Powerfully built, he could handle the heaviest coffins. Stocky Jack Cronin was working his way through law school. Sweet Pietro Verona, a gentle fellow of Italian descent, tended the gardens. In charge of this crew was our funeral director, elegant in his cutaway and bowler hat.

I spent my mornings at the Catacombs, watering ferns and generally keeping the place clean. Once my chores were finished, I'd settle into a wicker chair and read H. G. Wells's *Outline of History*. The only interruption came from talkative visitors whom I did my best to avoid. One widow, in particular, would come early, before there had been any chance to store away watering can and hose. Davis had told me to engage her in conversation, discreetly emphasizing the advantages of a Catacombs burial. The permanence of the structure, secure even from earthquakes, always impressed visitors.

I regret to report I did not carry out this part of my job too well.

Sometimes, in fact, I would suggest drawbacks, rather than advantages: "What would happen if the Japanese sent a warship to bombard San Francisco? In 1905, they destroyed the whole Russian fleet. One good hit and this place would be a shambles."

Such talk was my way of getting back at society. If there had been no revolution, I would have been starting a career in Russia as a graduate of the prestigious Corps des Pages. Instead I found myself in a cemetery, on the other side of the earth.

DEATH ARRIVED at Cypress Lawn every morning, promptly at 11 a.m. when the first hearse of the day pulled up at the front entrance. Behind the sleek limousine trailed several cars, filled with mourners. Davis would hop into the Model-T and lead the procession to the burial site. We would pause while the relatives assembled. On his signal, four of us would lift out the coffin. Often an invisible struggle would take place as each pallbearer jostled for position at the rear. This elbowing and shoving reminded me of a game of musical chairs. Since some coffins were heavy, shifting the weight could make all the difference. We would carry the coffin a few yards, then rest it on two wooden crossbars above a hole in the ground. If no minister were present, Davis would read a short service in a solemn voice. As two pallbearers on either side of the grave pulled on broad canvas tapes under the casket to raise it slightly in the air, the funeral director would reach down and remove the crossbars. Slackening the tapes, we proceeded to lower the casket into the grave.

Funeral services at the crematorium followed the same procedure as internment. As soon as the hearse arrived, we carried the casket to the auditorium and laid it on a conveyor belt near the organ. The mourners took their seats. Davis made a few remarks. Mrs. Duffy, the middle-aged organist, played "Nearer, My God, To Thee" while Davis slowly drew a curtain shut, hiding the casket.

After the mourners had departed, we'd throw out the wreaths and other floral tributes. Then we'd roll the casket to one of the ovens and push it in. A tall, thin, sallow-looking man named Jack Sims was in charge of the flame. The fire reduced the contents to ash, leaving only the skull and larger bones. After the oven had cooled, Jack would gather what was left and retreat upstairs where he would break up the bones with a mallet,

200

prior to grinding them into a powder. The screechy noise was like nothing I had ever heard before in my life.

In 1924, many Americans shied away from cremation. Davis had given the matter some thought and decided this resistance was not entirely due to religious beliefs. "In internment, destruction of the body is gradual," he told me. "Relatives can visit the grave, decorate it with flowers, and still think they are near their loved ones, which, in a sense, they are. That gives them more time to adjust to their loss."

Management had decreed personnel should look solemn during all ceremonies. Smiles were outlawed. Anyone caught cracking a joke within hearing distance of the public would receive a reprimand. This rule led to a game: we would all try to make each other laugh. Some of my colleagues were ingenious at it. Holding in for so long created a funny situation after each funeral. As soon as we were well away from the mourners, we would burst into uncontrollable laughter. At lunch, in a nearby restaurant, the joviality would continue. Davis usually led off with a few bawdy jokes. This excessive merriment was probably a facade to mask true feelings about the job.

WHILE AT CYPRESS Lawn, my off-hours were organized like a monk's. I would rise at 5:45. During the forty-five minute streetcar ride, I read books suggested by a local librarian. I kept a pad with me, and as the trolley climbed up and down the hills of San Francisco, I jotted down unfamiliar words. Even at work, I always carried a book around. On one occasion, when my chores were done, I settled into a freshly dug grave to get out of the wind and read *Wuthering Heights*. In the evening, I'd look words up in the dictionary. What stimulated this furious activity? English had become my life preserver. Concentrating fiercely on the language helped preserve my sanity. I kept telling myself that mastery of English would enable me to cope with life in my new country, perhaps even allow me to reach a social status similar to what my family had enjoyed in Russia.

On Sundays I allowed myself the luxury of sleeping late. I lolled in bed with the newspaper for a couple hours. Around noon, I'd eat a meal at a good restaurant and splurge on strawberry shortcake with whipped cream, my favorite dessert. I'd go out for a quick walk, then return to my studies, determined not to lose momentum.

Davis was the only person to whom I had confided my goal of becoming a writer. He promptly gave me Cody's *Self-Correcting Course in the English Language.* By then I had finished my screenplay and sent the draft to the Palmer Institute in Hollywood. I had even received a response, which bolstered my spirits: *Keep up the good work. Develop your talent. We're with you.* I immediately set to work on an eyewitness account of the first day of the Revolution.

IN THE FALL, I decided I had worked at Cypress Lawn long enough. I was now a full-fledged member of the American Federation of Labor Cemetery Workers and possessed a union card: Number 10634. Davis had even allowed me to lead a funeral procession. Best of all, after Mrs. Duffy retired, I was asked to take over her job.

One afternoon Davis took me aside. To get out of the sun, we strolled toward a nearby maple. I could see he had something special on his mind.

"I finally got around to reading your article on the Revolution. You should try to get it published," he said, wiping his forehead with a large handkerchief. "There's a job coming up. That Chinaman on the third tier up in the Receiving Vault—his family is shipping him back to Shanghai. By law, someone has to accompany the body. You interested? No special duties, all expenses paid, five dollars a day. Plenty of time on board to write. How about it?"

"Wish I could, but I'm off to Hollywood in a couple weeks."

"That hellhole? Why go there?"

I shrugged. I thought the movie capital might put me in touch with more companionable people, but didn't want to say so, lest the funeral director take offense.

A fortnight later, Davis and I drove into the city. After dinner, he dropped me off at Southern Pacific Station. "It's just as well you quit," he said as we shook hands one last time. "They were about to fire you. You were too conscientious about those ferns. Most of them will have to be replaced."

"But nobody said a word."

"Nobody ever does. You've got to find out for yourself in this life. But don't let it bother you. You're well out of here." Davis climbed back into his Model-T and honked the horn three times. "Good luck!" he called in that resonant voice of his as the car jerked forward.

202

6

IN 1924, CINEMA had already become the world's most popular form of entertainment. People flocked to Los Angeles to work in the burgeoning movie industry. As my bus passed low buildings, I looked up and saw the famous Hollywoodland sign, a reminder that fantasy can be turned into glamour—a marketable product.

Dan's mother Vivian had sent the name of a cousin, so I went right to Universal Studios where I obtained a temporary job, writing weekly book reviews. I dared to hope the reviews would lead to steady employment. Soon I had rented a room in a nice part of town. A movie star lived across the street. Matinee idol Conrad Nagel often returned home for lunch in costume, a pirate one day, a Beau Brummel the next. I settled in, glad to have both a salary and a place to live. Surely Hollywood couldn't be as bad as Davis had implied?

Unfortunately, reviewing books proved harder than I had expected. I decided to seek advice from Palmer Institute, where I had sent an early draft of my screenplay. The executive office was located near the expensive shops that cater to the nouveau riche, a section of Los Angeles where people gather at sidewalk cafés to swap movie gossip. As I walked past H. Grauman's Chinese theater, renowned for its premieres, in my mind, limousines rolled up to the curb, celebrities hurried along a roped-off red carpet, fans pushed against the ropes.

At Palmer, a receptionist told me the president was not available, but summoned J. P. Manker, his assistant, a man with bushy eyebrows and an enormous red nose. From the look on his face, I could tell he hadn't quite decided how to react to me yet.

"What can I do for you, young man?"

"Due to your correspondence course, I learned to write in English," I said. "Now I am stopping by to express some appreciation."

Manker led the way down a hall, past a room filled with women seated at typewriters. "Typing letters," he quickly explained. "We try to give each and every student our undivided attention."

I paused to take it all in. Until that moment, I hadn't realized hundreds of people received messages of encouragement. I followed him into an office where a man sat at a desk. The sign on the glass door read *Story World*.

"Meet one of our prize students, Jay. Down for a visit," Manker said, raising his eyebrows. "Take good care of him."

Jay Brian Chapman held out his hand.

"Paul Grabbe, Russian émigré," I said, shaking it. " I'd like to tell you about my experiences as a newcomer to your land."

Jay listened for several minutes without a word, then interrupted. "How about you write a short piece for our magazine, something on the order of how you overcame handicaps and, like Conrad, learned to express yourself in English? I bet our readers would be fascinated. We pay twenty-five dollars for two thousand words."

I rushed home and wrote "Drip, Drip, Drip," explaining there's a wealth of material to be found in daily life. I was particularly proud of the final paragraph, which made use of some of my new vocabulary: *Seemingly playing with us as though we were but mere puppets in a game of limitless magnitude, life is indeed the quintessence of the unexpected.*

Story World ran a rather posed photograph of me with the article. I felt elated. I had broken into print and even been paid. What's more, I began receiving fan letters. Heady stuff!

VIVIAN'S COUSIN soon phoned to say there was an opening on his staff. I rushed over to Universal. He handed me several magazines and asked me to write a short statement explaining why an article of my choice would be appropriate for adaptation to the big screen. I sat down at a desk outside his office and started reading an issue of *The Saturday Evening Post*.

"These stories are all so puerile," I said out loud.

The man at the next desk glanced at me. "What the public wants is precisely this kind of romantic, over-sentimental crap. You may want to take that into consideration when you do your write-up."

Six weeks later an executive in New York realized Universal had a second story department in Los Angeles and we were all fired. The experience wasn't a total loss though, because I had made a few new friends and met another émigré with whom I felt at ease: Vadim Pleshkov, a former cavalry officer, employed by Universal as a riding instructor. General Pleshkov insisted that, to remain whole, a person has to live according to his beliefs and principles, not by expedience—values I admired.

Soon I had moved into a cheaper room and found another job: processing film for the major studios, at twenty-five dollars a week. The darkroom, no bigger than a closet, had no ventilation and the manager refused to provide a fan. Even though I stripped to the waist, perspiration poured down my face. I had to quit after two months.

On the way home, I stopped in a coffee shop on Hollywood Boulevard where General Pleshkov often ate dinner. He greeted me warmly.

"How are you, Pavel Alexandrovitch?"

"Couldn't be better. I've given up a nasty job and have to move again to find a less expensive place to stay."

"How about the Rookery? That's what I call my rooming house. The landlady's a good sort. Molly Ryan. On the first floor, there's a young Pole who would probably jump at the idea of cutting expenses. Come along and I'll introduce you."

KAZIMIR VALSKY resembled a dandy with his slick hair and fine chiseled features. "I have pleasure greeting you," he said with a ceremonious bow.

"Pavel Alexandrovitch here is looking for a place to live," General Pleshkov said. "I thought you might want to share your room."

"Oh, yes!" Valsky took my hand and pulled me inside.

"How long have you lived here?" I asked, glancing at the single bed, the threadbare couch, the dirty kitchenette.

"Long enough for my visa to expire. I hope they do not deport me. I like America. You like America, too?"

Valsky made an attempt to be cheerful, but I could tell he was psychologically fragile and belonged to Hollywood's shifting population of aspiring actors who lived from hand to mouth. Although discouraged, miserable, and sometimes desperate, most of them persevered, reluctant to give up their dream. Sometimes I would accompany Valsky to the casting offices, but my own sense of identity was too shaken to allow me to enjoy acting. Sometimes I waited while he went to an audition. At one studio, they were giving away free postcards. I sent Helen Jones an image of the Metro-Goldwyn-Meyer gates, intimating all was well.

While Valsky continued his job search, I made the rounds of the employment agencies. Weeks passed and neither of us found steady work. Soon we were reduced to soup and bread, with hamburgers every other day.

I continued to accept General Pleshkov's occasional invitations to dinner. Worried about my condition, one day he took me to meet Uri

Blagoy, a former officer in the Imperial Russian Navy, who worked as a night watchman. The bungalow smelled of incense. I glanced at the walls, decorated with photographs of Russian ships and sailors in heavy gold frames. There was a silver icon in one corner. The Blagoys had a samovar and served us tea.

Uri and his wife Valentina Ivanovna were characters straight out of Gogol. Dark-eyed Valentina had studied drama at the Moscow Art Theatre and like so many young women in Hollywood, considered herself an actress. She wore bright red lipstick and dimpled whenever she spoke, but it was her husband who made the stronger impression. What attracted me to Uri was the fact that he was uncompromisingly Russian. When our host disappeared into the kitchen, he would always pause in silent contemplation before an enormous portrait of the late Tsar Nicholas II and bow his head. When Uri returned, he offered me some butter cookies.

Valentina had just complimented General Pleshkov on his thick blond hair. Her voice was surprisingly deep. "Uri has gone bald at only thirty-two." She snuggled up to her husband, tapping his head with her long red fingernails. "I do love him anyway."

My friend was quick to change the subject. "Pavel Alexandrovitch here is looking for work. He's fluent in several languages. He has even been published."

"I'll be giving a lecture to some retired naval officers on Saturday," Uri said. "I need someone to translate. Interested?"

"Why, yes. Certainly."

"Excellent!" Blagoy rubbed his hands. "Let me pay you at once."

With this advance, I was able to buy bread and kasha—buckwheat grouts—something Valsky had taught me how to cook.

BLAGOY WAS on his way to work when I dropped by later in the week with the translation. He suggested I accompany him to work. The warehouse was a grim place, lonely and impersonal. As we walked through endless corridors, he described a new scheme to bolster income.

"Wolfhounds, that's the answer. The stars all want them. Last fall we borrowed money and bought a Borzoi, a male with a pedigree, Uncle Vanya by name. Chaplin's casting director owns a female. As soon as he heard about Vanya's noble origins, he couldn't resist. In no time the bitch will be having puppies. To show his gratitude, he's already giving me acting roles."

I had to smile, imagining the scene. No doubt, Blagoy's accent and impressive manner had been instrumental in cementing the deal.

"Good for you. That's ingenious," I said, aware I could never have attempted, much less carried out, a business venture of this sort.

"You must meet Vanya and the others. We just bought seven more. Have a bite to eat with us? Say tomorrow?"

I was grateful for the invitation. I had to eat whenever the opportunity presented itself. I had even resorted to an unusual source of nutrition: walnuts. A former colleague at Universal allowed me to collect nuts in his side yard. I was soon walking over to his house and back whenever I had the strength. Sometimes Valsky came along.

"I've simply got to find work," my roommate said as we approached the Rookery. "I've already borrowed money from everyone I know."

"You two boys owe me rent," Mrs. Ryan called as we passed her kitchen door. "I should be putting you out on the street, but here's some minestrone. I made more than I can use."

Gratefully we accepted the jug of soup.

Around that time, I received a telegram from Marie de Mare, head of the *Alliance Française* in Denver: *Coming to Santa Monica for lecture Tuesday. Brunswig estate. Hope to see you there.*

I took the bus to Santa Monica. The venue was a mansion on several acres of well-tended grounds. During the reception, Marie introduced me to the Brunswigs' daughter, a comely blond, who lived in a cozy cottage on a secluded part of the estate. We chatted and Margaret invited me back for tea the following weekend. I couldn't get enough of the cucumber sandwiches. With the Nutcracker Suite playing on her Victrola, momentarily I forgot all my problems.

Margaret and I got together several more times. Luncheon was always served on the terrace, beside a formal garden. Gazing across the table as my hostess explained why she liked the sensitive writing of Lafcadio Hearn, my thoughts ran something like this: *She appears to like me. If I married her, she would make a good wife, and I would never have to cope with uncertainty again. But there would be pressure to join the family business. There was no way her brothers would approve of my becoming a writer.*

During a pause in the conversation, Margaret cut off a piece of chicken breast. I watched as she fed it to her poodle. Only the day before, I had walked miles to gather walnuts. In life, differences of all kinds—social, monetary, psychological—keep people apart, inhibiting normal response. Although I was hungry most of the time, I couldn't bring myself to call on Margaret again.

All I thought about was food. Money now meant nickels and dimes. A dollar seemed like a fortune. Every so often I went through the motions of scrounging through drawers and cupboards in the hope of finding something to eat, an old carrot, a potato, a crust of bread. It was during one such futile exercise that my landlady knocked on the door. "There's someone here to see you," Mrs. Ryan said.

Helen Jones stepped out of the shadows. How had she found me? Of course! That postcard, implying success. Her smile faded as she took in the tattered carpet, the peeling paint, the empty cupboards.

I pulled forward our one good chair. "Do sit down. This certainly is a surprise. What are you doing in Los Angeles?"

"I live in Santa Barbara now. Mother forwarded your postcard."

I wondered what had happened to Merck, but didn't ask. Instead I said, "How's Lolly?"

"Fine, fine. She looks forward to starting a new school." Helen had shifted her weight in the chair. There was an awkward silence. "Are you all right, Paul? You look so thin."

I nodded absentmindedly. I felt too embarrassed to speak. Helen went to open her purse and removed several bills.

"Please, let me give you this small loan."

"Thank you, no," I said, pushing away her outstretched hand. "Really, that's not necessary."

We sat there in silence a while longer. Finally Helen stood up. "Take care of yourself, Paul," she said softly.

As soon as I had closed the door, I collapsed on the couch, covering my face with my hands. All I had wanted was for her to leave. Consumed with shame, I hadn't been able to think of anything else, not even Valsky's hunger.

THE WEEKS dragged on. By now I had pawned most of my belongings. My wardrobe trunk was gone, as was my tuxedo, worn only once at the British Embassy ball in Copenhagen. A former colleague at Universal had bought the ruby and gold cufflinks, which Father had given me when we escaped from Riga. Hard-pressed for cash, I had sold them for twenty dollars. I felt particular distress at parting with Father's other farewell gift: the silver cigarette case. Selling it broke another link with the past.

My parents sent two hundred dollars, concerned because they hadn't heard from me in months. I didn't even bother answering their letter. I couldn't bring myself to admit I was losing the will to live. I had heard it said often enough that anyone could get a job in America if he tried hard enough. In Los Angeles, that simply wasn't so.

I still had one object left, my portable typewriter. I clung to it despite Valsky's insistence that it, too, be pawned. That Corona could provide income.

Months had gone by since my last paycheck. I wrote on a piece of paper, *Things I refuse to do: seek charity, enlist in the army, marry money.* At the bottom of the page I scribbled, *I have no regrets. The choice was mine. I'm ready to face the consequences.*

The next morning, half-awake, I noticed Valsky was dressing to leave. Weakened by lack of nourishment, he moved slowly. First he put on one shoe. He paused and sat up. Then he leaned down to put on the other. What was he up to? I watched him stand unsteadily. Tucking my typewriter under his arm, he made for the door. In an instant I was beside him.

"What do you think you're doing?" I shouted.

There came a sharp knock on the door and our landlady appeared. "What's going on in here? Now boys, you mustn't fight." Mrs. Ryan turned to me: "Paul, it's that employment agency on the telephone. You better hurry."

ELDERLY PLAYWRIGHT William Penrose needed a secretary. He lived in an unpretentious but comfortable house on Franklin Street, in one of Hollywood's older neighborhoods. The first thing the brusque old gentleman did was ask me to type a poem. Apparently I passed this test because he produced a bottle of sherry from the sideboard and said, "Play bridge, do you?"

"I do." Now was not the time to explain I hadn't practiced in years. I was determined to get the job since the agency had said Penrose was willing to pay eighty dollars a month, plus room and board.

"Every Friday night I play duplicate bridge with two friends, both crackerjacks. To cope with them I need a competent partner. Let's see how you'd bid these hands."

Penrose laid a handful of cards out on the table. My heart sank. I wasn't talented enough to succeed, even at ordinary bridge.

"The dealer will bid three hearts and make it."

"Sorry," he said. "I need a partner who's a whiz."

"I can learn by Friday," I blurted out, groping for a convincing argument. "Everyone in my family plays bridge. Ever since the Revolution, my uncle, formerly the Hetman of the Don Cossacks, has supported his family playing bridge in Paris."

Penrose scratched his head.

My voice grew more insistent. "Really, I can learn. I noticed some guidebooks in the hall. When I'm not typing your manuscripts, I'll be studying bridge, and, in a week, I'll be good enough to play with you."

"Highly unlikely. Takes time and practice."

"But I can. I know I can."

"All right," he said with a smile. "We'll give it a try."

That evening I moved into Penrose's house and ate practically everything in his refrigerator. "You certainly have a wonderful appetite," he commented enviously.

For six days I huddled at his card table dealing myself hands, taking notes, drinking lots of black coffee. At the end of the sixth day I told Penrose, "Okay. I'm ready."

Again he dealt the cards. Again I took a look. "This bid will be four spades, but you'll make only three."

"Good for you. Let's see how you make out with my friends."

For the next two months I typed Penrose's manuscripts. I could just about hold my own with his bridge pals who played by feel as much as by the rules. I settled in, began to relax, even took up the piano. Then Penrose caught pneumonia. A few days later the dear old gentleman passed away. I was aghast. Within a week I had to move. But where? Surely not back with Valsky![16]

MY NEWEST JOB had intrigued General Pleshkov who listened sympathetically as I reported its unexpected end. "Oh, Pavel Alexandrovitch! Life certainly has its ups and downs now doesn't it?" He thought a moment as the waitress brought the check. "Why not call on Uri? He seems to have started a press service. Maybe you'd fit in as translator."

Without delay I set off for the Blagoys. Uri was in the garden, pulling up weeds, and invited me inside for tea.

"I need to move," I said in a bleak voice. "My boss caught pneumonia and died. Can you recommend an inexpensive place to stay?"

Valentina settled onto the couch beside me. "Oh, Pavel Alexandrovitch, we were just talking about you," she said.

"Indeed. We were about to get in touch. We want to tell you about a wire service we've created, sending news to the Far East."

Valentina fixed me with her eyes, running the tips of her fingers along the plush velvet upholstery. "We want you to edit it for us."

"What I need is a place to stay."

"Let me show you what our stationery will look like." Uri drew a sheet of paper out of a battered briefcase. The engraved letterhead read, International News Service of Hollywood; Uri Blagoy, President; Paul Grabbe, Editor; Valentina Blagoy, Treasurer.

The wire service struck me as a harebrained idea. "What I need is a place to stay," I repeated.

Valentina patted my knee. "Stay here. Sleep on the couch."

I glanced around the cluttered cottage and wondered how they could possibly fit in another person.

Uri rubbed his palms together. "Excellent! Why not fetch your belongings straight away? I'll order a thousand sheets and a thousand envelopes and get us started."

As soon as I had moved in, I realized it was a mistake. Valentina saw herself as a *femme fatale* and often made veiled references to former conquests. She had the disconcerting habit of coming up from behind when my back was turned. I would feel her small hand on my biceps. "You must develop those muscles, Pavel Alexandrovitch," she'd say. "Women like their men strong."

One day Charlie Chaplin's casting director asked Uri to bring a friend along as an extra. A retake of a scene from The Circus gave us the opportunity to watch Chaplin at work. The scene was shot in front of a wooden pier where a number of people were to stroll back and forth. As the cameramen moved tripods into place, a long black limousine rolled up to the set. Out stepped the familiar little man in the oversized shoes and bowler hat. Immediately he set to work.

The action centered on a ragamuffin who was about to steal fruit from an outdoor vendor. We all watched the way Chaplin went about coaching the boy, explaining what was needed before having him act out the sequence. Finally Chaplin went through the scene himself while the boy watched. Then the boy was given the opportunity to imitate the director. It was fascinating to observe the sureness with which Chaplin turned the youngster's gestures into consummate acting. I was so taken that I almost missed my cue. Promptly at noon the black limousine reappeared. Chaplin got in, and the limousine drove off.

In due course, the stationery arrived. Two weeks passed, and there I was, still a house guest of sorts because all talk of the wire service had ceased. I volunteered to feed the wolfhounds. Soon I was also giving the eight animals their daily brushing and taking them for walks in exchange for room and board.

INNA WAS DARK, vivacious, and eager for new adventures. I liked her from the start. She must have liked me, too, because our friendship led to an affair. Yes, General Pleshkov introduced us. Sometimes Inna and I met to go hiking; sometimes we sat around and talked about our lives. The Russian we spoke brought us closer. Inna had also lived in Colorado where she worked as a dental assistant. I wished I had known about her beloved Dr. Morris two years earlier.

"It's never too late," Inna said. By then she knew I wanted to leave California. "Why not return to Denver? I'm sure I could get you a discount."

I didn't have the money for a bus ticket to Denver or any other place for that matter, but two months of eating with Penrose had improved my health; my social life now included Inna, and I had, at long last, met some interesting people. Dolores and Jaime del Rio were so utterly un-Hollywood that it was refreshing to spend time with them. I could always count on a cordial welcome at their handsome home in Beverly Hills. Dolores' father, a banker, was of Spanish-Basque descent; her mother, of ancient Indian ancestry. As for Jaime, he had been born into a prominent Castilian family and had trained as a lawyer. Both Jaime and Dolores radiated youth and prosperity.

Their story I pieced together gradually. Before Hollywood, the del Rios had lived in Mexico City where director Edwin Carewe had met

Dolores at a party. Enthralled by her ability to dance, he urged her to move north. At first the couple refused. They didn't particularly want to live in the United States, but were tempted by the opportunity to escape the staid atmosphere of Mexican high society. Once in Los Angeles, Dolores and Jaime discovered they felt ill at ease. Dolores had become aware of the superficiality of the motion picture world. Early in her career she was quoted as saying:

> *Hollywood, what a place it is! It is far away from the rest of the world, so narrow. No one thinks of anything but motion pictures or talks of anything else. And I too am getting like the rest. I have not read anything for a year. I do not know what is happening in the world or what people are talking about or even which revue is the favorite in Paris.*

The problem was that, while twenty-year-old Dolores rocketed to stardom, the industry shunned Jaime. He hated having to stand on the sidelines and watch Carewe pay attention to Dolores. To resolve this dilemma, Jaime decided to adapt Tolstoy's *Resurrection* as a vehicle for his wife, and asked me to collaborate on the screenplay.

Dolores always looked relaxed when she joined us on the veranda, even after a long day at the studio. On every visit, I found myself reluctant to leave, all the more so because I hated to return to the emotionally charged Blagoy household.

My living situation had deteriorated. One morning angry voices woke me up. Valentina and Uri stood arguing in the kitchen.

Soft-spoken Uri said, "Shut up, woman."

As I headed for the bathroom, Valentina picked up a plate and broke it against the countertop. She usually wore a neat bun, but her hair was disheveled and cascaded onto her shoulders. "Take that!" she shouted. "And that! And that!" With each exclamation, another plate crashed to the floor.

I saw Uri grab his briefcase. A door slammed. I waited several minutes before attempting to make myself a cup of tea. Valentina was nowhere in sight. Since I had laundry to do, I went out on the back porch, threw my clothes into an iron tub, and filled it with water. Suddenly, I felt a presence behind me.

"Let me do this for you," Valentina said as I turned off the faucet.

"Thank you but I can do it myself."

When I looked up, there she was, barely three feet away. Beads of sweat glistened on her olive skin. Valentina had changed into a tight black corset. In her right hand she held a whip used to make the dogs obey. There was a strange smile on her lips.

"Do you know what I'm going to do?" she asked.

"What?"

"I am going to whip you."

"You'd better not."

Slowly she raised her arm and brought the whip down across my back. As she stood there trembling, I realized I had two choices: take her to bed or leave. I chose the latter.

Packing took no time at all. I walked along Sunset Boulevard with my suitcase and typewriter, trying to come up with a plan. I was fed up with Hollywood, but needed more than thirty dollars to reach Colorado by bus. After almost a mile, I figured out how to finance my departure. I hailed a cab and rode over to the del Rios' to relinquish my share of the *Resurrection* screenplay.

Jaime accepted my offer and we drove to his bank where he cashed a check for two hundred dollars. On the way back, I asked him to stop at a music store where I bought Beethoven's Fifth, which I gave my Mexican friends after dinner. To me the symphony symbolized our mutual appreciation of music, of good manners, of gracious living. Still the gift didn't quite express how much I valued their friendship, so, in parting, I presented Jaime with my bamboo cane.

Fabled Hollywood! As my bus left Los Angeles behind and rolled past rows of orange trees, I felt indescribable relief. I now understood what Davis had meant when he called Hollywood a hellhole. Thanks to Jaime, I had escaped the sleaze.[17]

7

AFTER CROSSING Arizona and New Mexico, the bus finally reached Colorado. I headed straight for my old boarding house, eager for a bath. Frances Leatherman seemed happy to see me: "Welcome home! How was the trip? Hot, I bet. Bring me oranges?"

I hadn't, but my former landlady let me have my room back anyway. A practical matter had brought me to Denver. I immediately made an appointment with the dentist Inna had recommended. The next order of business was improving my living situation. Although Mrs. Leatherman had agreed to room and board in exchange for housework, I was not allowed near a broom.

"You must not clean," she said. "Absolutely not. What I want is for you to entertain during dinner. While my roomers eat, talk to them. They're high-school teachers. I reckon that won't be too hard."

"But why?"

"They'll enjoy the conversation."

"Mrs. Leatherman thinks having you at her table gives this place class," the kitchen boy explained later.

Permanent employment seemed the best solution. Should I search the classified? That hadn't worked in the past. I recalled Father's advice: *You must circulate, meet people. If no one knows you exist, how do you expect to find a job?* Yes, I'd start with someone I knew—Vivian Barney.

Friendly as ever, Dan's mother was eager to help, but short on ideas. "French lessons are out because Mlle. de Mare has moved. How about a job as a trailer conductor? Dan did that one summer."

I went straight to the Denver Streetcar Company where a clerk added my name to the waiting list. Then I called Tom and Miriam Campbell, whom I had met at the Cranmers. A Dartmouth trustee, Tom handled his mother's fortune. When I dropped by later in the afternoon, the Campbells acted cordially, but Tom's attitude changed as soon as I asked for help. "Why, sure," he said, fingering his lapel. "Let me ask around."

So...I went to work for Tom's plumber. Sawing through pipes, I hummed the lively Russian dance from *The Nutcracker Suite*, which reminded me of a happier occasion. At age ten, I had attended a matinee performance of the ballet at the Imperial Marinsky Theatre. What a fairytale place it was with tier upon tier of golden boxes, draped in turquoise satin. The sheer splendor had taken my breath away. Inside the boxes sat elegant people. Beyond the orchestra pit, a huge curtain, embroidered in blue, began to rise. The lights dimmed. Nils grabbed my arm. "Look over there," he cried in an excited whisper. "Somebody just entered the Imperial box. Maybe the tsar?" The conductor raised his baton, and the opening chords of Tchaikovsky's music floated through the theatre.

215

In my childhood, music was everywhere. During the winter months, Nils and I both took piano lessons. He practiced diligently. Not me. As soon as I heard the swish of my teacher's petticoats, I hid under the grand piano. Although I had refused to practice, I understood music was wonderfully nourishing, a tonic for the spirit. Since my move to the United States, I had been too busy looking for a way to make a living to listen to music. I had neglected it, repressed my need. By the time I had sawed through all those pipes, I knew what I had to do—get music back into my life. I racked my brain and came up with an idea: I would contact Martha Tate, a piano teacher I met at a party. Two years later I showed up at her door. Fortunately, Martha was delighted to see me. We had dinner together that very night. After I had played a few Russian folk songs on the piano, she offered free lessons.

EVERYTHING SEEMED to be falling into place. The only problem was mealtime. Making conversation proved impossible. I thought teachers would be interested in education, but Mrs. Leatherman's boarders didn't pick up on any of my leads. I tried literature and current affairs, but to no avail. At that point, Mrs. Leatherman carried in a homemade apple pie and said, "Ladies, did you know our Paul spent two years in Hollywood?"

"Hollywood?" Miss Sperry exclaimed. "Why didn't you say so?"

Lucy leaned toward me. "Oh, do tell us about the stars you met," she said.

"What movie sets have you been on?" asked Maureen.

The newest member of our household, a blonde who had not yet uttered a word, blurted out, "What I want to know is did Evangelist Aimée Semple McPherson really have her followers attach dollar bills with clothespins to a line over the pews of the Angelus Temple?"

Suddenly, they were all talking at once. How different had been my Hollywood. I thought of Dolores and Jaime. I had treasured their friendship. It had been so special that I didn't want to share the memory with anyone.

Looking back, I now realize what a vital period the twenties were— jazz, movies, radio, Gershwin, Hemingway, Fitzgerald, Cather. There was so much going on, so much to discuss. What a pity those teachers shied away from ideas.

TIME PASSED slowly. I spent many afternoons at the dentist. Every few days I would stop by the streetcar company office. "No openings yet," the clerk would say.

One day, a beautiful stranger opened the door to the dentist's waiting room and spoke briefly to the nurse. I watched out of the corner of my eye as the lanky brunette sat down on the edge of a chair and became engrossed in a letter. She was dressed with stylish simplicity: a white blouse, ornamented by a gold pin shaped like a four-leaf clover, a plaid skirt, and a paisley scarf that held back wavy black hair.

"Forgive me," I said finally, "but there doesn't seem to be anyone around to introduce us." Since this sounded ridiculous, I added, "I really want to meet you. My name is Paul Grabbe."

"If you insist, Eliza Martindell."

Once the nurse had handed Eliza a prescription, she started moving toward the door. The nurse gestured that the dentist was ready for me. I stood up and said in a lowered voice, "Please tell Dr. Morris I'm very sorry. Something has come up. I have to cancel my appointment."

I rushed down the hall, reaching the elevator just in time. My mystery woman looked surprised, but allowed me to accompany her outside. I noticed Eliza moved like a lynx. Unfortunately, she was on her way to the library, which was nearby, so that was the end of that, but I did manage to obtain her phone number.

HOW WELL I remember my first day of work at the Denver Streetcar Company. I stood on a raised platform near the coin box, feeling apprehensive. The job wasn't hard: all I had to do was answer questions, make change, issue transfers. These duties became more complicated when dozens of passengers, many pushing and shoving, tried to board at once. I got paid every two weeks at the rate of thirty-five cents an hour, always in gold and silver coins, a carry-over from mining days.

None of the other conductors wanted the route I liked best. On this run, the trolley left the barn at 5:45 and traveled empty all the way to Aurora, a distant suburb at the time, where we picked up commuters and returned to Denver. The sun had barely risen and the misty plain was still indistinct. The scenery reminded me of the outskirts of St. Petersburg in September, a bleak northern landscape I had seen many times as a boy from a window of the night train that carried my family back from Vasilievskoye. In the speeding trolley, feeling nostalgic, I could relive that boyhood experience and yield, however fleetingly, to the illusion I was going not to Aurora, but home to Mokhovaya Street.

I SAW ELIZA off and on for several months. We spent many pleasant hours together in her rose garden. She called me "Darling Paul" yet avoided all my advances. Meanwhile my study of music took a lucky turn. I expanded an exercise into a short composition, similar to something in *Le Sacre du Printemps,* and Martha allowed me free rein. Before I knew it, I had composed four pieces. Once I had mastered musical notation, I transposed my suite to manuscript paper and learned to hammer it out on the piano. This led to an odd discovery. In my head, I heard a symphony. Martha suggested I approach Horace Tureman, conductor of the Civic Symphony.

When I ventured up to the top floor of the Tabor building, Tureman was busy studying a score. "Have something to show me?" he asked in a friendly voice.

"It's a piano suite, but there's a problem. I don't hear a piano. I hear a whole orchestra."

I waited anxiously while the conductor examined my manuscript, humming from time to time. At last he raised his head. "Want me to teach you how to score that suite so an orchestra can play it? Here's some paper and a pencil. Now write this down. One piccolo, two flutes, two oboes, two clarinets, two bassoons...."

After Tureman had listed the string instruments, he gave me a pamphlet and told me to study the information it contained. "And get yourself some proper manuscript paper. See you here next week, Tuesday at four. Off you go."

"But I have no money to pay for instruction."

"Doesn't matter. You've got talent."

Slightly dazed at my good fortune, I spent the afternoon trying to imagine what different combinations of instruments might sound like. The following Tuesday I returned to the Tabor building.

Tureman frowned. "No, no. The oboe, here, doesn't go this low. You need an English horn." He walked over to a large cupboard, brought out an oboe, then an English horn, and played them for me, one after the other.

Despite the fact that the conductor marked up my manuscript with red ink, he invited me to his next rehearsal. I left feeling humbled, but hopeful. The private lessons continued for six months. Soon I was attending all the Civic Symphony rehearsals.

Once my whole suite had been scored, Tureman said, "There's an organization in town called the Denver Allied Arts. Mrs. George Cranmer is its leading spirit. I've written her about you. I'd appreciate it if you'd mail the letter. And, Paul, I really think you should send your suite to Juilliard. Apply for a fellowship in composition. They can take care of tuition."

I thanked him profusely and went outside where I opened the unsealed letter:

Dear Mrs. Cranmer,

Some years ago you asked me to refer to the Allied Arts such persons of exceptional talent as might require aid in their studies. I have never done so. Paul Grabbe will bring or send you this letter. It is my belief that he merits such assistance as the Allied Arts proposes to furnish....

What a dear man, I thought, as I dropped the letter in the mailbox.

When I reported these developments to Eliza, her reaction was typical: "Looks like we better get busy. Can't just sit around waiting to see what happens next."

"But what can we do?"

"Why drum up support, darlin'. Get testimonials."

My impresario swung into high gear. Eliza tackled every prominent musician who happened to be in town. Once, from her car, I watched with amazement as she approached Alfred Hertz, conductor of the San Francisco Symphony. Soon she was back, waving a piece of paper. It read, I have looked at your score with great interest and assure you that you have real talent.

"Admissions can't help but be impressed, and that's to your advantage," she said.

219

Eliza was right. I can still remember the sudden rush of emotion—two years to the day after my return from California—when the mailman delivered an ordinary looking envelope with my name on it. The letter inside stated Juilliard officials had decided to award me a fellowship in composition.

8

MY RETURN to New York in 1929 produced major change in my life. No more hard labor. No more caskets. No more adventures on Colorado's last frontier. I was convinced the Juilliard Graduate School of Music was much more in line with my natural aptitude than anything I had attempted thus far in America. My euphoria didn't last. As soon as I met the dean, I feared future difficulties.

"I need to know precisely what the school has to offer me," I said.

Ernest Hutchinson, a man in his late fifties, gracious and civilized, chose to ignore my insolence. He smiled in a way that made me think he was used to such remarks from young musicians. "The fellowship provides individual instruction not only in composition, but also with an instrument. What's your instrument?"

All of a sudden I realized you don't just turn up at Juilliard and tell officials you poke out tunes on the piano. "The instrument for which I have always felt a special affinity is…the cello. That's what I'd like to study. Yes, the cello."

"Very well then." Mr. Hutchinson glanced at his notes. "We'll make the necessary arrangements. Your instructor in composition will be Rubin Goldmark. As you may know, he has taught a whole generation of American composers."

That afternoon I contacted a friend from Denmark, Kai Winkelhorn, who worked for a Wall Street investment firm, and was able to move into his Greenwich Village apartment. By sharing the cost of lodging, I could afford to live on my monthly stipend from Allied Arts. But additional problems soon arose. From my first lesson, it became evident I had little aptitude for the cello. My teacher complained that I wasn't even holding it right.

Six fellowship students in composition attended Juilliard that year. Goldmark asked us to bring in a weekly composition that demonstrated increasingly complex aspects of musical form. These compositions were to be reviewed by our peers. This competitive situation inhibited me completely. I was convinced my classmates were all more qualified and soon fell behind in my assignments. I requested individual instruction, but the crusty old gentleman brushed my requests aside.

Rather than admit musical impotence, I submitted a letter of resignation, which was met with shocked disbelief. Goldmark urged me to reconsider. By then I had grown fond of him. I realized, however, that my musical knowledge and preparation was not sufficient for study at Juilliard. Furthermore, what I wanted to do was write prose, not compose music.

During this period, I was so preoccupied with my personal problems that I hardly noticed the economic crisis unfolding around me: the Wall Street Crash had jolted the country and affected almost everybody, including my roommate. No one realized a depression was already under way. Soon there would be soup kitchens, long unemployment lines, haggard men and women selling apples in the streets. Against this background of uncertainty, I continued to study music on my own. Detachment was possible because I did not feel personally threatened. My stipend check arrived on the first of the month, and the national economic picture remained too bewildering to grasp.

WHILE AT JUILLIARD, I had become friends with Paul Nordoff, a talented pianist with a flair for modern music. Nordoff's distinguished piano teacher, Olga Samaroff,[18] liked to entertain, and he often took me along to her musical soirees.

One day Olga called to invite me to a luncheon. The other guest turned out to be Sergei Prokofiev. Before dessert, our hostess left the room so the eminent composer and I could converse in our native tongue. We talked about our homeland and what it felt like to be an émigré. Prokofiev said that he had grown increasingly unhappy living away from Russia and yearned to return.[19] I told him I shared this feeling, but resisted the impulse lest I land in a labor camp.

At the time, I felt bitterness about my predicament, deep resentment not only against Russia, but against anyone who didn't need to worry about money. I was on my own again, with no job prospects at all. I tried to contact the Kates and discovered they had moved to New Orleans. There was no one to turn to. Well, almost no one. Mother and Father had written of having met one J. McBride Hubbard, who managed a dozen tenements between 10th and 11th Avenues, an area known as Hell's Kitchen.

Hubbard, a dapper man in his mid-sixties, threw me a sharp look as I entered his office, then got straight to the point: "I need a rental agent. The work's not hard. You collect back rent without promising any repairs. Pay is twenty dollars a week."

Immigrant Italians, Poles, and other Europeans, too poor to find lodging elsewhere, inhabited the neighborhood near the West Side docks. Greeks added color with their vegetable stands. The area was known for drunken brawls between local toughs and sailors on shore leave. Honking delivery cars jammed up 11th Avenue as I strode from tenement to tenement. My sympathies went out to the immigrants, families close to destitution, jammed into apartments in disrepair—leaky pipes, broken toilets, missing electric bulbs, mildew, fallen plaster all over the floor. The four-story buildings lacked conveniences: no hot water, no heat. Yet, Hubbard wanted me to cajole these poor people into paying back rent, even threaten them with eviction.

An Italian couple with a sickly child particularly moved me. The wife could barely speak English. The husband had no job. Their old kerosene stove gave off little warmth. They carried water in from a neighbor's kitchen and probably didn't have enough to eat. Despite this hardship, when I turned up to collect rent, they always acted friendly and slipped me two or three dollars on account.

I saw many cases similar to theirs.

Finally, I got up the nerve to raise some of my concerns. Hubbard showed no interest whatsoever. He couldn't have cared less about his tenants' welfare. All that mattered was making a profit. His attitude only left me feeling more despondent. Then I met Laura and everything changed.

Antlers Hotel on Pike's Peak Avenue in Colorado Springs, with snow-covered Pike's Peak in background.

Author as a waiter at Cragmor Sanitarium. (1923)

Author in Helen Jones's darkroom in Colorado Springs. (1923)

Exploring Garden of the Gods with Helen Jones. Note camera in foreground. (1923)

Gibbs House, where author lived in Cripple Creek, Colorado. (1923)

Author as miner at the Cresson Gold Mine. (1923)

Author at The Catacombs, a stained glass-domed community mausoleum for above ground entombment, Cypress Lawn Cemetery, San Francisco, CA. (1924)

Cypress Lawn pallbearers, waiting for funeral. Author, third from left. (1924)

226

Elvin Davis, funeral director, Cypress Lawn Cemetery, with Model-T Ford used to lead funeral processions. (1924)

Author, in Hollywood. Photo taken for article published in *Story World*. (1925)

Count and Countess Alexander Grabbe, Cazenovia, NY. (1936)

Laura Harris, author's first wife, Cazenovia, NY. (1936)

Author marries Beatrice Chinnock in Montclair, NJ. (1944)

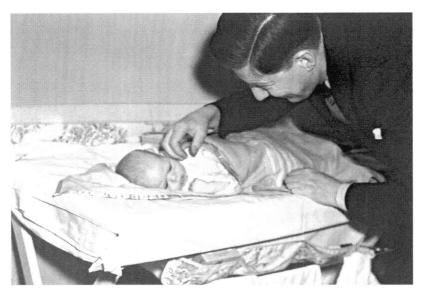

Author meets daughter Alexandra. (1947)

Author with Beatrice on Brandywine Street, Washington, DC, at house purchased with royalties from books on music. (1952)

Author with Beatrice in Wellfleet, photo taken for promotion of their book *Private World of the Last Tsar*. (1986)

Alexandra Grabbe with son Paul Boutin, Wellfleet, MA. (1970)

Author with son Nick and grandson Alex, Wellfleet, MA. (1990)

Author, in his eighties, when he wrote Parts III and IV of this memoir.

PART IV

Reaching
for Broader
Horizons

1

I HAD A standing invitation from some Denver friends to visit their Greenwich Village apartment. When I dropped by, a party was under way. Several guests were crowded onto a sofa. A couple more were perched on the upright piano. Everyone had a drink in hand. I crossed the smoky room and recognized George Willison, a Rhodes scholar from Colorado. Since I hadn't read the book he was discussing, I wandered into the kitchen where I found myself alone with a small woman who had a streak of white in her hair. Laura Harris told me she worked as a junior editor at Grosset & Dunlap. In describing her job, she gestured as if to draw attention away from her upper lip where I noticed a scar, visible despite plastic surgery. I disregarded this facial deformity, impressed by her lively mind and exuberant personality. Quickly, we discovered a mutual interest: music. I didn't see Laura for a few weeks. Then she phoned. One thing led to another and soon we were living together.

That same month my friend Paul Nordoff received a Guggenheim award. The three of us celebrated with a bottle of wine. I hadn't intended for anyone to take my affair seriously and, for days, experienced a kind of malaise. Finally I wrote Nordoff a note in which I made disparaging remarks about our erstwhile hostess. As soon as I had mailed the letter, I regretted sending it. Laura had sterling qualities which I had chosen to disregard simply because she was not the chic young thing I envisaged by my side. Clearly what I had done was wrong and deserved amends. But how? Ask her to marry me? That would demonstrate high regard. Without further hesitation, I proposed. Even now I don't entirely understand my motivation. I only know it was a difficult period of my life. Laura, a kindred spirit, assuaged my anxiety.

The week before the wedding, I managed to deposit thirty dollars at Bank of the United States. When I mentioned my coming nuptials to Hubbard, he assumed he would be invited. I tried to explain the wedding was to be an intimate affair, and got fired. That afternoon the Bank of the United States closed its doors and the Great Depression started. The prospect of looking for work was demoralizing. Laura suggested teaching Russian. The Soviet Government had begun its five-year plans of industrial development, and many Americans wanted to learn the language. The lessons brought in fifteen dollars a week, which, combined with Laura's forty-five, provided enough for us to get by. Of course, we were always on the lookout for a new source of income. An opportunity presented itself unexpectedly soon after Nordoff's return from Germany.

Laura was breathless as she entered our apartment. "Guess what I heard today? Mr. Grosset is looking for someone to write a book on opera. Couldn't you do it?"

"How would we get them to hire me?"

"You're right," she mused. "They wouldn't consider an unknown author, especially someone married to an employee."

"Why not ask Nordoff for help? He's got the credentials."

"He could pose as the potential author. I'll introduce him to Mr. Grosset...."

"...and once Nordorff signs the contract, I'll write the book."

We looked at each other. Laura hugged me. We both knew the undertaking involved risk. If Alexander Grosset were to learn Laura had maneuvered me in through the back door, he would probably fire her on the spot.

Luckily our plan worked better than either of us could have imagined. Grosset gave Nordoff an advance of two hundred dollars, which he split with us, and I began work on the book. After a while, Laura introduced me to her boss. Still later, Nordoff bowed out, claiming musical commitments. In superlatives, he recommended me for the job. I took over officially and was listed as co-author. *Minute Stories of the Opera* soon became a bestseller. Our gamble had paid off.

Once sales had topped fifty thousand, Grosset decided there might be a market for another book on music. "What we need now is something that appeals to concert-goers," he said, rubbing his hands.

I happened to be meeting Laura for lunch that day and overheard the remark. "How about symphonic music?" I suggested from the doorway. "Symphony orchestras draw a large audience these days."

"Let's do it. We'll call this addition to our music library, *The Story of 100 Symphonic Favorites.* Want the job?"

Of course I said yes, although I had no idea what those hundred symphonic favorites should be. A rapid calculation had told me I'd have to write a fixed number of words per day to make the deadline. I got right to work, consulting the programs of prominent symphony orchestras and compiling lists. I spent mornings at the New York Public Library, doing research. By afternoon, I was ensconced at The Gramophone Shop on Fifth Avenue, listening to records. Every night my quota had to be on paper before I let myself go to bed. For three months I stuck to this routine.

As soon as *The Story of 100 Symphonic Favorites* appeared in bookstores, people bought it. The fifty-cent volume fit snugly into a pocket and could be taken to concerts. The book seemed to answer a need no one had anticipated. Critic Deems Taylor called it *a factual, sympathetic, and unsentimental guide to music.*

"Your new career has begun," Laura said.

I knew this was an exaggeration. Turning me into a writer was not going to happen overnight. Still, such startling success bolstered my spirits. I agreed to write a companion volume, *Orchestral Music and Its Times.* Not that I expected to get rich from the sales—I was paid a royalty of two cents a copy—but becoming a published author did carry a certain prestige. And then, there were other benefits.

After I mailed *The Story of 100 Symphonic Favorites* to Serge Koussevitsky, eminent conductor of the Boston Symphony, he invited me to his Brookline home. I arrived in Boston in time for the orchestra's fall season. My host could not have been more cordial. Off and on we had long conversations in Russian. During one rehearsal, he took me to a first-tier box to gauge how the orchestra sounded at that distance.

"These are remarkable musicians, Pavel Alexandrovitch. Here they are playing a piece by Albert Roussel, a piece they have never seen before, and they play it flawlessly. Without a conductor."

"Do they need one?"

He thought a moment. "As you must realize, conducting is not a question of waving your arms around. Marking time and all the other signals the conductor gives the players, the mechanics of it, must become automatic before any attention can be given to the music. But what the conductor really does is pull the orchestra along, up to the tempo he perceives as right. I must tell you, the one thing I dare not do while conducting is show lack of interest. Even a suggestion of boredom and the musicians would react. They'd catch my mood, and you can imagine what would happen to the music."

After this visit, every time the Boston Symphony played Carnegie Hall, I received a note stating a seat had been reserved for me. I met Aaron Copland, Gregor Piatigorsky, and other famous musicians in the conductor's box. Our conversations further contributed to my education.

ÉMIGRÉ

I BECAME an American citizen in 1932. I had filed for citizenship in the twenties and promptly forgotten all about the application, so I was surprised to receive a summons to appear in court for naturalization proceedings years later. At the time, I thought of Communism as a temporary aberration and hoped I might some day be able to return home to St. Petersburg. I considered naturalization no more than a routine procedure set up for foreigners, an administrative convenience, like passport renewal. I had no doubt about my allegiance. In fact, the idea of becoming an American upset me, since I had been raised to believe giving up one's nationality was a form of betrayal. That I might want to relinquish the quality that made me Russian had never crossed my mind. Still, on the day indicated, I showed up at the District Court of New York in Lower Manhattan with the summons in hand.

An agent interviewed me and led the way into a hall where I found myself in the company of thirty other applicants. After a while, a judge swore us in. "Congratulations!" he said. "By becoming citizens, you are assuming a special responsibility because our country is in the throes of a revolution...."

Revolution? I glanced around the room. Everyone wore a puzzled expression. The others probably had as little understanding of American society as me. Laura explained later that the judge must have been referring to the Great Depression and what might happen once Franklin D. Roosevelt had taken office.

I left the courthouse feeling something important had been accomplished: no longer would I be considered an alien. I realized I would have to learn more about the United States if I planned to become a permanent resident. One of my Russian students offered to teach me about my new country. Professor Henry Pratt Fairchild imparted a vision of America as a land of courageous immigrants who had demonstrated that a free people, even when starting from scratch, could reach for and achieve the impossible. How fortunate I was to have been befriended by this fine man, perceptive enough to sense the hidden tears in my psyche, caused by exile, and intent on reassuring me in every way possible.

I MUST ADMIT that during these same years my marriage was encountering difficulties. Somewhere I had picked up the notion that for a man to keep his self-respect, he should support a woman, not the other way around. As the discrepancy in our salaries grew, my discomfiture increased.

Laura and I had another problem: I had never said I loved her. She kept nagging me about it until I declared, "I don't know what the word means. I don't believe in love anymore than I believe in God. We're far better off without false labels."

Although outwardly rational enough to become a citizen and thus take a first step toward building a new life, inwardly I was in deep mourning for the country I had lost. Russia, my homeland, had ceased to exist. The Soviet Union had taken its place. Rootless in a culture not my own, I suffered from depression. Some days I would sit for hours, motionless, in a chair, unable to move.

Meanwhile Laura's publishers were beginning to appreciate her accomplishments. Almost single-handedly, she had created a children's department and introduced several successful series, including the Nancy Drew books. Recognition and a raise came after a *Publisher's Weekly* profile. Bolstered by the publicity, Laura put up with my moods. Always an astute editor, she helped me a great deal with her criticism and suggestions.

LIFE SEEMED to be running smoothly until the day in 1936 when I received a letter from my parents who had moved from Germany to Monte Carlo. I read parts out loud to Laura: *We have been invited to spend two months in Cazenovia, New York. I'm sure you remember cousin Tania Wright who married an American stockbroker? Can you meet us when the* S/S Conte di Savoia *reaches New York?*

I threw the letter on the floor.

"Golly! Aren't you feeling dramatic. What's so awful about your parents coming to visit?" Laura said.

"Don't you understand? They're invading my territory. I put an ocean between us, gaining a sense of freedom. Their arrival will probably reactivate old inhibitions and other psychological problems."

"Seems you still have a lot of resentment."

"When I think of all the years I've struggled … Father should have transferred money abroad when he had the chance. Did he? No. As a result, my parents are broke, and I barely earn enough to get by."

"They're your parents, Paul. They need you to be there for them."
We argued for some time. Finally I agreed. Still, it was with trepidation that I left for the pier on their day of arrival. Spotting the parents at the guardrail only intensified my anxiety. Mother seemed the same, but Father had aged greatly and looked a touch rueful, a change probably due to resignation at life's exigencies. I feigned happiness and escorted them to Hotel Algonquin. What a relief when they left for Cazenovia.

A few days later, I received an invitation from the Wrights to spend a weekend in the country. There was nothing to do but accept. Tania had arranged for Mother and Father to stay in a separate cottage on the estate. When I did the introductions, Laura acted distant, taking her cue from me, which made the situation all the more difficult. Although I hadn't seen my parents for fourteen years, I couldn't wait to leave, and drove back to Manhattan without stopping once, except for gas.

IN ORDER TO finish the second edition of *Orchestral Music and Its Times*, I found it necessary to go to Washington to do research at the Library of Congress. Worried that her job interfered with our marriage, Laura left Grosset & Dunlap and followed me south. It wasn't easy finding a small apartment in the overcrowded city. We were having dinner with friends when the radio first broadcast news that Hitler had invaded Poland. We knew at once that a disaster had occurred, probably leading to world war and all the misery such an event involved.

Soon after that, Laura began to show signs of strain. She felt ill at ease in the housewife role and decided she was socially inept as a hostess. One night our marriage fell apart. We had been to a movie.

"Was that ever stupid," I said when we got home.

"It was a comedy, Paul," Laura said. She paced back and forth for several minutes. "You're so serious all the time," she blurted out. "I can't take it anymore. I'm going back to Manhattan."

Two months later Laura asked to see me. A painful scene ensued in which she expressed regret at our separation. I found it difficult to tell her that I wanted a divorce, and harder still to put her on the next train to New York.[20] I might not have had the strength to do so except that in the meantime I had met Beatrice.

2

EVERYONE OLD enough to remember Pearl Harbor knows exactly what they were doing the day news of the Japanese attack came over the radio. I was in McLean, Virginia, reworking the final pages of *Orchestral Music and its Times*. When I drove to the Library of Congress the next morning to check a few facts, sentries already guarded Memorial Bridge. On the way to the catalog room, I overheard three men discussing the war.

"Think we're going to be drafted?"

"Not while in college."

"I'm going to volunteer," the third said. "That way, my cousin says, you can choose which branch of the service you want to be in."

Should I, too, volunteer? I stopped by the Navy's recruiting office and picked up some pamphlets.

At home, in the mail, I found a job offer to become head of the Graphic Unit at the newly created Office of Facts and Figures. Indeed, it turned out some Government official had seen *We Call it Human Nature* and decided my use of graphics might prove applicable to reports. I told the war agency representative that I wasn't an artist. He said that didn't matter, so I accepted the job. It was fortunate I did.

The azaleas were in bloom the day I met Beatrice, a svelte blond with intense, cornflower blue eyes. I was attracted to her at once. She headed up the Radio Section, which reported on how war news was being presented to the American people on the radio. We had been introduced at a meeting with a number of other people present. Ever since, I had looked forward to the opportunity of getting better acquainted.

The Government had set up its war agencies practically overnight. Due to a shortage of office space, the Library of Congress Annex served as headquarters for Facts and Figures. There were seventy of us, crammed into one large L-shaped room. We received temporary civil service status although we had little or no knowledge of the most rudimentary ways of government.

Since smokers were required to smoke outdoors, I left my desk five or six times a day. I would grab a few documents and walk briskly down the aisle. I hoped no one would notice that instead of heading for the door, I made a detour past Beatrice's desk. I walked fast, as if intent on some important task. What I didn't realize was that my frequent appearances had piqued her curiosity. It wasn't long before she waylaid me to find out why I kept striding by.

"What do you do here?" she asked.

"Come over to my desk and I'll explain."

As she followed me, I wracked my brain for an adequate response. It certainly wouldn't be appropriate to admit I had done nothing so far but read reports and attend staff meetings. I glanced down at my watch. "Nearly noon," I said, as if with surprise. "Should you happen to be free for lunch, there's a little place nearby, fairly quiet."

We easily found a table at a Greek restaurant. I ordered sherry for us both. "It's gotten cooler today," I said, leading her eyes toward the window. "Seems there was a shower." I studied my companion and hoped she wouldn't think I was staring. Beatrice looked unusually attractive in her suit of charcoal gray, accented by an orchid pinned to her lapel, and a chartreuse sweater. Perched on her head was a saucy little hat to match the suit. There was a silence while the waiter brought drinks.

"You were going to explain your work," she reminded me, taking a sip of sherry.

During lunch, I described some of the jobs I had held before the war and explained my bafflement at the ways of government. Beatrice listened closely and asked several questions. Then I suggested she tell me about herself.

"I graduated from Vassar ten years ago. After that I worked as a producer of educational programs for CBS radio."

"So you came down here to help in the war effort?" I said, urging her on.

She minimized the importance of what she had done, but I was impressed. Time flew by. We parted, promising to see each other again soon.

A few days later, as I was about to call Beatrice on the intercom, she called me first. Her voice sounded ebullient. "I'm giving a party next Friday and hope you can join us. I've invited a glamorous Spanish girl you'll enjoy meeting."

Didn't she realize I was interested in her? I scrambled for an appropriate response. "Friday?" I said, trying not to reveal my disappointment. "I would have loved to come, but unfortunately already have an engagement. It's a shame." I felt I couldn't let it go at that, so I added, "How about supper some other night, say next week?"

It turned out we lived in Georgetown, only a few blocks apart. We walked over to Martin's on Wisconsin Avenue. After dinner, we went for a stroll along the Chesapeake Canal. It was June, and the warm summer evening lent special intimacy to the occasion. Looking sideways at my companion, I thought surely she must be the most alluring creature I had ever known—apart from Veta. But Veta was long ago and far away, while Beatrice was here and now. On impulse I told her about my marriage to Laura and our imminent divorce.

We paused to watch the city lights reflected in the Potomac. There was no one around. We could barely hear the sounds of distant traffic. I felt a sharpening of all my faculties, a sudden keen awareness of the woman at my side. I counted to four, trying to quiet the pounding of my heart, and took her in my arms.

DIFFICULTIES AROSE at the office. I thought I was supposed to introduce visuals that would clarify the weekly report. Editorial writer Bartley Moore disagreed. He insisted I had been hired to design covers and clarify statistical comparisons through charts. His tone became defensive whenever I attempted to discuss the matter. I went to find R. Keith Kane, Chief of the Bureau of Intelligence. Kane told me to work things out myself. I hadn't had enough job experience to realize that, in America, people are supposed to solve their own problems, or find a way around them, not run to superiors for help. The situation posed a real dilemma, because Moore did everything in his power to prevent me from doing my job.

About that time, I began suffering from insomnia. I couldn't get to sleep until three or four—problematic when work starts at seven-thirty. Beatrice suggested I seek psychoanalytic help. Something had to be done and fast. I called the Washington School of Psychoanalysis, which had a reputation for favoring a less rigid approach than the Freudian method. In this way, I started seeing Dr. Benjamin Weininger.

I took a notebook to my first appointment in order to write down impressions and judge whether the five-dollar sessions would be worthwhile. Although I would have been the first to speak up for psychoanalysis in any argument, I felt skeptical about its benefits in my particular case. As soon as I stretched out on the couch, however, it became obvious that certain critical aspects of this form of therapy had eluded me. Psychoanalysis was beneficial not only in relieving my insomnia, but also in providing insight that helped correct irrational behavior.

During this period Beatrice and I grew closer. I recall one morning on the way to work, we happened to be on the same streetcar. We exchanged greetings, and I remember feeling glad I was wearing my favorite navy blue linen suit.

Another memory: We strolled along a gravel path in Dumbarton Oaks, past beds of roses in full bloom. Neither of us had ever seen so many varieties before. We sat down on a bench, enjoying the pungent scent of the neatly clipped boxwood. The serenity seemed such a contrast with wartime Washington.

That day Beatrice asked me, "Why do you have such a negative view of the world?"

I hesitated before answering, "I still feel bitter about being forced out of my native country. In order to endure the pain of separation, I guess I repressed my longing for Russia and tried very hard to adjust to America."

"Strange. You act as if you were born in Hartford, Connecticut. If you want my opinion, you need to get in touch with your roots."

BEATRICE WAS offered a new job at Time Inc. and decided to move back to New York. By then I knew I was in love and said I wanted to marry her, but she declined: "You're not mature enough to venture into a second marriage, and, for that matter, I'm not ready to get married myself."

I remember the day I drove her to the airport. I watched as the plane taxied down the runway and rose into the air. I searched the sky, straining my eyes to keep that plane from disappearing. "No, no, no!" I repeated under my breath. "I won't let her vanish from my life." Overcome with emotion, I had difficulty remembering where I had parked the car. I returned home reminding myself I could visit Manhattan anytime. I must have made the trip at least a dozen times.

Soon my divorce had come through and I got a research assistant job offer at Dartmouth. Finally Beatrice agreed to marry me. Here was an opportunity to start married life in comfortable circumstances as members of a college community. And, so it came about that in June, 1944, I headed for Montclair, New Jersey, Beatrice's hometown. After a Nantucket honeymoon, we set off for New Hampshire.

During this period the war was very much on everyone's mind. The

Dartmouth quadrangle had become a parade ground with people in uniform everywhere. Shortages increased in local stores. Products such as butter and cheese became scarce. Gasoline was rationed.

By mid-April the end of the war seemed imminent. Each day brought more promising headlines: Red Army Reaches the River Oder, Russians Penetrate Berlin's Suburbs, City Encircled; Fierce Battle in the Streets. It was clear that the struggle to repulse the Nazis was being carried out not just by the Soviet Army alone, but by all the Russian people. When the Red Army launched its drive through East Prussia, I began to feel an increasing pride in what my former countrymen were doing. I hung a map of Eastern Europe on the basement wall and followed the steady advances with colored pins.

IN EARLY AUGUST, Beatrice and I gathered up our gasoline coupons and took a short vacation. Somes House on Mount Desert had been recommended as a picturesque place overlooking a fjord. For several days we had been enjoying this retreat, when something unforgettable happened. At dinner, animated voices caught our attention. The man at the next table leaned over and said, "An American warplane just dropped an atomic bomb on Hiroshima!" We were struck with horror. It was as if some evil genie had been let loose on the world, a genie that could some day destroy us all.

On the ride back to Hanover, we witnessed an unusual event. What seemed to be the entire population of Conway, New Hampshire, had come out in the street to express pent-up emotion and joy. Everyone was doing a dance similar to the bunny hop, snaking up onto the sidewalk around a stop sign, and back onto the pavement. We stopped to watch and learned then of the Japanese surrender.

At home we found a letter from a friend at AT&T asking me to take part in a conference in Manhattan, organized for company personnel. Beatrice and I discussed the offer, and I decided to accept. Who knew what opportunities might be available now the war was over?

3

IN MINUTES I would address dozens of executives on the problems facing a personnel department. A rush of anxiety washed over me as I realized I knew next to nothing about the subject and should never have agreed to participate in the AT&T symposium. My speech simply wouldn't do. What in the world was I going to say? Reluctantly, I stepped up to the microphone.

"Gentlemen, my knowledge of Bell System personnel policies is necessarily limited, for I'm an outsider here. It would seem best, therefore, not to venture an opinion on the programs so far discussed. On the other hand, I do have a few general observations, which may prove useful. I would like to suggest, for instance, that any process involving people, be it training or counseling, should rest on a foundation of good communication if it is to engage everyone's support and achieve its goal: two-way communication, to be exact."

I managed to speak for the appropriate length of time and felt incredible relief at leaving the podium. Soon the conference ended. As I stood up to go, several men approached me.

"I enjoyed your talk, but wish you could have elaborated more on two-way communication," said a fellow wearing a crisp bow tie. With a quick nod, he was gone. Apparently I had touched a nerve.

A thickset man with an enigmatic smile then introduced himself: "Cleo Craig, Vice President of Personnel. Great speech, Paul. Really enjoyed it. How about you walk me up to my office?"

After we had stepped into the elevator, Craig said, "The process of two-way communication to which you alluded certainly needs improvement here. Management's message is often distorted as it travels down the line. There's little feedback. I make a decision and expect something to happen, but it doesn't. Not what I intended anyway."

Once we had reached Craig's office, he bowled me over with an unexpected offer: "I'd like you to work here as a consultant. Your job would be to advise me on how communication could be improved at all levels of the Bell System. We can offer you a three-year contract. Think about it and give me your answer within a week."

I stood there, dazed by this development. Cleo Craig had impressed me as a person of superior intelligence. There was no doubt in my mind that I should accept his offer, for it meant a 25% increase in salary.

WITHIN TWO MONTHS, Beatrice and I were back in Manhattan, installed in a cozy apartment on East 86th Street.

AT&T was located at 195 Broadway. On my first day of work I paused in the lobby to admire the towering ceiling and marble columns, which made the place resemble an Egyptian temple. In the center stood a five-foot sculpture of Alexander Graham Bell. I knelt down to study two bronze medallions embedded in the floor. They showed Mercury, bearing the message of the gods. I ran my fingers across the inscription, *Universal Service.* I had the feeling these symbols of Bell's dominance in the field of communication conjured up not only universal service but great power, the might and solidity of the world's largest corporation.

My office was on the fourth floor. Never before had I commanded such an impressive set-up. Craig had even made a secretary available. He stopped by shortly after my arrival. "Remember, you don't have to go through anyone to see me. Not even the Assistant Vice President for Personnel. Got that straight?"

One of the country's top business executives had given me a task whose ramifications I hardly understood. Could I rise to the challenge?

After some soul-searching, I pulled together a few ideas and took them up to the 22nd floor for his go-ahead. I knew I had to sound sure of myself so I spoke with as much confidence as I could muster. "First I'll go to Cleveland, two to three weeks at the most. There I'll have some sessions with an old-timer who can enlighten me in plain English regarding the inner workings of relays. I need to know basic telephone technology before talking to telephone installers, repairmen, and maintenance technicians. Once back in New York, I'll learn to operate a switchboard, prior to interviewing chief operators and their assistants. Discussing satisfactions and frustrations on the job will help me learn about two-way communication. I also plan some sessions with middle management on the district and sub-district levels. With regard to the methodology and the statistical part of this investigation, I'll need the help of a consultant, one afternoon a week. I know the perfect man. Gene Hartley. We worked together during the war. Can you authorize me to get in touch with him?"

"Proceed," Craig said. A twinkle had come into his eye. "I'll alert the people involved. Don't forget to keep me posted. I want to see you once or twice a month to hear how you're doing."

Over the years I had formed an image of the heads of industry as ruthless men with no humor, driving grimly forward, but Craig did not fit this stereotype at all. There was a gentler side to his nature. With people who functioned at a slower pace, he could be patient. When he showed up at the annual Christmas party, for instance, he went around acting as if he were one of the boys. Naturally, nobody thought of him that way. His behavior was a gesture, part of the etiquette of equality that, in this country, is most scrupulously observed by persons of superior status in their relationships with the less privileged.

WHILE WORKING in Manhattan, I decided to look up someone I'd met at Dartmouth, Dr. Alan Gregg of the Rockefeller Foundation, a big man with bushy eyebrows, a ruddy complexion, and a lion's mane of white hair. We got into the habit of having lunch together in the executive dining room at 30 Rockefeller Plaza. During these lunches, Gregg sometimes reminisced about his life. One day we discussed the immigrant's problems of assimilation, and mine, in particular.

"Sometimes I feel ill at ease among Americans because some of their reactions baffle me. For instance, in the company of someone unfamiliar, I often fumble, trying to find something to talk about. Americans have no such constraint. They are able to make contact right away, even with total strangers."

Gregg nodded sympathetically.

"There's something else. In Russia, people thrive on a serious exchange of views, which is what happens automatically when they get together. But here, say at a party, if the conversation takes a serious turn, everyone seems to lose interest. I'm afraid making sense of the thought processes and behavioral patterns of Americans remains a challenge. This bothers me because my life, or what remains of it, won't give me enough time to really understand this culture."

Gregg drew his chair a little closer. "How so?"

"One way to understand would be to pool my observations and insights with those of other European immigrants. In fact, I have already found a few such people to interview."

He replaced his cup on its gold and white saucer and looked at me expectantly. "What will you ask?"

"First off, whether there's anything that makes them feel ill at ease in everyday dealings with Americans. 'I'm an immigrant, too,' I'll say. 'Here's what bothers me.' I'll then ask, 'How about you? Is there anything that still makes you feel like an outsider, despite all those years in the United States?'"

"What makes you think you'll get answers?"

"I can't be sure, but I can try."

"Hmm," Gregg mused. "Pooling insights. Sounds like an interesting approach." He lowered his eyes, deep in thought. "Look, tell you what. Why not write up your project and send the idea to Roberts who heads our Social Science Division? In the meantime, I'll have a word with him. Make sure the scope is small. It should be an exploratory study, not over eight thousand dollars, so it doesn't require submission to the Board. And, be sure to mention you've already gone ahead, entirely on your own."

I FELT CONFLICTING emotions as I entered the familiar lobby for the last time. Craig had offered me a permanent job, which I had refused. During my three years at AT&T, Beatrice and I had lived frugally and were able to put aside a little money. The week before, I had submitted my report. It had confirmed that employee morale and plant productivity increased when the impersonality of the workplace was counteracted and workers were made to feel their opinions made a difference. Good two-way communication tended to encourage an impression of increased participation, producing more feedback. In this way, management was kept in closer touch with employee needs.

The elevator raced past the floors that contained ordinary offices and stopped at the very top of the building. The door slid open noiselessly. Behind a desk sat a middle-aged secretary. As I walked toward the couch, I noticed a watercolor of a Marin seascape. I had seen a reproduction of it somewhere. At one o'clock sharp the secretary opened a massive oak door, and Craig got up from his desk to greet me. A table had been set for lunch near the picture window, overlooking the Hudson. "Thought we'd eat up here where we can talk undisturbed," said the newly appointed president of AT&T.

I looked around at the comfortable furnishings, the oriental rugs, the paintings. How did Craig endure such an exclusive atmosphere? Maybe isolation was bureaucracy's means of minimizing interference from above and preventing the people on top from knowing too much? Perhaps the real reason Craig had taken me in was that, even as vice-president, he was groping for a way to break through the bottlenecks in internal communication? My former boss must have read my thoughts. He was the one to begin our conversation: "I now feel that we made a mistake when you joined us. We should have set you up near the Long Island General Manager, say in the office next door. That way maybe some of your ideas might have rubbed off."

Back in the lobby an hour later, I stooped to touch the bronze medallions one last time. I felt confident my decision not to seek further employment at AT&T was sound. The temptation to create a niche for myself had been great, but the industry simply did not appeal to me. Yes, it was the right decision.

SOMETHING ELSE unusual happened that year. I saw Veta Bezobrazova again. She had come to New York for a visit and contacted me. I took her out to lunch at one of the restaurants in Rockefeller Plaza. We picked a table near a window where we could watch the ice-skaters. As we sat down, I couldn't help but notice how attractive she still was. My childhood sweetheart knew that I had married Beatrice and that we were expecting a baby. During lunch I learned Veta had been married a number of times and had raised three children. Denmark seemed so long ago. Hearing the details of her life was a bizarre experience.

"I was widowed when Hans died after an operation. I remarried a Russian named Rebinder, and later a Norwegian doctor whom I divorced. I worked at the Danish Ministry of Foreign Affairs, then in the Intelligence Service of the Danish Ministry of Defense...."

As we sat opposite each other in that restaurant, we were not altogether at ease, unable to recapture the past and incapable of finding common ground in the present, so we stopped talking for a while and watched the skaters.

"You're different now," Veta said finally in Russian. "More manly, more capable, but so serious, so very serious. Why? You used to be happy-go-lucky."

"Was I?"

She was right. I had changed. My life had been very different from hers. It was impossible to explain. Instead, I said, "I hope you've been happy." She looked at me without answering.

I hesitated. "There's something perhaps you don't know. That evening in Hans's car on *Kongens Nytorv.*" The expression on her face told me she remembered. "You said he had proposed and asked what to do. I was taken aback. I didn't know what to say. Didn't you know how much I cared for you?"

Veta looked off into space, then said in a low voice, "But you never asked me to marry you."

I was silent. Until that moment I had blamed circumstance. Now I knew that the opportunity to marry her had existed, only it had come at the wrong time in my life.

The waiter, who had hovered nearby for several minutes, brought the check. We paused, our eyes drawn to the skating instructor as she demonstrated a figure eight.

"She's graceful," I said. I felt as if I was talking against time.

Veta nodded. We watched the girl pirouette on the shining ice. Still we lingered, loathe to part. On Fifth Avenue, I hailed a taxi and held the door open. She climbed in.

"I hope you have a pleasant journey home."

"Don't forget me," she said, fixing me with those languorous eyes of hers. "In case you ever come to Denmark…."

The noise of the traffic drowned out the rest of her words.

I struggled to control my feelings. Was I still in love with Veta or was it our Russianess that drew me to her? In the wake of the Revolution, we had been parted not only from each other, but from our earlier selves. Still the emotion had not changed.

I closed the door and waved as the taxi pulled away from the curb, remembering how, twenty-four years earlier, I had waved goodbye to a group of friends gathered on a pier in Copenhagen. That past now seemed so very far away.

4

"DURING WORLD War II, my parents moved here from Monte Carlo. We found them an apartment, not far from our own. After many years of precarious status as refugees, they were pleased to become U.S. citizens." I paused and looked at my new psychoanalyst. Dr. Meyer Maskin was watching me reflectively. "Do you think people ever forgive their parents?"

"Have you forgiven yours?"

"I suppose so. Sometimes I think I have." It was difficult to find the right words to express my feelings. I fumbled on. "Childhood memories fade. Memories of those unhappy times when my father and mother belittled me. Painful incidents like my pet pig being served for dinner or the time my mother phoned my school, questioning the high mark I had received for good behavior.

"Some of my resentment is also directed at my father. He was away so often. When home, he always sided with Mother as if to get unpleasantness out of the way as soon as possible. One incident stands out." Sudden emotion overwhelmed me. I had to pause until I felt calm enough to speak. "Apparently, for over twenty years, my father tried to collect money from the National City Bank of New York, money he had deposited in Petrograd prior to the Revolution. When he finally won the case, somehow he neglected to tell me. I didn't even know he was suing the bank or that a prominent attorney had represented him. He didn't tell me after he won a sum of money large enough to get a life annuity from a Canadian insurance company. A cousin did. This slight was deeply embarrassing. When people asked about the victory, I felt humiliated. I interpreted his secretiveness as a sign of mistrust. Was he afraid I'd want to share in his good fortune? Spend some of the money? Why couldn't he trust me?"

Dr. Maskin said nothing. Outside, rain began to pound at the window.

"I've often wanted to get the matter into the open, to talk to him about it, especially now that he's in ill health. I've never been able to. I'd like to think I've forgiven him. But, have I?"

Dr. Maskin stood up. The session was over. I felt immense relief. As I sloshed home through the rain, I wondered whether people ever know forgiveness. Did Father forgive me?

MARCH 15, 1947, was the day the obstetrician said our baby was due to be born. Father, now eighty-two, wasn't well. He had ruptured his spleen in an accident on a crosstown bus and, after several transfusions, refused to return to the hospital. We knew he did not have long to live. In the middle of the night, Mother called to say he wanted to see me. I rushed over to their apartment where he lay in bed. He lifted his wrist to wave as I entered the room.

"Pavlik! You've come. Could you help me get more comfortable?"

I found his body heavy. As I lifted him, he looked up, and, at that moment, we knew we forgave each other for whatever hurt we had caused.

By then I had come to realize how difficult Father's life had been: forced absences from home on military duty, demanding years with the tsar, a life's work annihilated by Revolution. I was still holding him when he sighed and slipped from my grasp.

THREE WEEKS later Beatrice woke me up shortly after midnight. "It's started," she said, wincing. "We better call Dr. Corwin."

Up until that moment the arrival of a baby had been an abstract concept, something I knew was coming, but didn't quite believe would happen. In ten minutes we were on our way. From East 86th to the Presbyterian Hospital on West 167th was quite a trek. As the taxi crossed Central Park, Beatrice grasped my hand and squeezed. "A spasm. It's gone now." Then she added, "I'm really sorry I couldn't attend your father's funeral. There was no telling when this would start. You see how painful it is."

"Are you very uncomfortable?"

"Yes, and it's getting worse."

Dr. Jean Corwin must have alerted her staff because a nurse met Beatrice at the front desk. While I paid the taxi driver, she disappeared, swallowed up by the immense institution. Another nurse directed me to a waiting room where two men sat in armchairs, flipping through magazines.

Around two, the nurse brought us a pot of black coffee. "It will be a while yet," she said.

"How long?"

The nurse shrugged.

I tried to distract myself by leafing through *Time*. I thought of a Danish friend who had told me he had been allowed to stay with his wife during their baby's birth. He had held her hand and spoken to her reassuringly. When she screamed, he said he had felt like screaming, too. Better to be involved that way than excluded, here in this wretched waiting room.

A couple of hours passed and still nothing happened. When a nurse called to one of the other men, I asked if there was any news for me. There wasn't. I settled back in the chair and tried again to concentrate on the magazine.

I had all but dismissed the idea of becoming a father until I met Beatrice. After our marriage, I had sensed I couldn't hold on to her unless I changed my attitude. Even so, I had only the faintest notion of what having children might involve. I had come to look upon kids with apprehension. I avoided them, in fact. To me, children were not little darlings, but rather demons who broke things and made noise.

My watch now said 5:15. No doubt the hospital staff had forgotten me. Hoping to hail someone, I looked up and down the passageway, but it was deserted. For some time, I paced the floor.

An hour later a nurse stuck her head in the door. "You still here? We thought you'd gone home. Your wife's okay, but it's taking longer than we expected. We'll give you a ring as soon as there's anything to report."

I went home to bed. The telephone woke me up.

"Congratulations!" said a cheerful voice. "You have a daughter. Mother and baby are doing fine."

I felt intense relief. I got dressed and returned to the hospital to meet Alexandra.

IN THE SPRING of 1948 we gave a cocktail party to celebrate the 25th anniversary of my arrival in America. During the party, somebody asked how I had gotten on initially in this country. "With difficulty," I responded. "It took time to get my bearings, to find ways of coping in a culture so very different from my own. It wasn't until I had learned English well enough to write for publication that things began to change."

Soon after that party, I found myself in need of a job, as the Rockefeller Foundation had not yet approved my plan to study European-born Americans and their reactions to this country. The situation was familiar, but now I had a family to support. Fortunately, this crisis did not last. Gene Hartley, my former assistant at AT&T, called to report a vacancy in his department at what was then called the City College of New York. He had recommended me: "We need an instructor in industrial psychology, and your experience seems just right."

Although the job was temporary, Beatrice and I decided to have another child, for Alexandra's sake as well as our own. Six months passed. I was worrying about where to find the money to pay the doctor's bill when the phone rang. On the line was a General Motors personnel chief whom

I had met while doing research for AT&T.

"I've just discovered that we used some of the visual materials you developed without paying for them," he said. I held my breath. "So, this morning, I put a check for one thousand dollars in the mail with our thanks."

Miracles do happen!

After several months of unemployment, I decided to contact two friends from my Office of Facts and Figures days, who were now working for the State Department. They told me the head of Visual Services was looking for a project director. I applied immediately.

On Lincoln's birthday we again had cause to celebrate. Beatrice gave birth to our second child, a boy. We named him after my paternal grandfather, a cavalry general distinguished for taking several divisions across the tallest range of the Caucasian Mountains. From behind a glass panel, I watched Dr. Corwin lift up Nicholas. She smiled and waved, and I gestured back. Could this possibly be my son? As I gazed through the glass, I wondered how I would make out as a father. How could I ever make up to my children for not being native-born?

THAT SUMMER I had become increasingly concerned about Mother's health. The doctor had said she suffered from uremic poisoning and didn't have long to live. I remember sitting in the dark, looking fixedly in the direction of the dining room where she lay in a coma. We were alone. As hospital appointments were hard to schedule, Beatrice had been obliged to take Sandra, now four, to have her tonsils out. Baby Nick was asleep in another part of the apartment. It must have been three or four a.m.

Mother was breathing heavily in a deep-throated way. I still felt ambivalent, but it was too late to settle anything now. Over the years, I had come to believe many of my problems related to her inability to provide mothering, allowing nurses, governesses, and tutors to assume my care. Not that I blamed Mother for this choice—such behavior was typical of her class. Still I did regret the way she had treated me as a child, lavishing all her attention on Nils. I doubt whether she ever realized how rejected I had felt.

As my thoughts slipped into the past, I recognized a new emotion: pride. When the Revolution came, Mother had proven she was not helpless in the least. From having everything done for her—she had not even brushed her own hair until we left Russia—she had adjusted to a whole new way of life. Not only had Mother learned to cook and keep house, but she had given English lessons to the French and French lessons to the English. She had learned to carry her own load and never complained, not once.

I sat there in a daze, juggling these mixed emotions. Presently Mother stirred. She moved her legs, as if in slow motion. I watched her pause at the edge of the bed, sitting perfectly still. After a while, she stood up and shuffled toward the bathroom. Soon she returned to bed. Her breathing became raucous. It got louder and louder, then suddenly stopped. There was absolute silence. I kept thinking *my mother has died.* I have to go see… make sure…yes, I have to go see. But I didn't move. I couldn't get up from the chair.

We buried Mother in Kent, Connecticut, next to Father, in the Congregational Cemetery that overlooks the Housatonic River, near a clump of birch trees. Nils was the only member of the family to return to the Russian earth.

5

BEATRICE AND I decided to move to Washington, DC. My luck changed as soon as we made this decision: the State Department accepted my job application. That same day I received a telegram: the Rockefeller Foundation had finally agreed to finance my study. Which to choose? I wanted to do both. The problem was solved more easily than expected. The State Department agreed to hold the job open while I did the immigration study. I was, therefore, able to complete the interviews before leaving New York. We bought a house in Wesley Heights, using my royalties as a down payment, and I started work in downtown Washington.

SENATOR MCCARTHY'S virulent anti-communist campaign made 1952 a tough year to be in government. As if seized with paranoia, the Senator repeatedly pointed a finger at the State Department, asserting that here, in our midst, was a veritable hotbed of communist sympathizers. He even claimed to know the names of *dangerous elements* and vowed to ferret them out. McCarthy would call up individual workers for questioning and subjected them to brutal, wholly irrational accusations. There wasn't much use in defending oneself. The Senator always seemed able to produce evidence, supplied by anonymous informers, and his victims lost their jobs.

Personnel notified my boss that he was next on McCarthy's list: "Be prepared. We don't know exactly what accusations the Senator might level, but think it has something to do with the fact that, as a Rhodes scholar, you struck up a friendship with a young Englishman who later published several Marxist-oriented tracts."

Jim Willis became a different man. He would sit at his desk for a while, then withdraw from the world. I stood nearby as he lay motionless on the couch.

Suddenly he opened his eyes and said, "Tell me, Paul. How would you respond if you were in my shoes?"

I shrugged, unable to come up with an answer.

"What upsets me the most is that, if called upon to testify, I'll carry the stigma forever." With a sigh, he closed his eyes again.

I assumed as much of the workload as possible. Since the Division Chief happened to be on vacation, helping Willis, in fact, meant running the Division. Fortunately, things were rather slow, and I didn't encounter any problems. When the phone rang, I would say, "Mr. Willis is out of the office at the moment. Would you care to leave a message?"

Days went by without any news on the subpoena. Weeks passed. Then, one morning, as I opened his door, I knew something had changed. Willis rose to greet me. "You'll understand, I'm sure, when I say I've had enough of this." His voice was steady and he wore a smile. "No longer will I be intimidated. My first obligation is to my family ...to safeguard them and myself...against the consequences of what this man might do. So, I've decided to leave the government. Yes, I'm resigning and going into business for myself."

I inherited his job. This promotion became official upon the division chief's return. A year later I was advanced again, this time to deputy chief. I'm not sure whether these promotions signified I was considered ready for more responsibility or whether higher management favored the candidacy of a Russian émigré with a background that guaranteed unfailing anti-communism. Indeed, there was no way for me to become McCarthy's next target.

IN 1955, I transferred to the United States Information Agency, a fortunate assignment because I already knew my new boss. Indeed, I had once provided him with charts, which he had used to advantage at a congressional hearing. He expressed his appreciation by giving me a blank check: "I've decided to name you special assistant. Officially, we'll call you agency adviser on Visual Projects. The title is vague enough so that people won't know exactly what you do or whether you're important. This ambiguity will make them more willing to work with you."

Soon after my transfer, President Eisenhower asked the agency's director, Theodore Streibert, to deliver an hour-long report on communist propaganda. Streibert chose me for visuals.

"Let's use several film clips, one of the Kirov Ballet, another of a symphony playing to an enthusiastic crowd in Japan," I suggested once the script had been approved. "The point we must emphasize is that the Soviet Union is mobilizing every means available to promote its image as a peace-loving nation, rather than as an instigator of world revolution."

We ran several rehearsals, the last one in the cabinet room itself. My charts were set up on an easel to one side of the podium. Two technicians stood ready with the film clips and soundtrack. I felt nervous as I watched cabinet members take their seats. Everyone was waiting for the president. I looked around with awe, thinking momentous decisions affecting the country and the world were made at that conference table. Soon Eisenhower appeared. He seemed tired, but moved briskly toward his seat. He leaned over to say something to the secretary of state in an irritated tone of voice. Eisenhower motioned for us to begin. For a while the presentation ran smoothly, then there was an interruption. An aide whispered in the president's ear. He stood up and left the room.

"Sir, should we continue?" Streibert asked.

"No," John Foster Dulles said. "This is too important. I want the president to hear it all. Wait for him to get back."

The rest went off without a hitch. Streibert received compliments from a number of Cabinet members. Before leaving, Eisenhower told us he wanted the event repeated for the bipartisan members of Congress.

This second presentation took place a week later in the Old State Department Building. About thirty officials from various government agencies were also present. Afterwards several people stayed to have a word with Streibert.

I was watching from a distance when a broad-shouldered, middle-aged man approached me. I recognized him immediately as Nelson Rockefeller, Chairman of the Presidential Commission on Organizational Reform. "I'd like to express my appreciation," he said, shaking my hand. "I'm a great believer in visuals and particularly liked the way you used those film clips to make the talk come alive."

Several days later, Abbott Washburn, USIA's deputy director, called me into his office. "Seems the White House was very pleased with your work," he said. After a moment of hesitation, Washburn handed me a letter and motioned for me to read it. *I've decided to retire from the Federal Government. My assistant is looking for a new job. Since Nadia Williams has a talent for turning complicated factual data into simple visuals, there probably is a place for her in USIA.* The letter was signed, *Cordially, Nelson.* At the bottom, there was a handwritten postscript: *Please give my best regards to Paul Grabbe.*

I handed the letter back to Washburn. He was looking at me quizzically. "Guess it might be a good idea if you were to meet this Nadia Williams."

Washburn hired Nadia as my assistant. This remarkable woman was a great asset to me in future assignments.

The letter produced another totally unexpected result. Its contents were soon common knowledge throughout the agency. Rockefeller's name carried so much weight that the mere possibility we might be friends placed me in a special category. I was now able to tackle things that needed to be done, but, for one reason or another, had never been undertaken— projects I would not have been allowed to touch under ordinary circumstances. One such job was production of a reference manual for senior officers. This Public Affairs Officers' Handbook became one of the main training tools for officers assigned abroad.

BEATRICE AND I lived in Washington for almost twenty years. Toward the end of my career, USIA directors asked me to represent the State Department at a traveling show from the Soviet Union, which opened at the Time-Life Building in New York. When I met the Russian coordinator, he immediately asked, "Where did you learn such good Russian?"

The graphic artists couldn't have been friendlier. They even apologized for slipping in propaganda films, outlawed by a prior agreement, and added that this transgression had nothing to do with me: they were simply obeying orders.

The show was about to close when Lee Harvey Oswald assassinated President Kennedy. That night the streetlights of Manhattan dimmed, theaters and restaurants shut their doors, and, in a great outpouring of emotion, normal life seemed to stop. In this atmosphere of crisis, the co-ordinator asked permission to fly the Soviet flag at half-mast. Time-Life officials panicked and demanded the flag be removed altogether.

As an intermediary in the negotiations between Soviet authorities and Time-Life management, I found myself in the middle of this dispute, unable to get instructions from Washington because the circuits were all jammed. For several hours, I became the sole official representative of the United States government, responsible for resolution of one specific international conflict. Fortunately, I was able to contain the crisis long enough to get the exhibit to Philadelphia. However, the strain did not leave me unscathed. I suffered a heart attack and had to be hospitalized.

At 68, I retired, glad to leave Nixon's universe and the traumatic events of the nineteen-sixties behind: the burning of the capital, muggings in the streets, the continuing nightmare of Vietnam. Once the children graduated from college, Beatrice and I moved to Cape Cod. Originally a fishing village, Wellfleet was far enough out of the way to be relatively unaffected by drugs and pollution. Here, in 1970, freed at last from job-related anxieties, we bought a two hundred-year-old house and settled down to spend our remaining years writing, enjoying nature, and tending a garden. A generous government annuity allowed a comfortable life.

6

LIKE MANY OTHER retirees on the Cape, Beatrice and I are drawn to the sea. I park our old BMW near the edge of a dune at Newcomb Hollow beach and look out across the boundless expanse of water. We find the ocean endlessly fascinating. Its timeless ebb and flow somehow transcends human concerns. Wellfleet seems the perfect place to write a memoir. Under a clear blue sky I find the leisure to reflect on life. My thoughts turn back to childhood.

I remember St. Petersburg with its row of palaces fronting the Neva, its churches and monuments, its many canals, crowded with skaters. The first hard frost came in September, marking the beginning of the long, dark winter. On December mornings it was pitch black outside.

I remember how Father would come and go. His arrivals were memorable because he unlocked his desk and showed me his collection of watches and other gadgets. Father invariably arrived home for Christmas and left a few days later. He would be back briefly at Easter, but not for my birthday in February.

I loved Russian Easter with its excitement and gaiety. Easter meant staying up late for the midnight service. It meant greeting people and being greeted in turn with the words *Christ has Risen*, followed by a threefold exchange of kisses on both cheeks. Easter, celebrated with *paskha* and *koulich*, foods not eaten at any other time, marked the end of winter. It was then that ice came floating down the river, bringing a wonderful freshness to the air. The snow in the streets turned to slush. Coachmen put away their sleighs and brought out little carriages to which horses were hitched.

In my mind I see the butcher shops with rabbits, geese, wild ducks and other game hanging on metal hooks outside, the glitter of the audience at the Marinsky Theatre during a ballet performance, the pedestrians crossing themselves as they pass a church. I remember Koukoulya, my wonderfully kind and compassionate tutor.

Sitting there beside the sea, I think back to the white nights of early summer when I would play tennis outdoors past ten p.m. and the golden-haired teenager with whom I danced all evening at my first and last costume ball. I cannot help but wonder what became of her. Did she, like so many others I knew, perish in the turmoil? Or did fate lead her to safety, as it did me?

WHEN THE BOLSHEVIKS seized power and my family fled to Denmark, people would say, "Don't worry. You'll soon be going home. The Soviet regime won't last."

They were wrong. The Communists remained in power, and the Soviet regime wrought great devastation. I bear witness to the losses in my own family: my brother Nils, dead after he enlisted to fight Bolsheviks;

Uncle Kolya, thrown into the Moika Canal; Cousin Nika, arrested on suspicion that he was a counter-revolutionary, then shot at Kronstadt prison.
The Revolution disrupted my life in other ways, too. I was deprived
not only of my homeland, but also of financial independence and social
status. My education ceased when I turned fifteen. But no longer speaking
my native tongue overshadowed everything else. Living as I did, first with
Danes, then with Americans, I seldom had the opportunity to speak Russian. I could tell that my fluency was gradually slipping away, a wrenching
loss because people never feel quite the same in another language. Some
indefinable part of one's inner self ceases to function. I have not used Russian for more than half a century now. How to express what a wrenching
loss that continues to be? The absence of that special confidence, which
the mother tongue provides, has proved to be an incredible handicap.

On an even deeper level comes the spiritual damage uprooting cre-
ates. When an injury of this type is inflicted in the formative years, the
personality, stunted, may fail to reach its potential. Other changes may
follow, if my experience is any indication. Veta, who had known me as a
teenager, remarked that I had lost my *joie de vivre* when we met later in
life. She was right. I often felt as if I had lost the capacity to experience joy.

As the years passed, the illusion of being a visitor in a foreign land
became more and more difficult to maintain. The Soviet government, after
all, had lasted quite a while. Ten years passed, then twenty, then thirty. I
began to realize I might never return to my homeland, a reality that was
hard to accept.

Friends have sometimes asked whether I derived anything positive
from the cataclysm that was the Revolution. The end of the world I had
known forced me to reexamine assumptions and values. After I left Russia,
only one constant remained—the guidelines I had picked up in childhood. They made it possible to recognize what was important and kept
me strong while I groped for new bearings. My loss of status and security
was the driving force behind my determination to redress the balance,
insofar as possible, and rise above the humdrum existence I saw unfolding
before me. To a certain extent, I think I was able to meet this challenge.
Still, changing cultures is not easy. One of the most difficult aspects was
learning to relate to my own children.

When I conjure up an image of my father, I see him standing resplen-
dent, as in a fairy tale, being fitted by a tailor for his parade uniform—a

crimson tunic with sparkling silver epaulets. He bends toward me, smiles, ruffles my hair. What's missing is intimacy. A measure of formality underlies our relationship. This restraint between parent and child, I have been led to understand, is proper in the social milieu in which my life is cast. As a child, I must have learned my lesson well, for now that I myself have become a parent, half a world away from where I once belonged, I find it difficult to shed a certain impersonality of manner.

There are experiences I cannot share as an American-born father might: playing Wiffle ball in the back yard, helping with school work, or just relaxing on a Sunday afternoon with the comics. Although I get myself two books on baseball, Nick's favorite sport, its appeal remains a mystery. Watching the huge crowd in the bleachers shout and wave, I realize that for many Americans baseball is an emotionally charged experience. I feel frustrated in my effort to understand something that engages my son so deeply.

Similar constraints affected my relationship with Sandy. It wasn't until she married a Frenchman and, while living in Paris, became nostalgic for the United States, that we were able to truly connect.

During their childhood, a disproportionate amount of my energy simply had to go into holding onto a job. I think both my children understood these limitations and tried to make allowances insofar as possible. They were aware of my concern for their welfare and returned my feelings of affection.

Perhaps I have not said much in this memoir about Beatrice, but then again, perhaps I have, for she is an invisible presence in my saga. When we met, she said a wooden quality would set in, if I didn't get closer to my Russian roots. In this, and in many other ways, she is and has been, to quote that curious American word, my *soulmate.* To her I owe a great deal. Beatrice helped mitigate the trauma of exile and made me more human.

PEOPLE HAVE OFTEN asked why I didn't return to St. Petersburg, if only for a visit. In 1971, I did go back to Europe after an absence of forty-eight years. During the crossing, Beatrice and I met five Soviet Russians, returning home from assignment in the United States. They seemed fascinated to meet a representative of another Russia. I was, after all, an actual eyewitness to the Revolution. I was equally intrigued at the opportunity to get to know them. We shared a table in the dining salon of the Italian liner, conversed in Russian, got on well.

"Why not visit Leningrad?" one of them said. "The government would not hold émigré status against you, since you were a teenager when you left."

"Perhaps. We'll see," I equivocated, unable to bring myself to tell them why I had no wish to return.

I used to think going back to Russia would be dangerous because of my father's association with the tsar, but gave up that idea as the years went by. Now I'm sure visiting the Soviet Union would be quite safe. Safe, but not without pain. I'd find my home occupied by strangers. It's unlikely that they would know my family name. I would probably want to avoid certain parts of the city, like the Moika Canal, where my uncle was stoned to death. There is something else, too, besides troubling associations. I know all too well that losing one's homeland leaves a wound that is slow to heal. To return might open it, a risk I do not intend to take. No, I will never return to Russia. I have accepted that now.

Although I applauded *glasnost* and hoped Gorbachev would succeed in vitalizing the Soviet economy and reactivating the country in a human way, I am not convinced that the revolutionary pendulum has ceased swinging. There is no guarantee that it will not reverse itself again. I wouldn't even feel comfortable contacting those Soviet Russians that I got to know in 1971. Our association might have negative repercussions. While I was recounting happy memories of birch trees flying past on the train ride home to St. Petersburg each September, we all knew I would never see that landscape again. My descendants, however, are not subject to the same constraints.

In 1989, our seventeen-year-old granddaughter called from Paris to inform us of her imminent departure for Leningrad with a school class. "I'd like to visit your house, Grandpa. How can I find it and do you think the present inhabitants would mind?"

"Yes, do go. Judging from the photographs which the American consul was good enough to send, the exterior has not changed at all, but, who can tell what it's like inside? The rooms may be in terrible condition. After all, I left seventy-two years ago, and that's a long time."

I'M 95 NOW. Good Doctor Millhofer says modern medicine will help me live to be one hundred, but I'm not sure that's such a good idea. Sandy has come back from France to care for us. She takes me to the clinic in a wheelchair and has found a walker so I can get around the house on my own. I do well on all Millhofer's tests. I tell him what my name is, remember the date successfully, count all the fingers he holds up.

On Wednesdays, I go to Sally Hall, my therapist, in Orleans. My new son-in-law, Sven, drives me there. On the way, we listen to classical music. Sometimes we hear that piece Nils used to play back in St. Petersburg: Schubert. I can't hear so well anymore, so Sven turns the music up loud.

On Thursdays, I look forward to seeing Melissa, the visiting nurse who comes to give me a bath. We both know my life is drawing to an end. Her cheerfulness helps me forget.

Recently, Beatrice and I celebrated our 55th wedding anniversary. I worry what will happen to her. I sleep a lot now. Sometimes I wake up, still in a dream. I can tell my absentmindedness distresses her.

I can't see too well anymore, but try to read *The New York Times* every day and discuss articles with Beatrice. I don't feel especially good about the news. The world seems to be going backward, rather than forward. During my lifetime, man's inhumanity has increased appallingly. As complexities develop here and abroad, there are signs that governments can no longer cope. When the established order is weakened, democracy is threatened. I find this reality upsetting. At least, in the United States, I feel free to speak my mind. No one will stop me from voicing concern for the nation—this nation that has become my home, if not my homeland.

In conclusion, I'd like to express my thanks to America for having treated me so well. When I came here as a youth, I had no job skills and was woefully unprepared to make a living. Some of my jobs tested my strength to the utmost, but very few turned out to be a waste of time. Each was a learning experience. Those attempts that misfired did so mainly because of a lack of readiness on my part, or a boss's neurosis. However, throughout my life, at every step, there was always someone there to extend a hand, so that I could negotiate the bumps more easily. I was able to keep going without jeopardizing my health or my integrity.

I now wind up my life here in Massachusetts with a family that cares for me. I have two children, five grandchildren, a beloved wife. They helped repair the damage done to my psyche after I was thrown off-balance by the Revolution. With their support, the wound inflicted when I was uprooted, gradually healed. This process also made me mature. For that, I am deeply grateful. I realize that I am one of the lucky ones in the violently disoriented world of the twentieth century. I survived.

End Notes

1. The Russian nickname for Pavel (Paul) is Pavlik.

2. Elizaveta Alekseyevna Orlova-Denisova was the granddaughter of a fabulous merchant, Savva Yakovlevich Yakovlev-Sobakin, who came out of nowhere to push a fish cart on the streets of Moscow. Soon he had created a chain of liquor stores and cornered the customs concession in the capital. Linen factories and gold mines followed. A robber baron of his time, he bought his way into the nobility with a loan to Peter III.

   Countess Orlova-Denisova's father was no less remarkable. Aleksei Petrovich Nikitin, a member of the lesser nobility, was an orphan educated by Catherine the Great. At age thirty-six, as colonel of artillery, he commanded the Raievsky Redoubt at the Battle of Borodino. Despite wounds in both legs, he and his battery held back Napoleon's advancing forces long enough to give Kutuzov's army a chance to regroup. For this deed, he was officially declared a hero of the Napoleonic War. This exploit is described in *War and Peace*. It is not generally realized that many titles trace back to some outstanding achievement. Nikitin is an ancestor of whom I have reason to be proud.

3. A leading biographical source traces the Bezaks to Lusatia and gives the name as Bezatsky, that of an old Slavic family. Uncle Sasha looked into earlier antecedents and found the de Besacks were French Huguenots from Toulouse who took refuge in Austria-Hungary. A branch of the family found its way to Anhalt, Lusatia. Christian, a professor of philosophy at the University of Leipzig, came to Russia at the invitation of Catherine the Great. He soon had learned the language well enough to write several books. Over the years, he rose in the civil service. On becoming a college councilor, he attained the privileges of hereditary nobility. Mother's grandfather had the same need to excel. As governor-general of Samara and Orenburg, Aleksander Pavlovich became a key figure in Russia's expansion into western Turkestan. After a stint in the senate, he served as governor-general of southwestern Russia, where he introduced peasant reforms of considerable importance and had a railroad built, connecting Kiev with Moscow.

4. Kolya had a reputation for cutting people down if he didn't like them or thought them stupid. Friends warned that his barbed remarks might lead to trouble, or even involve him in a duel. Instead of curbing his tongue, he practiced daily with rapier and pistol.

His reputation for acerbic wit made him a familiar figure at the English Club and the Café de Paris. Among those who found his conversation rewarding was Maurice Paleologue, the last French ambassador to the Russian Court. In *An Ambassador's Memoirs*, he gives his impression. Particularly striking, he writes, was Kolya's "paradox-loving imagination (which) he occasionally reveals with the spontaneity and genius of a Rivarol." One day, when the ambassador was giving Kolya a lift home, the chauffeur drove past Falconet's famous statue of Peter the Great. To Paleologue's surprise, my uncle called Peter "the greatest revolutionary of modern times," not a true reformer. Why? Because Peter attacked national traditions and customs, and was intent on destroying the past. "A true reformer," Paleologue quotes Kolya as having said, "allows for the past...is cautious in his changes and paves the way for the future."

5. Recent information indicates only the greenhouses burned. The manor still stands today and is used by local government.

6. General Count Pavel Khristoforovich Grabbe's ancestors had come from Sweden, presumably descended from a partisan of Gustav Vasa, one Nils Grabbe, who brought the Reformation to Finland. Pavel Khristoforovich took part in a historic meeting when he was only twenty-three. Napoleon was at the gates of Moscow. Field Marshal Kutuzov had called a council of war at Fily, on a hill above the city. The question was whether to stand and fight or to retreat. Some of the people present were in favor of battle. French historian Alfred Rambaud quotes artillery officer Grabbe as having said, "It would be glorious to die under Moscow, but it is not a question of glory" (Russia, vol. 2, trans. Leonora B. Lang New York: Peter Fenelon Collier, 1898, p. 183). In making this comment, he not only dared to oppose the advice of the illustrious General Barclay de Tolly, but also showed his grasp of the real military need: to keep the army intact. Even General Ermolov favored a last battle. Kutuzov listened to them

all, then ordered the retreat.

Reading through my ancestor's memoirs, I tried to understand the course his life had taken. Here, Pavel Khristoforovich tells what happened when, as a young military attaché, he presented his credentials to Prince Baryatinsky, Russia's envoy to Bavaria:

The butler escorted me to the English garden where we found the prince strolling, alone. I had several packets of letters and dispatches for him, and, as we met, with scarcely a word of greeting, he began reading, tearing open the envelopes and throwing them on the ground.

He was a tall, stately man with graying hair, pleasant features, quick, impatient gestures. Apparently not everything was to his liking in the letters, particularly the relative freedom of action I was given, independent of his control. This could be guessed from the fact that several times he interrupted his reading and gave me a stern, searching look.

Once he had finished reading, he inclined his head and, pointing with his gaze to the discarded envelopes at his feet, ordered me to pick them up. I knew the moment was decisive. Meeting his gaze for a second, I turned my head toward the butler, who had remained standing a short distance away, and motioned to him to pick up the envelopes. Not a word was spoken as we watched the butler hastily gather up the pieces of paper, but this quick, silent exchange was sufficient to establish our future relations. From that point on, they became and remained most cordial.

Pavel Khristoforovich was a heroic, even a tragic, figure. He took part in every military campaign that occurred during his lifetime (twenty-eight) and was wounded several times. Every existing decoration for valor was bestowed on him. He was promoted to the rank of general. And yet his espousal of liberal causes got him into serious trouble with the government. At thirty-six, he spent four months in jail for associating with the Decembrists. After he reached the age of fifty-three, he lost the favor of the military high command and remained without assignment for extended periods of time. His financial situation was such that he could not afford to pay for treatment for his wife, whose nervous condition led to suicide, possibly induced by the death of two sons in battle. At sixty-one, Pavel Khristoforovich made this touching entry in his diary: "A letter from Paris informs me of my election as Honorary President of the International Society for the Abolition of Traffic in Negroes and Slavery.... Spent all day at home, ill. My old wound is bleeding profusely. Lacking money to pay for treatment, I am not calling the doctor." At long last, at age seventy-three, recognition came to the old soldier. He was appointed Ataman of the Don Cossacks. When he retired four years later, he received the hereditary title of count, as well as Russia's highest honor—the Order of Saint Andrew. What changes brought about this belated recognition, I do not know. Thereafter, until his death at eighty-six, Pavel Khristoforovich lived quietly on his small estate in southwestern Russia, riding out into the open country every morning. Father remembers him as "a proud old man sitting erect on his horse."

7. *The Letters of The Tsaritsa to the Tsar,* 1914-1916, introduction by Sir Bernard Pares (London: Duckworth, 1923), and *The Letters of the Tsar to the Tsaritsa, 1914-1917* (New York: Dodd, Mead, 1929). In 1923, a friend sent Father a Russian translation of the letter from the German edition. Father, who often saw Nini in our home, may well have said that he hoped Aleksandra Feodorovna would stay away from army headquarters. He was certainly fed up with her disruptive visits there. Nini undoubtedly repeated this comment to her husband, the much-hated Voyeikov of my youth, now palace commandant. And since he was in the same Rasputin-oriented circle around the empress as Virubova, Voyeikov, in turn, soon passed along the remark. Seeking revenge, Virubova must have jumped on Father's comment to make plausible the idea she was promoting with the empress that Father wanted Aleksandra Feodorovna away so he could introduce Mme. Soldatenko to the tsar.

8. By March 12, 1917, a serious crisis had developed in Petrograd. Father reports how events were affecting the tsar at general headquarters:

Mogilev, March 12, 1917. All morning we (the tsar and his aides) sat in the governor's palace, and several times General Alekseyev came with telegrams from Petrograd where the situation has grown alarming during the past several days. In the afternoon, we stayed indoors, waiting for more news. In the evening, Count Fredericks and Voyeikov came in while we were having tea and called the tsar out into the adjoining room. We assumed they wanted to tell him something particularly important as they usually never came at night.... When the tsar came back into the dining room, it was barely noticeable that he was upset. In about twenty minutes, they came again, and we took our leave, surmising that something really serious had occurred. The fligel adjutants went to their quarters, but I waited in Dr. Feodorov's room while he stayed upstairs in Voyeikov's quarters to find out what was gong on. In about thirty minutes, the doctor reappeared. When I asked him what had happened, he called out to me as he rushed past, "Tell you later. You'd better pack. We're leaving in an hour." In the train we learned that revolution had broken out in Petrograd. I must say, it is surprising that one can be so close to the center of things and yet find that everything is concealed, that one isn't informed, and one learns of such momentous events almost by accident.

March 17, Mogilev. Toward evening, the train bearing the (Dowager) Empress Maria Feodorovna, who had come to say goodbye to her son, arrived from Kiev.

March 18, Sunday, Mogilev. In the morning, the tsar, as usual, attended mass at the cathedral, which was jammed with people.... Many cried.... The tsar complained that General Alekseyev did not report anything to him anymore. He spent nearly the entire day with Maria Feodorovna.

This, no doubt, was the occasion on which Nicholas told her, "Even Grabbe has turned against me."

March 19, Monday. The tsar sorted out his personal effects and, after lunch, went to the building that housed the general staff, where all officers and men (who worked there) had been assembled. In a touching speech, he thanked all for their service and said goodbye to each one individually. The meeting left a painful impression.

March 20, Tuesday. The deputies of the Provisional Government (A.A.) Bublikov and (N.V.) Nekrasov arrived during the evening.

The former tsar had been in Mogilev five days when a delegation headed by A.A. Bublikov, sent by the Provisional Government, arrived to take him to Tsarskoye Selo. It was not until then that General Alekseyev, chief of staff, was told that the Provisional Government had decided to put Nicholas under arrest. Almost immediately they started back, taking the former tsar and a company of ten soldiers placed under their orders by General Alekseyev. Father writes that General Alekseyev was "undoubtedly leftist in his views." Since "he still had complete authority to command and to direct reliable troops," he bears a share of the responsibility for the course of events. Father adds, "Alekseyev quickly perceived all the falsity of his politics…but it was already too late."

March 21, Wednesday. In the morning, after tea, the tsar got ready for the journey. He said goodbye to the officers and men of the *Konvoy* and thanked them for their services. Then he joined Maria Feodorovna, where he waited for the time of departure. He would be accompanied on the journey by Bublikov and Nekrasov, who made all the arrangements and indicated who would be allowed to go along.

Maria Feodorovna's train stood nearby, and one cannot (calmly) recall that terrible moment when the tsar, having said goodbye forever to his mother, crossed over to the train that was waiting for him. There he found himself at the complete disposal of the (Provisional Government's) deputies, who admitted (to the train) only (Prince Vasili) Dolgoruky, K.A. Naryskin, and the duty officer, Fligel Adjutant Duke N.N. Leuchtenberg.…

On March 21st, the tsar signed his last order to the troops in which, among other things, he asked them to obey the Provisional Government. This order was not given to the troops by General Alek-

seyev in accordance with instructions from Guchkov....

...The (military) representatives of the Allied Powers who were at general headquarters wanted to accompany the tsar's train (to Tsarskoye Selo) to ensure his safety, but General Alekseyev declared to General Williams that there was no necessity to do so since the train would reach its destination safely....

...The news that some representatives of the new government had come to fetch the tsar was concealed. That is, it was not known that, from that moment on, the tsar found himself under arrest and lost his liberty. All instructions now came from the deputies who had arrived....

...Only after the tsar's departure from Mogilev did it become known that the Provisional Government had arrested him. Such a base decision could be carried out only because of the secretiveness surrounding the government's plans. But if knowledge of this (intent) had come earlier in Mogilev, neither those in charge (of the military establishment), nor the garrison, nor the inhabitants of the town, would have so easily let the tsar go. One can assume that General Alekseyev, knowing about the orders of the Provisional Government, was already beginning to have second thoughts about his false orientation.

The oath of allegiance to the Provisional Government was taken only the day after the tsar left (Mogilev), but, if the directive regarding the arrest had become known not at the moment of the train's departure, but even an hour earlier, then, despite the tsar's words of farewell in which he told (the troops) to "serve the Provisional Government," etc., one can be entirely certain that this order would not have been carried out, and they would have acted differently.

9. Many people thought Father should have gone with Nicholas when the former emperor was taken from Mogilev. They questioned Father's loyalty, perhaps unaware that he was not allowed to go. It's now known that the representatives of the Provisional Government delib-

erately kept the tsar's arrest secret until the last moment, telling only General Alekseyev. And it was certainly not by accident that Father was excluded from the train. He was the only one in the entire entourage who had a military force at his command. For all they knew, he could have had a contingent of the *Konvoy* outside the station, waiting to rescue Nicholas. In the years to come, Father would find himself pursued by the allegation that he had been remiss in his loyalty. The former ruler's comment to his mother—"Even Grabbe has turned against me"—suggested to her—hence, spreading the rumor—that Father had deserted him. Maria Feodorovna had no way of knowing the context of the comment. Her son probably had in mind Father's criticism in the dining car on the day of abdication.

10. Grand Duke Georgi Mikhailovich decided to return to Petrograd where he was arrested, imprisoned, and eventually shot. His brother Grand Duke Nikolai Mikhailovich was executed at the same time.

11. Fedya did not succeed in getting both his brothers out of Russia. Kolya was arrested at the English Club during a bridge game. While being led away, he was picked off the street by an angry mob, thrown into a canal, and stoned to death. His death came but a few days after he missed the special train on which he was to leave communist territory. Sasha made his way to Nice, France. He was offered a job by Thomas Cook, but refused to sell his travel experience, preferring a hand-to-mouth existence.

12. At first Father could not understand why his name should have been on the list, since he had shunned political activity all his life. Then he remembered that, in 1905, his brother Michael, a Cossack colonel, had been sent with a contingent of Cossacks to quell disorders in Estonia and Latvia. Apparently the family name was still remembered for the harsh treatment Michael had given the local revolutionaries. Father thought that perhaps he had been mistaken for his brother.

13. By taking the hand of St. John the Baptist to Denmark, I inadvertently became a link in a chain of events going back to early Christian times. Today it is difficult to realize that, during the Middle Ages and

even earlier, relics of saints were of profound importance in people's lives. Throughout Christendom, churches vied for fragments of the Holy Cross, bones of saints, even bits of raiment. Relics were placed in the most consecrated parts of cathedrals and churches for the veneration of the devout. The hand of St. John the Baptist, in particular, has a long history, notable for political intrigue.

According to St. Mark (6.14-29), when John was beheaded, his disciples retrieved the remains and put them in a tomb. Legend has it that St. Luke, fearing desecration, tried to remove the body. Surprised by guards, the physician apostle succeeded in cutting off the hand that baptized Jesus. Luke took it to his hometown of Antioch where it remained for many centuries. Eventually, the revered relic was brought to Constantinople.

In 1453, with the capture of that city by the Turks, the hand became part of the booty seized by Sultan Mohammed II. Some years later, in exchange for some crucial help, Mohammed's son gave the hand to the Knights of Malta, then known as the Knights Hospitallers of St. John. They were based, at the time, on the island of Rhodes. Henceforth, the hand of the patron saint became the sacred relic of the Order. Eventually driven from Rhodes, the Knights moved to Malta.

In 1798, when the French captured Malta, the Knights had to move again. As Bonaparte seized the bejeweled gold reliquary, he is said to have exclaimed, "Here! Keep your carrion!" But he did have the gold melted down to pay his troops.

The Knights sought refuge in Russia where their relics were kept under the protection of Paul I. There the hand was encased in a new gold reliquary, and the Madonna received the necklace of Ceylon sapphires, which had so attracted my eye. At this point, the Madonna was now partially adorned with embossed silver in the manner of a Russian icon.

As Prince Isheyev told me, a Russian priest rescued these objects and took them to Estonia.

Prince Isheyev turned out to be Count Alexei Ignatieff who, as he had said, was a friend of my family. The patriot who brought the sacred objects to the convent in Estonia was Father Bogoyavlenski. Edgar Erskine Hume reports these details in his book, *Medical Work of the Knights Hospitallers* (John Hopkins University Press, 1940). Mr. Hume died in 1952 and never learned my part in the story, which is told here for the first time.

What happened to the bejeweled reliquary and the hand of St. John the Baptist after Larsen and I delivered them to the Danish Ministry of Foreign Affairs?

Maria Feodorovna had them in her possession for seven years. On her deathbed in 1928, she entrusted these sacred objects to the patriarch of the Serbian Orthodox church, who placed them in the chapel of the royal palace in Belgrade. Mr. Hume states that Prince Paul, regent of Yugoslavia, gave him permission to have the hand photographed. The picture was taken on September 10, 1938, with the first secretary of the American Legation as witness. The picture shows a right hand with several fingers missing. The reliquary appears to be the same. To my knowledge, it is the only photograph ever made.

They remained in the Royal Chapel in Belgrade for thirteen years. When the Nazis invaded Yugoslavia, the hand was moved for safekeeping to the Ostrog Monastery, near Niksic, Montenegro. It is reported that a renegade monk revealed the hiding place, and the Nazis were able to capture the treasures.

Is the hand still in Montenegro? Or somewhere in Germany, perhaps in some little church in the Bavarian Alps? According to another source, the hand is safely hidden away in a Spanish monastery. And the icon of the Virgin Mary, the Madonna of Philermo? Has she perhaps quietly found her way to the Vatican? Surprisingly, a rivalry between the different branches of the Knights of Malta still exists— Orthodox and Catholic. So, these secrets may be well kept, and we shall never know.

14. Elena Böhme did not return to Copenhagen until after I had left for the United States. I wrote her later from Colorado Springs. By then she had moved to London and suggested I join her. A year had passed, but apparently the relationship had meant something special to her, as it had to me.

15. At age 39, George died of pneumonia in the French Alps.

16. With my first paycheck I had paid my debts. It was my intention to lend money to Kazimir Valsky, but the impulse to push out of one's mind miserable times is so strong that I had not yet gotten around to it. I have felt guilty ever since about this moral lapse, especially after I learned that he had been deported back to Poland, pronounced unbalanced, and institutionalized.

17. A year later, the Denver *Post* reported that Jaime had gone to New York to collaborate on *From Hell Came A Lady*, which failed at the box office. In December 1928, the Del Rios were divorced, and Dolores married Carewe. Not long afterwards, Jaime died in Germany—according to rumor, a suicide. Some said he had lost the will to live. Dolores eventually went back to Mexico where she was largely responsible for giving new life to the Mexican theatre and establishing the film industry there. She did much to make Mexico City the cultural center it is today.

18. Olga Samarine was not Russian. She had changed her name to sound Russian.

19. Eventually, Prokofiev returned to Russia. He was denounced in the Soviet press as a decadent formalist, an accusation he must have taken very hard.

20. Laura Harris moved to London to work for a British publisher. That's where I thought she was until 1955 when, one day, I heard her voice on the telephone. "I'm coming to Washington. Could we have lunch?" Of course I agreed. We made a date to meet in a restaurant near the Department of the Interior. We had cocktails and discussed our work. Laura had earned quite a reputation as an editor of books for children. I noticed that her hair was whiter than I remembered and that she was more stylishly dressed. We parted casually, as if we had both come from one of Washington's suburbs and would meet soon again. More time passed, then Laura's sister called. She told me Laura had died of cancer. Later I learned Laura had known her illness was terminal and had come to say goodbye. But she hadn't given me the slightest clue that anything was wrong. It crossed my mind that maybe I was in

some way responsible for her illness. Certainly the difficulties in our marriage had caused her pain, even anguish, and may have weakened her desire to live, but it couldn't have been all my fault. Still, I was glad to recall that, at the time of our divorce, I had arranged to share half of my book royalties with her.

Acknowledgments

I WISH TO thank everyone who encouraged me to publish my father's full memoir, including my brother Nick Grabbe, who never shied away from answering editing questions, my sister-in-law Betsy Krogh, and my friend and proofreader Carolyn White-Lesieur. Thank you to photographer Steffen Thalemann for stopping by to shoot both my father's key collection and the portrait, given to my parents by Johanna Cecelia Hansi Bohm in 1974. Thank you to Maryellen Kelley at Hi-Def Photo Imaging for doing such an amazing restoration job on dozens of old photos. Thanks also go out to my historian husband Sven Rudstrom for his encouragement, and to my children, Stephanie, Paul, and Natalie Boutin, for their patience. Finally, thank you to Angela Tavares and Sue Williams at Here Booky Booky, who helped complete my father's dream of sharing the full scope of his experiences, both in Europe and America, so other immigrants would know it's possible to leave everything behind and start over in a new country.

Alexandra Grabbe
Wellfleet, MA
September 30, 2014

Made in the USA
Charleston, SC
05 January 2015